SOLD OUT

HOW TO SELL OUT ON THE WORLDWIDE SHOPPING CHANNEL STAGE

Alli Mang

"The limits of the possible can only be defined by going beyond them into the impossible."

- Arthur C. Clarke

Published by Authority Press, Inc.
7777 N Wickham Rd, # 12-247
Melbourne, FL 32940
Authority-Press.com

Copyright 2014 © by Alli Mang

All Rights Reserved

No part of this book may be reproduced or transmitted in any form by any means: graphic, electronic, or mechanical, including photocopying, recording, taping or by any information storage or retrieval system without permission, in writing, from the authors, except for the inclusion of brief quotations in a review, article, book, or academic paper. The authors and publisher of this book and the associated materials have used their best efforts in preparing this material. The authors and publisher make no representations or warranties with respect to accuracy, applicability, fitness or completeness of the contents of this material. They disclaim any warranties expressed or implied, merchantability, or fitness for any particular purpose. The authors and publisher shall in no event be held liable for any loss or other damages, including but not limited to special, incidental, consequential, or other damages. If you have any questions or concerns, the advice of a competent professional should be sought.

Manufactured in the United States of America.

ISBN: 978-1-62865-088-4

For Wayne and Alice

Thank you for teaching me to never, ever, ever give up.
You are my shining stars!

ENTREPRENEURS MAY CHANGE HATS, BUT WE NEVER STOP GROWING!

1986
National print ad campaign for a jean company

1988
My mom's favourite musical – A Chorus Line
I played Val (3rd from the right)

1989
2nd Season Co-Host of Wild Guess with Host Neil Crone

1990
My agent called me the 'Commercial Queen' in the 90's

1992
Guest Starred with Mr. T and Alex Amini on the TV Series – T and T

1993
National print ad campaign for a paint company

1994
Guest Starred on the TV Series – Friday the 13th

1995
I was an Ivory Girl in an ad campaign in Canada and the U.S.

ENTREPRENEURS MAY CHANGE HATS, BUT WE NEVER STOP GROWING!

2007
30th Anniversary of the Chicago Marathon. I'm in there somewhere with 50,000 other runners

2008
Mississauga Marathon. My personal best time

2011
Performing at a concert celebrating the music of Oscars and Hammerstein for DZ Entertainment

2010
I decided to celebrate being over 40

2013
Fashion Designer and TV Personality Steven Cojocora and I at TSC

2012
Stedman was one of the key people who encouraged me to write SOLD OUT

Author and Keynote Speaker Stedman Graham and I at a Sirius broadcast

James and I enjoying some R and R

2014
Hosting When Every Minute Counts

2014
Life is Good. I am so grateful!

Contents

Foreword 13
Thank You 15
My Story 17
Introduction 21
Setting The Scene 25
The Customer Is King 27
Why Should I Buy It This Minute? 27
An Example of a Great Retail Sales Experience 27
Similarities of Different Types of Command Performers 30
An Anecdote on Focus 32
Top-Selling Record Breakers of Products Sold Out within Minutes ... 33
The Perfect Storm Brings Best Practices Together 33

SECTION I
The Home Shopping Industry

CHAPTER 1 The Home Shopping Experience 39
Nomenclature 39
The Phenomenon of Home Shopping 41
Home Shopping Industry Roots 42
The Top Three U.S. Shopping Channels 43
Direct Response Television (DRTV) 45
Seamless Multi-Level Marketing 46
Dollars Per Minute (DPM) 47
Future of the Online Industry 49
What Is Special about Home Shopping? 52
Transparency Is a Key Marketing Tactic 53
Home Shopping Website Reviews 54
Predictable Show Structure 55
Matching Time Slots to Customers' Buying Patterns 56
Need for Speed 56
Brand Theatre 57
How to Get Products on the Air 59
Massive Access 61
Vendors' Eyes Wide Open 62
Pitching Your Product to Buyers 64
Leave Your Porsche at Home 65
The Importance of Face-to-Face Meetings 66

The Trifecta of Marketing - Brand Awareness, Recognition and Insistence....... 67
Recap 73

CHAPTER 2 THE GUEST EXPERT **74**
Rules and Regulations 78
The Chosen Ones... 79
Notable Actor Turned Electrifying Guest Expert and Host 84
Do Great Products Find You or Do You Seek Out Great Products to Sell? 84
Category Expertise 85
Crossing Categories... 85
Overexposure 86
Networks... 87
Time Management.. 87
Know Your Entertainment Style 88
Modeling with Etiquette 89
Finding Your Own Unique Voice 90
My Two Favourite Books.. 91
Toolbox to Create Your Vision Statement 92
Recap 97

CHAPTER 3 TO WEAR OR NOT TO WEAR, THAT IS THE QUESTION **98**
Change It Up 100
Body Language.. 101
Two-Dimensions of the TV Screen I 102
Categories Home Retail Networks **Do Not** Sell 103
Emergency Wardrobe Tool Kit Checklist... 104
Style Options of Dress That Best Complements Your Category 105
Wardrobe Considerations Before You Pack 106
Questions to Ask before Final Wardrobe Decisions................................... 107
Wardrobe Overall Don'ts 109
Point of View (POV) Wardrobe Guidelines for Women 111
Point of View (POV) Wardrobe Guidelines for Men 115
Recap 117

CHAPTER 4 THE JOB OF GETTING THE JOB **118**
The Job of Auditioning... 118
The Audition Starts at the Front Door of the Building 123
Due Diligence 124
Audition Perspective 125
Principles to Live by 126
The Power of a Strong Image in an Audition or Interview 127

Contents

The Power of One Image in the Boardroom 128
My First Shopping Network On-Air Audition 128
HB Pencil 130
Glass of Water 130
Quiet Before the Storm 131
Stay Calm and Carry On 132
3 Questions in Life 133
I Got the Job, Now What? 135
It's Not Where You Start, It's Where You Finish 136
Basic Business and Negotiation Principles 136
Stick to Your Numbers 139
Negotiating Guidelines 140
Recap 148

CHAPTER 5 IT'S SHOWTIME, FOLKS 149
A Truth About the Business of Performing 149
Nerves Are a Good Thing 151
Suggestions on How to Manage Your Nerves 152
Stay Hydrated and Well Fed 154
Celebrity Effect 155
Sales Means You Have to Put the Puck in the Net 157
Life Cycle of the Guest Expert 158
Never Say Never 159
Lifecycle of a Product 160
Recap 163

CHAPTER 6 THERE'S NO 'I' IN TEAM 164
Relationship Capital I 165
The Buyers 169
Buyers and On-Air Guests 170
The Hosts 170
Dances with Hosts 172
Show Producer 174
Multiple Guests on One Show 175
Chaos Is Possible 175
Order Is Also Possible 176
Your Peers 176
The Viewers 177
Product Competition 177
Internal Customers 178
Recap 180

CHAPTER 7 YOUR CUSTOMERS **181**
How Do You Make a Connection if You Can't Talk to Your Customers? 183
What Is Your Customer's Experience? 184
Assume Your Customers Know As Much As You Do 185
Principle of the Anchor 187
Anchor Seven™ 188
Anchor Seven™ Discovery 189
Questions on the Path to Creating Your Anchor Seven™ Customers - Chart ... 194
Example Anchor Seven™ 196
Recap 200

SECTION II
SALES

CHAPTER 8 DIET Your Way to Sales Success™ **203**
ABC's of Sales 204
Our Bread and Butter 204
Salespeople Can Learn from New York Cabbies 205
The Perfect Storm Brings Best Practices Together to Become: The Sales Equation
 DIET Funnel 207
Sales Success Depends On How Well We **Listen** to Our **Listeners** 208
Stage I - The Define Listener: 210
Stage II - The Inspire Listener: 210
Stage III – Execute the Plan: 212
Stage IV – Trust is the Result of Executing the Plan Successfully: 212
D I E T Leads to Trust Chart 214
T-R-U-S-T 215
Sales Equation DIET Funnel 216
Define your way with TRUST 217
Inspire your way with TRUST 224
Execute your way with TRUST 235
Trust your way with TRUST 243
Recap 246

CHAPTER 9 THE LILY PAD STRATEGY™ **247**
Formulating Your Pitch 250
Pitch Pad 251
Breaking Down Each Pitch Pad 252
HOOK THEM 253
The Host Has Introduced You, Now What? 254

Contents

Opening Statement 254
Personality Driven Opening Statements 255
Opening Statement Guide... 256
Anchor Yourself... 257
Anchor Statement Guide... 258
Chase Thought.. 259
The Out of Town Guest Expert Advantage 259
FULFILL A NEED.. 261
ILLUMINATE THE EXPERIENCE... 262
Understanding How to Answer Objections 263
RISE ABOVE OBJECTIONS 264
Component I: I Don't Trust the Product 265
Immediate Results Demonstrations... 269
Component II: I Don't Trust Home Shopping 273
RISE ABOVE APATHY 275
Intention and Pace 277
ASK FOR BUSINESS 278
Successful Call-to-Action... 278
Closing Statements Guide 280
Maybe To Yes Transition 282
THANK YOU 283
Recap 285

SECTION III
ACHIEVING PEAK PERFORMANCE

CHAPTER 10 The 3 P's Preparation, Practice, Performance........................289
PREPARATION.. 293
Script Writing 293
Key Words and Phrases 293
The Voice Recorder is Your Best Friend 294
When Do I Start to Record? 295
At-A-Glance Script.. 296
Preparation Guide to Get You Ready for Your Show................. 297
PRACTICE 298
Tools to Get You Show Ready 299
Practice, Prepare, Rehearse. Practise, Prepare, Rehearse............. 302
Visualize Success Throughout Your Day 303
Preparing Your Voice 304

Speed of Turnover 305
Stay Hydrated and Well Fed 306
PERFORMANCE 307
Habits are Habit Forming 308
Performing Demonstrations 309
Pre-Show Set check 311
Two Dimensions of the TV Screen II 311
When Demos Don't Go According to Plan 311
The Camera and You 313
Visual Tools 314
A and B-Roll in Home Shopping 315
To Use Cue Cards or Not to Use Cue Cards 316
Use of Large Visual Boards 316
Pace Yourself on a Long Show Day 317
Phone Calls to Air 318
The New World Approach 319
Two Fantastic Guest Experts Who Are New World Specialists 322
When the Unexpected Happens 324
Recap 326

CHAPTER 11 ASSESS YOUR SUCCESS 327
Understanding the Long-Term Process of the Goal to Sell Out 329
Feedback from Your Measurements 331
Identifying INtangibles You Can Measure 331
Quantifiable Matrices 333
Performance Self-Evaluation Template 335
Sales Tracking Worksheet Template 337
How Did the Numbers Help You? What Did You Get Out of It? ... 338
Establishing Your Good, Better, and Best Goals 338
Recap 341

CHAPTER 12 HAVE YOU GOT YOUR GAME FACE ON? 342
Give Them All You Have to Give 343
10-Point Checklist 346
Pre-Host Meeting 347
The Power of the Green Room 347
Relationship Capital II 348
The Keys to Success 350
Recap 353

GO BEYOND THE FINISH LINE 354

FOREWORD

Selling is both an **art** and a **science**. Putting the science of selling into words is one thing, but putting the art of selling into useable, practical and informative words is quite another. In her book *Sold Out*, Alli Mang plays the role of sales coach providing an encyclopedic how-to guide on every aspect of selling. Besides this book being a thorough source for every new and seasoned home and Internet shopping sales expert, this book is written for anyone looking to improve their sales and marketing capabilities including keynote speakers and other performance based professions. By applying the many principles outlined, this book will help the reader reach for a new and higher dimension of achievement.

The structure of her book is crafted in such a way that mirrors a similar framework of home and Internet selling. It keeps the reader engaged and makes for an easy read to get the information you want quickly. In biblical times, teaching was done through the use of parables. Alli, in her book, uses today's version of the parable by telling stories to illustrate and relate her views on the importance of connecting directly to your customers and delves deeply into every important aspect of the pitch, the performance and the journey on how to capitalize on the opportunities given to you. The stories that Alli tells are born of real-life personal experiences she has endured throughout her career coupled with stories and anecdotes of many professionals within the world of top performance.

When you get to know Alli through reading her book, it is not long before you recognize how much she cares about your experience as the reader. You'll find she's talking directly to you as she shares her wisdom in an entertaining, informative and highly detailed manner.

If you want to get to the root of how best to achieve top performance in anything you do professionally, read *Sold Out*. It truly is a "must read."

-Raymond Aaron,
New York Times, Best-Selling Author

THANK YOU

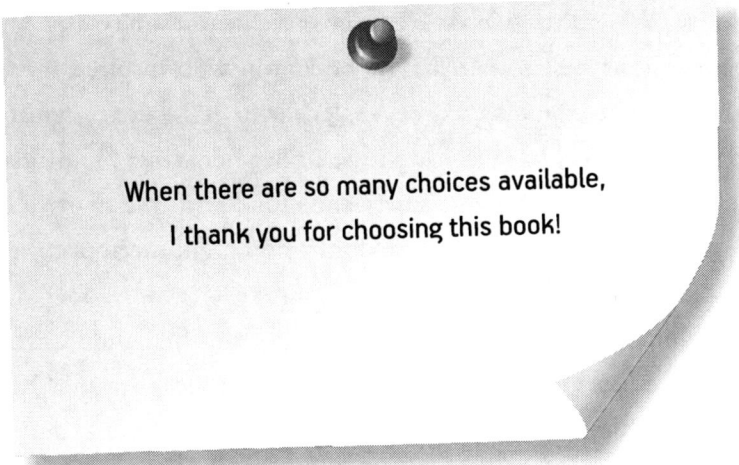

There are many people who have helped provide their own insights on the business of selling and performance throughout the next few hundred pages. I am delightfully grateful to them all for sharing their expertise and have highlighted many throughout this book. From the bottom of my heart I thank you all.

There are a few people, however, that I'd like to give a standing ovation to as their influence and encouragement has been most important to me. Thank you to both my mother and father. They set the bar extremely high as I grew up and have been my biggest supporters and mentors throughout my life. My mother was an entrepreneur who knew how to light up a room and assess situations in a heartbeat. My father was a fiercely strong leader and strategic thinker well ahead of his time. Throughout his career, he enjoyed professional highlights such as hosting and honouring President George H. W. Bush Sr. and his wife Barbara,

Canadian Prime Minister Brian Mulroney, and moderated a significant keynote speech of the late Prime Minister of the United Kingdom, Baroness Margaret Thatcher. Many of the customer and sales principles in this book have been inspired by my Dad's leadership and forward vision throughout his fifty-five+ years of business.

Thank you to my husband James who has stood by my side supporting my dreams and endeavours since the first day we met. Your creative vision and ability to see beyond what seems possible inspires me every day.

Thank you as well to Mr. Raymond Aaron who inspired me to write something I knew about; Forbes Riley, who has been a great coach; Dallas Prince, who graciously took me under her wing; Sandi Hall, who first trained me to be a guest expert and stood with me many a day and night rehearsing; and Kimberley Seldon, who taught me about the importance of knowing my numbers.

Other important contributors include the beautiful Sandie Savelli, John Harten my editor, Andrea Boyle my book architect, Virginia Rodriguez my graphic designer, Bruce Dean my agent for many years, and Jennifer Le my publishing administrator. Christine Bryant, Darrin Baker, Susan Yull, David Hogan, David K. Hurst, David Rogers, David Sigal, Denise Wade, Dennis Pellaren, Duane Andrews, Gerda Tanti, Greta Culliford, Hugh Wilson, Jaymz Bee, Jeannette Lee, Jerry Philippeau, John Sebesta, Carrie Olver, Krista Maitland, Carol Mair, Laurie Sorensen, Lella Liuzzi, Linda Brooks, Lisa Griffin, Maria Aranha, Mark Cassius, Nancy Forsyth, Norm Murray, Alex Mustakas, Peter Franceschini, Rebecca Poff, Renee Torrington, Rob Hoene, Rosalie Brown, Sandra Smith, Sandy Martin, Sharon Snider, Stacey Schieffelin, Richard Nester, Tiffany Jones, Todd Noel, Burt Weisner and Donald Lowes. Last but not least, my marathon coach Fiona (Gray) Whitby who, when I interviewed her, gave me the key insight to delivering high performance: **Execute the Plan You've Built.**

Alli Mang
New Year's Day 2014

MY STORY

It was a beautiful, crisp January morning in 2008. I was driving like a madwoman trying desperately to arrive on time for a planning appointment with my triathlon and running coach of many years, Fiona. I first met her in 2001 while managing a local retail triathlon store. As I walked up the front entrance of her beautiful home, she met me at the front door wearing cozy slippers, lulu lemon pants and a fleece top. I turned the corner to take off my salt stained boots and noticed a shiny silver engraved platter draped by a colourful Hawaiian lei sitting proudly on her living room mantel. She won 3rd place in her age group at the Ironman World Championships in Kona, Hawaii in October of 2007. Although Fiona has logged a few age group wins at Ironman competitions throughout the world, this race was one of her most cherished accomplishments. Her deep humility and grace left me wanting to know about her process of pulling out a winning performance.

What made this race the winning one for her?

I have gleaned a lot from Fiona over the years and have learned that the sound principles from one discipline can be transferred to another completely different discipline with relative ease. She's helped me to understand that every time you put yourself out there there's always a risk that it won't work out the way you had planned. Outlining the finish is important but there really is no black and white answer to the game of winning. It's about finding a way to get the best out of ourselves while we're in the middle of doing what we're doing. As we chatted that day, she shared, "It's impossible to predict outcomes because there are so many variables that may impede the fullest performance on any given day. My only job on race day is to trust that I did all I could to get to this day and then respond and manage my thoughts, actions and reactions to whatever arises on the day the best way I can. I remember during that race, I took a look at my direct competitors to assess how I was doing in comparison to them as we neared the end of the marathon (about seven hours into the race). If I was going to make a move to win, I knew it would have to be now. After a moment of assessment, I proceeded to go for the win. That is what racing is all about. You execute your entire plan to the best of your ability making the most of each moment. Then you move on to the next challenge."

She won third because she was racing for gold.

I first started running to get my head centred again after the shocking passing of my beloved mother. I was desperate to figure out how to walk forward when all I wanted to do was stand still and hide. The energy and engagement I felt during even a short run seemed to help me rebuild my world with hope again. My first half marathon (13.1 miles) coincidently fell on my mom's birthday. My first marathon (26.2 miles) happened to fall coincidently on Mother's Day and my first 70.3 Ironman (1.2 mile swim, 56 mile bike, 13.1 mile run) was run on the anniversary of mom's passing. As you can see, endurance sport has been present during some of the most significant moments in my life and perhaps is why I have such kinship with it. Just to set the record straight, I do love the benefits of running, but it is a rather unnatural task for me. I'm relieved I don't have to make a living doing it or I'd starve!

My drive to understand the ultimate secret of top performance was found through the power of repetition, training and setting both lofty and attainable goals. Training benefits everyone because it prepares us to work through the tough times as well as capitalize during the triumphant times.

I have learned the power and freedom this framework provides. It pushes us beyond what we think is our limit and helps us to see our gifts in ways we might not have imagined.

Since I started working as an entrepreneur and actress in 1986, I continue to discover even more to learn about the craft of performing and delivering on command. I love working in this industry because of the high pressure to execute and deliver all that you have to bring when it really counts. That's why I love it.

I am a runner, a performer and a sales guest expert. All three disciplines have interesting similarities within their vast differences. You will notice my use of sport and theatre performing as a way to explain the vast scope of what it takes to perform on demand. From time to time, I will use these three disciplines and others to represent the degree of focus and strategy required. I know of no other way to describe the amount of whole *body* and *soul* attention required to prepare to sell out your product. It is one of the toughest endeavours to achieve and is similar to the kind of pressure to cross the finish line of a marathon or performing on stage on Broadway. It doesn't just happen overnight. There are no second chances and every minute does count.

I do understand very well that not many people may be able to relate to sporting analogies and so have used other relatable topics as well. The focus of the book is the function and art of selling. To make this art form effortless, takes a lot of effort. I plan on tossing every possible example I can throw out to you, to help unleash even more of your natural ability to sell. I'll also throw out a few remarks to make you laugh and perhaps to think a little more deeply about your current and next steps towards building a lasting and exciting career for yourself to benefit you and others too.

As we work together throughout this book, I ask you to trust in this process. The technique of selling has no guaranteed outcome, but every personal story of mine and those of the experts I interviewed, the quotes, exercises, ideas and charts will most definitely help inspire your own personal and professional excellence. Let's get ready to explore it together!

INTRODUCTION

"I love the pressure of having to be your best in the biggest moments."

-Jennifer Jones
2014 Women's Curling Olympic Gold Medalist

The goal to thoroughly understand how to access our own best performance is the assignment of life, I believe. It is the one thing that many of us ponder; often keeping us up at night before the big meeting, competition or the big interview. The goal of this book is to inspire exceptional sales execution. Everyone in business today needs to know how to sell ideas, themselves and products.

To be the best in the chosen field of on-air selling is to understand the power behind the artistry and technique of performing and selling. Performing is opening up your soul and energy allowing it to pass through your body with ease. Selling is the ability to understand the power of what you are communicating and how you are connecting to your audience with likeable confidence and personal style. In the home shopping world, a sales expert must survive the first few minutes on-air or the guest expert and product is *pulled*. The sales volumes that are achieved in those first minutes dictate whether you continue or whether you are shut down. And believe me, the pressure to sell out is felt from all sides as you approach your selling day. The standout difference between home shopping retail and almost any other business is the time allocated to produce top sales results. It is one of the most heightened performance environments and mirrors the type of pressure that Super Bowl competitors and Olympic athletes face. Delivery has to be instantaneous. (There's no luxury of time to take files home to mull over, strategize and assess when in the live studio). It's a real time exchange of ideas where both the sales professionals and the customers work together in a rapid fire manner.

For this reason, selling live on-air is one of the most competitive and transparent selling jobs in business. Customers can shut you down with one click and never have to let you know about it. The biggest difference between a shopping channel guest expert and other sales professionals is our pitfalls are broadcasted on national TV and the worldwide stage of the Internet where multi-millions of people are watching and millions of dollars are on the line every minute. It is not a role that can be picked up in a moment, like a suit jacket or sneakers. This is a profession that is thrilling, exciting and lucrative. It is for new and veteran guest experts, models, hosts, actors, speakers, sales people, athletes and other professional endorsers, teachers and tradeshow sellers who are looking to be inspired further and to excel at this art form.

The home shopping world is unique but the principles and winning prescriptions can be applied to any business and sales environment in any market. In today's society, everyone is fighting for those big opportunity jobs. High achieving new graduates with Honours MBA's and Law degrees seem no closer to getting work than people with lesser education. Diploma-carrying-twenty-somethings face the highest student loans in history, leaving young people little choice but to take any work that comes their way instead of finding work in the field in which they were educated. No matter what profession you are in, you need to know how to catch the attention of every buyer that walks past you. More importantly, you have to know how to apply your highest level of performance when it counts.

INTRODUCTION

I have often asked what kind of training and work has to be done in order to fully arrive for that important 10 AM job interview, or the presentation that is scheduled next Thursday when delivery has to be 100%. Is this a teachable skill? I wanted to understand if this *it* factor of delivering on command could be identified and packaged in such a way that we regular people could learn, emulate and apply this focus and drive. When everything is going well in our careers, we have no real need to dig deeper. The need comes when we are being pressed and challenged from all sides of our profession. This is when we often go back to our technique and tools to get us through the rigors of fulfillment.

The tools and techniques in this book have been created specifically for this very purpose.

This is a reference book and compilation of sales tips, analogies, and proven techniques created from my own experience and built from extensive interviews of top experts in the field of performance, including CEO's, CFO's, elite endurance athletes, broadcasters, film and theatre actors, artistic directors, casting directors, infomercial directors, as well as shopping channel hosts and the top selling guest experts and pitch people on-air today. It is for this reason I wrote this book. I have developed unique performance and on-the-job training sales tools to redefine what exceptional selling is. This is not a book of guidance to produce a mediocre professional at selling on-air, but rather a book to assist you to become your own authority on the subject.

One of the many reasons why home and online shopping is alluring and has a strong place within the world of retail is the unique and intimate way we get to tell stories and relate one–on–one with customers. We also know that customers may be tuning-in and out and need to hear about the merits of the product (more than once) to really trust that it is a good choice to buy it. Pitches and programming are often repeated and product offerings are re-configured to attract as large a viewership as possible. This book mirrors a similar framework unique to shopping channels worldwide. Each section is therefore devised to be a complete work in its own right, allowing you to flip from one place to another based on your needs and requirements at any given time. I also provide some teases along the way that may lead you to read more of a certain subject. In order to maximize your usage of the book, I've added a one page recap to sum up each chapter to help you get the inspiration and answers you want when you want them. Although the framework is targeted to becoming an exceptional on-air sales expert, the principles of selling and the importance of customer focus applies to everyone in business today.

The most important elements in any sales environment are your customers and knowing how to create a most inviting experience for them. The next element is to decide on the type of performer you are and to figure out what will ignite the fire within you.

SETTING THE SCENE

"To be a consistent winner means preparing not just one day, one month or even one year - but for a lifetime."
-Bill Rodgers

Bill Rodgers is a legendary long-distance runner and 4-time Boston Marathon winner

You arrived at the network building yesterday at 16:00 hours and you haven't stopped moving since. You've already met with your buyers, producers and stagers to discuss your show, your set up, and any last minute requirements. This place doesn't seem to have normal business hours. It's a fast paced 24-hour, 365-day-per-year world where literally every minute counts.

Fast-forward 10 hours to 2:45am. You stand in a dark control room with 18 TV monitors blasting different shots and everyone is wearing headsets. They are all laughing about something the host has just said on camera. You are given a microphone and an IFB (interruptible foldback ear piece) to wear in your ear. Within a few minutes, you are wired up for sound. "Check, check… Everything sounds great, have a good show," the sound technician shouts as you vacate the room. As you walk down the hall into the studio, you check your makeup for the

14th time that hour. You check to see that your Spanx (body shaping undergarments) are in place and then you push the studio door open and walk through. Butterflies wave through your body. One of the stagers puts her pointer finger over her mouth as if to say, shhhhhh. The lights are alarmingly bright. This is it! You are about to go on national television and the Internet worldwide to sell yourself and your product. The last show is just winding down with the host doing a recap of the features, product numbers and prices. Earlier in the day, you met with that same host to go over your products and to get to know each other briefly. The celebrity who was just on for the past hour had staggeringly high sales! How is that possible? Is that possible? How will my show go? Will they pull me? Will anyone buy? How does my hair look? I'm drawing a complete blank ....Take a deep breath and focus up your thoughts. You go through your routine and remind yourself of your anchor statement, the three minute loop and the seven minutes allotted to you and you trust that all you've worked so hard for is available to you. You declare quietly, *I am ready*. You know every side of your co-star (your product) the set looks beautiful, the host will do her job and your job is to connect it all together. Just like opening night on Broadway where there are no second takes, it's showtime!

The Customer Is King

Sales begin and end with the customer. If we are not spending almost every waking minute figuring out who our customer is, what they look like, what they adore, what they can't live without, what they'll experience when they open the box to use our product, we as sales experts are not doing our jobs to the fullest.

When customers decide they need something and are looking to purchase – whether it's a hard good (hot-tub, printer, engagement ring, house etc.) or soft good (vacation, event, retreat, etc.), they want answers and solutions. The way the answers are packaged can often depend on two major factors – available *current* currency and what their lead personality trait is. An example of a personality trait would be analytical or emotional, impulsive, pragmatic, critical, or socially aware. They might research their options by going online or they may drive to a store to feel it and touch it. With each person, the kind of answers they will be looking for will have to be framed in the right way for them to relate to and ultimately to make that switch from "Maybe" to "Yes, I'll buy it". No matter how they go about getting the answers they need, the only question they really want answered is this:

Why Should I Buy It This Minute?

Without a convincing and strong answer to this question, there would be no business. In order to excite and urge customers to take action to "Buy now", the sales expert needs to become exceptionally adept at describing and defining the product while inspiring customers in as many ways as can be imagined. The better we become with these skills, the clearer our execution and message will be and the more trust we'll create with our customers.

An Example of a Great Retail Sales Experience

Recently, I had one of the most amazing retail experiences. I went into a store that I had purchased from before. The sales staff welcomed me with sincerity and made me feel like they were genuinely pleased to have me drop by. My agenda was that I had a bit of time before an appointment and thought I'd drop in to see what was going on. I went directly to a certain brand name of dresses. I found that this particular designer knew how to fit a woman's body so well without any fussing and thought. I'd see if there were any new designs. The sales person came over and said, "Is there anything you were specifically looking for?"

I said, "No, not really. I don't have any time to try on things today. I was just looking for more dresses from that designer I love so much!"

"Oh yeah, she is wonderful. We just got some new dresses in of hers. I haven't even taken them out of the packaging yet so you're the first to see them. I'll check my records to confirm your size." The sales person continued, "You are size small. Here are the dresses. Look at this one – it has the most flattering lines."

"I really don't have any time to try it on but it looks lovely. I'll come in again."

"Take it home and try it on there. If you like it, give me a call and you can give me your credit card number, and if you don't, just bring it back the next time you are in the area," she said.

WOW. That was a call to action I couldn't refuse. Risk free and I'd be able to try it on in the comfort of my own home, with the right shoes and my own mirrors and reasonable lighting.

Do you think I bought that dress? Do you think I'll do more business with this particular store again? Yes to all. And why? Because they delivered a great retail *experience*. The salesperson made me feel special, she offered a risk-free trial and she let me know that she trusted me to take care of the dress and to return it if I wasn't completely satisfied. In return, the store gained my trust. I will be going back to them because of that fantastic experience and because I love the products.

In this next segment, I highlight a championship runner, a guest expert and a theatre performer to point out that although the disciplines are obviously very different, the way in which each performer shows up for their performance day has surprising similarities.

Performing on command isn't a skill just handed over to you because you have decided to try it. It is earned through overcoming many trials and challenges, doing drills, falling down and translating experience into improving your position and abilities. Talk to any film, TV, or theatre performer or high achieving athlete and they will all agree. So what does training for endurance sport and rehearsing for a Broadway opening have to do with selling? It teaches the principles of consistency and working the plan to manage and execute when called upon to do it.

Similarities of Different Types of Command Performers

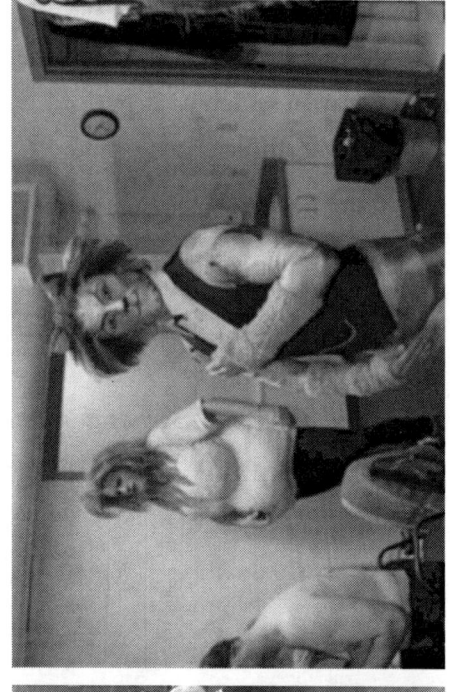

Theatre Performer
Todd Noel - Backstage getting ready for the 2nd Act as Skimbleshanks from Cats
Picture used with Todd's permission

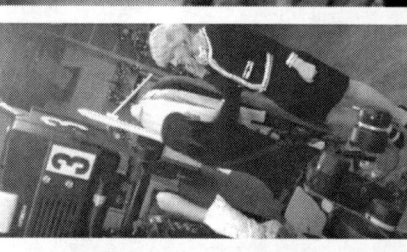

Guest Expert
Alli Mang - 5 minutes away from showtime!

Marathon Runner
Priscah Jeptoo - Winner of the 2013 New York Marathon
www.mydailynews.com

Similarities of Different Types of Command Performers

MARATHON RUNNER

1. You're only as good as your last race
2. Set Meaningful and Attainable Goals

Good	Better	Best
Place top 10 to secure current sponsors for next season.	Achieve Personal Best Time with top 5 finish.	Win the Race, Break a Record.

MARATHON RUNNER

3. **LAST FEW HOURS BEFORE YOUR RACE:**
- Wake up early enough to take in 500 calories of nutrition and stay hydrated
- Wake up your body, your legs and your heart by running a few kilometres
- Ensure all of your gels, hydration and equipment are ready to go
- Put on your time chip and attach your number to your race-belt
- Apply glide to protect your body from chaffing and blisters
- 30 minutes before your race, walk over to the start line and visualize a successful performance
- Relax, take it all in and smile. You have made it to the start line of the biggest race of your life. You are ready to run!
- **Execute your planned Performance**

GUEST EXPERT

3. You're only as good as your last show
4. Set Meaningful and Attainable Goals

Good	Better	Best
Get Another great product to sell and get booked again.	Crush your sales targets with minimal product returns.	Sell out your product. Gain the trust of returning and new customers.

GUEST EXPERT

3. **LAST FEW HOURS BEFORE YOUR SHOW:**
- Have a light snack and stay hydrated
- Confirm with all parties – stagers, producers, directors, buyers that production requirements are in place including b-roll and demonstrations, pristine well lit products
- Walk through the choreography on set to ensure you feel completely comfortable and ready to soar
- Meet with the host to establish rapport and overall selling tactics
- Get IFB and wired up for sound
- Apply last minute makeup or powder to reduce glare for the HD cameras
- 10 minutes before your show, you walk into the studio to get acclimatized and visualize a successful performance
- Relax, take it all in and smile. You have made it to the largest selling platform in the world.
- You are ready to perform and entertain!
- **Execute your planned Performance**

THEATRE PERFORMER

1. You're only as good as your last show
2. Set Meaningful and Attainable Goals

Good	Better	Best
Get another great show and get another job.	Give your audience a performance of a lifetime. Leave nothing in the dressing room.	Win a Tony for best Performance. Win the respect of your peers and critics.

THEATRE PERFORMER

3. **LAST FEW HOURS BEFORE YOUR SHOW:**
- Have a light dinner and stay hydrated
- Check that all of your costumes, wigs, props and accessories are in place and ready
- Walk through the choreography of your track. Ensure you feel completely comfortable and ready to soar
- Put on your mic pack, spanx, your wig and tape up your mic in your hairline
- Get dressed in your opening costume, hosiery and shoes and apply last minute lashes and makeup. You want the second row balcony to see your eyes too!
- At the 5 minute call, you walk past the orchestra on the stage right side to the wings for the top of Act I. Visualize a successful performance
- Relax, take it all in and smile. You have made it to opening night on the biggest stage of your life. You are ready to perform and entertain!
- **Execute your planned Performance**

An Anecdote on Focus

Recently, a friend of mine told me of a unique event his golf club offers every fall. Weather permitting, they organize a round of night golf where the tee-off times commence at 9:30 pm. Players are equipped with glow-in-the-dark golf balls, glow sticks to hang around their necks and their bags and a horn to signal to the upcoming group when it's clear for them to tee off. The fairway and the flagpole are the only areas lit up by light sticks and everything else is pitch-black except for the faint illumination of the moon. Just like night skiing, where there is an extraordinary amount of peace and elegance, this event shares a similar charm. My friend explained that most everyone who played hit the fairway with more ease than ever before.

In fact, one of the junior members played a first-time par round. The stories bantered around back at the clubhouse were ones of surprise and amazement on how well they all played. It was surmised that without the regular distractions and noise of the day, the sand traps and ponds in sight, the tall grasses that could easily pull mental and visual focus, the members just focused on the task at hand to hit the ball at the sweet spot of the club and aim for that light stick (refer to Chapter 8, Trust is Earned) highlighting each hole. Because there was nothing to

> "It's one of the greatest feelings in the world to see those numbers on the screen climb up as fast as lightning. There's a wonderful, almost perfect storm scenario that happens when you sell out the product. One of our biggest challenges as owners and on–air guest experts is to figure out how to duplicate the experience again thereby taking away the mystery of the sell out. We do know that everything and every department have to work seamlessly together. The timing and seasonality has to be spot on. It's got to be an exciting product with a recognizable brand attached to it, and there has to be a huge amount of urgency attached to the product and price to be enticing enough for our customers to buy it now. It doesn't happen every time but we all know it is possible and that's what keeps us fighting for the next sell out opportunity!"
>
> **-Jerry Philippeau,** *long time entrepreneur, owner and guest expert of twenty+ years at QVC. Refer to point five (on the next page) for Jerry's inspiring sell out experience.*

see except the lit up ball they were hitting, their swing technique and *feel* for the appropriate force was the only thing that mattered and all they had to do was trust in the process, keeping the goal in sight.

Top-Selling Record Breakers of Products Sold Out within Minutes

1. 1992 on QVC, Joy Mangano sold 18,000 mops in 20 minutes.
2. Oct. 21, 2006 on QVC, Barry Manilow performed live from Chicago, breaking QVC records for highest single-hour music sales of over 43,000 units sold. Barry Manilow, performing live from Chicago, breaks a QVC record for the highest single-hour music sales event. More than 43,000 units of his album *"The Greatest Songs of the Sixties"* were ordered.
3. July 16, 2007 on HSN, when Joy Mangano partnered with chef Todd English to create GreenPans, with Thermolon technology, they sold 24,000 pieces in 4 hours.
4. September 10, 2009 on QVC, Celtic Thunder sold out their CD's the first minute it hit the air. [1]
5. March 11, 2010 on QVC, long-time guest expert Jerry Philippeau sold out 12,000 decorative tube lights in less than 9 minutes. [2]
6. January 31, 2010 on HSN, Joy Mangano broke an HSN record by selling 180,000 units in one day of The Forever Fragrant line of home odour neutralizers. *The all-time best-selling product in HSN history with more than 300 million sets sold are Joy Mangano's Huggable Hangers. Her hourly sales regularly top $1 million.
7. Tuesday, February 18, 2013 on QVC UK, the first ever airing of *Sugru* (a fantastic customizable household rubber product) sold out in 4 minutes and 37 seconds. [3]
8. October 2 – 9, 2013 on ShopHQ, 102 hours of selling *Invicta* watches were simulcast from Las Cabos, Mexico. It was the network's biggest event ever. [4,5]

The Perfect Storm Brings Best Practices Together

You may remember one of the most recognizable opening scenes from the TV Series *Get Smart*. Agent 86, Maxwell Smart, walks down a corridor where steel plate doors open up as he walks toward them and then slam shut behind him as he walks through.[6]

It portrays a strong image of specific stepping stones that need to be completed in order to earn one's way.

When you want to perform at your best, there is a certain building order that constitutes effective preparation. If you are an Olympic athlete for instance, winning a gold medal would be your ultimate goal. If you were selling on a shopping channel, again, your ultimate goal would be to sell out the product that day. These ultimate goals have merit but need to be *parked* in order to deal with the initial work. Consider any round-robin and tournament-based sport like tennis, basketball, rowing, sculling, swimming, curling, hockey or soccer as strong examples to illustrate how the wins are accomplished in small morsels, building a succession of wins seamlessly toward the ultimate goal. Everyone wants the win, but not everyone understands the behind-the-scenes process of how that win will be achieved.

One day when I was considering how best to capture the dynamic action of the totality of what selling involves, I was filling up the oil in my truck. I'm always sloppy at this maneuver, especially at the beginning until the flow of the oil in the container gains momentum. I noted how well the funnel worked to capture all of the oil thrown into it at the top and how it gently pours with exacting ease in the direction you want it to go without waste or spillage. It seemed to represent a striking image to illustrate the continuous flow of focused energy.

Each descending field in the funnel physically mirrors a zeroing-in process.

Throughout the book you will see the development of the funnel image. In the diagram on the next page, I provide the example of what endurance athletes of any kind often use. It represents a periodized program dictating the stage and focus of each step to help them gain stamina, strength and a deeper belief in their abilities. In this case, I use what a marathon runner would rely upon to get them race ready.

Performing strongly (no matter the discipline) is a direct result of how well the tools, coaching, and key milestones are applied and executed.

The meaning of funnel according to *Webster's Encyclopedic Unabridged Dictionary* is:

"To concentrate, channel or focus."

Marathon Training Funnel

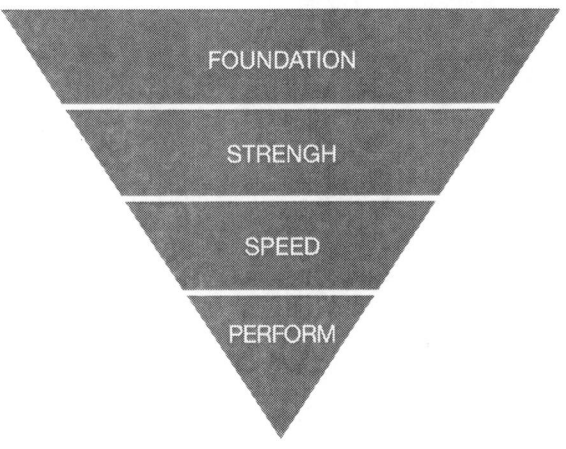

Starting in Chapter 8, DIET Your Way to Sales Success™, this exact funnel will be transformed and applied to a high-performance sales model.

SECTION I

The Home Shopping Industry

This section takes you through the entire world of home shopping. We start with an overview of the business, the history, direct marketing, how products get on the air, and a window on the world of today's market and how it is evolving for the future. Then we provide a step-by-step guide from customer intimacy to solution-based guidelines on everything you need to develop your ability to sell out.

CHAPTER 1

The Home Shopping Experience

Nomenclature

The most significant promotion on any home shopping channel is a twenty-four-hour special value product that is exceptionally priced and available only while quantities last during one 24-hour period. This is where the potential to sell millions of dollars in one day lies. (At times throughout the year, some shopping networks may enhance their programming by highlighting even more than one product). Most every home retail customer knows about these daily specials and will sign up to be alerted when their favourite product line and/or celebrity/guest expert will be on so they can be among the first to get in on the deals. The only goal of this promotion is to sell out the product before time is up. That's the goal and everyone knows it.

The big four shopping channels use the following names for this promotion:

QVC: Today's Special Value
HSN: Today's Special
ShopHQ: Today's Top Value
TSC: Today's Showstopper

To alleviate any confusion in this book, the following *fictional* name will represent this specific promotion. From now on, I'll call this promotion: Greatest Value Special, or **GVS**.

It's an extremely competitive and high stakes proposition to be the vendor of choice who is the GVS for the day, and as such, each product is meticulously scrutinized to be an almost guaranteed sell out. Brand awareness is a good start, but because of worldwide competition, it has to be a recognized brand before it is considered to be a promising GVS for the networks. It not only drives the major sales of the day, but a large degree of the advertising and pre-promotion campaigns as well. The focus of each network every day is to rally customer anticipation to a fever pitch so by the time the GVS airs there is a mad race to the phones and website a la the familiar Black Friday craze.

> "Consumers now spend their money on either 'super high fidelity experiences' (i.e., exclusive or limited products or services) OR 'super high convenience experiences.'"
>
> -**Doug Stephens**, *Founder & President, Retail Prophet* [7]

The San Francisco 49ers new Levi's Stadium is set to launch the 2014 National Football League (NFL) season. It is a state-of-the-art sports and event stadium. When they started planning in 2006, the goal of the 49ers' front office and that of their architectural firm was to create the highest fidelity indoor experience possible for their ticket holders because that is what the fans want now. "The seating design of the stadium puts approximately two-thirds of the fans in the lower bowl. It will be one of the largest lower bowls in the entire NFL." [8]

While at the game, fans have wireless, unlimited access to inside player information, statistics, play-by-play commentary and other real-time information to suit each individual's interests. This, as well as many other customer focused initiatives, gives fans the unprecedented opportunity to navigate their own experience while at the game. Experiential, emotional and entertainment marketing is a driving force within every facet of business today so it seems. This type of essential customer connection is not any different than what the great experiential retailers such as Abercrombie and Fitch, Starbucks and Tommy Bahama are also doing. They all create way more than just products to buy. They create an experience that makes their customers feel known and special and each nuance from live music playing at Tommy Bahama stores to the Abercrombie and Fitch night club style equipped with bouncers and scantily clothed twenty-year olds greeting you at the entrance. The black American Express card and the new black Visa card are additional examples of creating an exclusive experience that is guaranteed to connect with their unique customers.

The Phenomenon of Home Shopping

Home shopping is an experiential business too and is one of the fastest growing retail industries today. In principle, the home shopping experience and the 49ers fan experience have great similarities. They both know that providing a tailored and up-close customer experience, unique loyalty to the organization is enhanced.

Is there anything more comfortable than sitting in familiar surroundings, on your favourite couch or chair, drinking your favourite cup of aromatic tea or glass of vino while you shop and browse for stuff online or on TV? You may be looking to get ideas on décor, how to make your life a bit easier, your health and body more beautiful, etc. It's a time to relax, unwind, dream and wish with all the entertainment, research and value specifically delivered right to you in the way that you choose to receive it. It might be to see your favourite star sell purses or makeup, to get that great product that will save time coupled with value-adds like easy payment plans, free shipping, gift with purchase, or perhaps the product comes with 100 recipes that can't be found anywhere else but with the purchase just made. It is a 'super high convenience experience' and is the key differentiating factor that vastly separates it from any traditional retail experience.

Tuning-in either on TV or on the Internet may be part of a daily or weekend ritual. (Just like turning talk radio on in the morning or checking-in with your mom to find out what the day entails.) If the viewer had a good experience the first time watching, chances are that same person may choose to watch again and again and with that *buy-in*, or as I call it, *tune-in* cycle, you will get that customer to switch from MAYBE to YES sooner than you think.

People want to navigate and decide when and where they want to shop and every consumer is fully informed on price, features and options. Whether they are decorating and outfitting their first apartment or trying to decide on the perfect kitchen product for the upcoming holiday event – it's often the most cost effective way to shop. It appeals to shift workers and busy families that don't want to fight the crowds of the mile long malls. Parking half a mile away from the department store entrance only to get back in a car that has been sitting in the heat or cold for hours is becoming less and less enticing. We now know we have more options to get the same products with a whole lot less effort and possible aggravation. So of course, do the department stores.

Home Shopping Industry Roots

The home shopping industry commenced in 1977, when a Florida-based small market talk radio show host, Bob Circosta, was asked by the general manager of the radio station at the time, Lowell (Bud) Paxson, to sell can openers live on the air.

"I thought it would be unethical because I was trying to be a serious host," said Circosta.

The story goes, according to a colleague close to the station at the time, that an advertiser traded a limited amount of can openers (112) instead of paying their late advertising bill. Circosta was obviously reluctant to proceed, but when they came back from a break, he started to describe the openers and within an hour, they had sold out! Paxson sensed the vast sales potential of home-based commerce, and founded the world's first shopping channel on cable television, later launching nationwide with the Home Shopping Network (re-branded as HSN).

"HSN, Inc. (Nasdaq:HSNI) is a $3.3 billion interactive multichannel retailer with strong direct-to-consumer expertise among its two operating segments, HSN and Cornerstone. In addition to its existing media platforms, HSN is the industry leader in transactional innovation, including services such as HSN Shop by Remote®, the only service of its kind in the U.S., the HSN Shopping App for mobile handheld devices and HSN on Demand®"[9]

The Top Three U.S. Shopping Channels

HSN (based in St. Petersburg, Florida), **QVC** (headquartered in West Chester, Pennsylvania), **ShopHQ,** formerly Shop NBC (based in Eden Prairie, Minnesota) are fierce competitors. In a report from *Home Textiles Today*, July 22, 2013, their combined total revenue in 2012 was over 8.5 billion dollars.

HSN: "As of December 31, 2011, the HSN television networks reached approximately 95.5 million homes, of the approximately 114.6 million homes, in the United States with a television set." They currently rank 26th as one of the top 500 Internet retailers. [10]

QVC (Quality, Value, Convenience) was founded in 1986 and broadcasts in five countries as QVC US, QVC UK, QVC Germany, QVC Japan and QVC Italy to 200 million households and is No. 8 in the Internet Retailer Top 500 Guide as of 2012. QVC is live 24 hours with 27 hosts to keep up to the demands. Over the past 26 years, QVC has shipped more than 1 billion packages in the U.S. alone. [11]

> "Our strategy is much more about the psychographics than the demographics because it's really about what's going on in a customer's life as she's approaching her 30s, and what is changing. She has a lot less time. She's married and having kids. And she doesn't have the free time to wander through an entire mall and hit all the specialty stores, so she's shopping the end-caps. She's shopping with us at that point because she can do it on her own time at any time, and on any device."
>
> -**Bill Brand,** *Chief Marketing and Business Development Officer at HSN Inc.*

At the time of print,
- QVC U.S. broadcasts live 24 hours each day and reaches over 262 million households.

- QVC U.K. broadcasts live 17 hours each day and reaches over 24 million households.
- QVC Germany broadcasts live 24 hours each day and reaches over 40 million households.
- QVC Japan broadcasts live 24 hours each day and reaches over 17 million households.
- QVC Italy broadcasts live 17 hours each day and reaches over 18 million households.
- QVC China (a joint venture) broadcasts live 12 hours each day and reaches over 40 million households.

QVC ranks #5 overall and #2 among multi-category retailers in the 2013 *Internet Retailer Mobile 400 Guide.* [12]

ShopHQ is headquartered and broadcasts in Eden Prairie, Minnesota, approximately 15 miles outside of Minneapolis. It ranked 91st in the *Internet Retailer Top 500 Guide* as of 2013 and continues to perform strongly.

"On May 22, 2013, the Company announced that its multichannel retail platform will begin operating under a new name, ShopHQ. The new ShopHQ brand leverages the core identity of *Shop* and layers on simplicity, comfort and strength. The new ShopHQ brand also clearly states the aspiration of making ShopHQ a shopping destination. ValueVision has an active and loyal community of 1.2 million customers who shop the categories of Jewelry & Watches; Beauty, Health, & Fitness; Home & Consumer Electronics; and Fashion & Accessories. On a daily basis, we interact with customers – whenever and wherever they may be through a *Watch & Shop Anytime, Anywhere* experience – with unique product, special offers, entertaining hosts and guest experts, and educational demonstrations."[13]

TSC is based in Mississauga, Ontario and is Canada's largest and the only nationally televised 24-hour shopping service. Formerly known as the 'Canadian Home Shopping Club', it began in January 1987. Initially it didn't have a license to broadcast and therefore went on-air as an alphanumeric service. In 2013, it celebrated 25 years and "...has become a true multi-channel retailer and distributor through its leading online presence. The Shopping Channel today is recognized as Canada's premier success story in electronic and diversified retailing and is Canada's only 24/7, nationally televised shop-at-home service. Vendor products are featured on The Shopping Channel Web site, one of the top ecommerce sites in Canada generating 40+% of its annual sales. Currently, "The Shopping Channel reaches over 8.5 million households in Canada and is actively watched by more than 1.5 million viewers weekly. Our viewing audience is approximately 30% male and 70% female. Our customers range in age from 25 to 55+ and live in urban/suburban households. They are also very well-informed and savvy, and they know what they want. They will often do research and price comparisons before making a purchase." [14]

Direct Response Television (DRTV)

From the home of "But wait, there's more!" and "Call within the next 15 minutes and you'll get a second set absolutely free!", DRTV started in 1984 and became a household name by 1990 when many brand manufacturers began to use DRTV as part of their advertising mix. Many manufacturers found it to be a great lead generating initiative to either sell via the infomercial itself or couple that along with the retailer carrying the product. They found it gave options to their customers that really worked. It caught on quickly, and soon manufacturers, retailers and even services like insurance, mortgage and credit card companies added this initiative to their marketing budgets.

Direct Response TV is a significant partner within the home shopping/electronic retailing industry. Like the popular infomercials *Proactiv, Tony Horton's PX90* and the newly famed *My Best Pillow*, they all have positioned themselves to act as a reciprocal middleman between the traditional retailers on the one hand and the home shopping retailer on the other. As a consumer, one can purchase all three products either through DRTV, traditional retailers and/or shopping channels. The differences between each selling platform depends on the taste of the customer and perhaps the different configuration that it offers. This is one of the ways the DRTV world of sales differentiate themselves from other mainstream retailers. The only significant limitation to both the shopping channel and DRTV medium is that customers can't feel, touch or try the products before they buy it. This is of particular importance when it comes to bigger ticket items like mattresses, jewelry, fashion or home theatre electronics (to name a few). Knowing this sales constraint, the home retail arenas provide added flexibility and peace of mind with a no questions asked/no obligation thirty to sixty day (or longer) money back guarantee.

Strong media support is particularly crucial to DRTV. The average media buy is somewhere in the neighbourhood of $2 million per week. If you see a product regularly sold via infomercial, you know it is a campaign that is making money and working. (As a matter of context, as of 2012, Coca Cola's yearly worldwide marketing budget was said to be close to $2 billion).

Seamless Multi-Level Marketing

How many times have you been to a big box store only to find three or four different ways to get information about a product without having to move or even ask an attendant for assistance? Recently I was looking for some kitchen cupboards and took note of a great example of this:

> "In our business, we have to come up with interesting angles to make a compelling offer to our viewers. But what we're finding now, more than ever, is that that same customer travels back home to purchase that exact same product online instead of at the traditional store because our products are less expensive or we have added some type of *and you gets* which have tipped them over the fence to purchase."
>
> **-Duane Andrews,** *Director of Creative Services KingstarTV*

The product I could feel and touch was there in every colour and grain imaginable, made by a certain name brand I trusted would manufacture a product that would last. That exact product was advertised on a local

CHAPTER 1 — The Home Shopping Experience

breakfast morning show on TV, which made me feel like I was making a good choice – if the pros are endorsing it, it must be good. Finally, if you choose to, you could use your smartphone to potentially win a prize and get more information blasted right to the smartphone or tablet just by holding it up to the QR code. This type of availability allowed me to get immediate information in the form I chose to get it. The information was useful, clear and clearly the future of seamless multi-level marketing. The San Francisco 49ers are doing the same kind of communication with their stadium.

Traditional retailers (like it or not) are becoming the retail showrooms for the infomercial/online home shoppers. The home shopping customer may see a product in the store, then see it being offered on an infomercial at perhaps a better price but they still won't purchase it there. They will deliberately seek it out on their favourite shopping channel to make their purchase because they have a relationship and familiarity they are most comfortable with and perhaps are members of a loyalty program that earns them points.

Dollars Per Minute (DPM)

Every large retailer in the world is data driven. Every quarter, with microscopic accuracy, these numbers and comparisons build a history of trend behaviour of their customers' buying habits. Corporations and companies establish predictable markers to assist program planners, logistics, managers, buyers, human resources and merchandise managers alike to stay ahead of the business at hand. In the traditional retail stores, measurements range from pinpointing which teller at checkout is used more

> "A sense of autonomy has a powerful effect on individual performance and attitude. According to a cluster of recent behavioural science studies, autonomous motivation promotes greater conceptual understanding, better grades, enhanced persistence at school and in sporting activities, higher productivity, less burnout and greater levels of psychological well-being."
> **-Daniel H. Pink,** *Drive*

frequently, which SKU turns over the quickest and identifies peak hours for product purchases (to name only a few).

It shouldn't be a surprise then that the home shopping business is meticulously reliant on the buying history of their customers, trend products, host preference, guest preference and the product performance per product, per day, per minute. One of the most important measurements by far is what is referred to as 'dollars per minute' or DPM. The main factors include average ticket price, CPO (cost per order), return ratios (which can be higher than 35% with some categories), if it is a regular stock item, if the product is the network's own brand, if it's a GVS, etc. Home shopping channels normally look at a GVS average ticket price ranging from $29 - $199. Obviously there are exceptions, particularly in the electronics world, but on average, this is the general range. And there are statistics to back up these seemingly pleasing number combinations. Therefore, the higher the average ticket price, the higher the DPM is set for.

QVC (the highest daily target budget in the world) bases their DPM somewhere in the range of $6,000 to $10,000 per minute, depending on the unit price of the product sold. As stated earlier, if sales aren't tracking the targeted DPM within the first few minutes, the program planners and producers will already start moving their on-deck products into a new programming cycle and your product and the guest expert are yanked. No network can afford to be losing money when every minute counts. 'Time is money' is a cliché that is applied to many industries, and, like every sales environment, there is no 'time' to waste in home retail either. If you make the DPM, the programming will adjust accordingly. The guest expert and the product both earn their stripes to get more and more air time as targets are consistently hit. No matter whether you 'get the hook' after three minutes or after three shows, it's never a great feeling to get pulled and you wonder how you, as the guest expert, hindered or helped the sales that day. (More in Chapter 11, Assess Your Success.)

Future of the Online Industry

In a CNN news report during the 2nd Inaugural speech of President Obama, they compared the number of tweets in 2013 (1.1 million) to the tweets in 2009 (82,000). The same social media platform within four years has increased usage by over 700%. This vast change has forced every business to take notice of what is happening in the world of social media and with the dominant users who are 20 – 35 years of age. In fact, the grassroots tactics of marketing products via social media with guerilla-like commercials, *mom blogs* and other close-to-the-customer communication is now one of the most viable and recognized marketing options. What was once considered a non-traditional mode of entertainment not too long ago is now considered commonplace.

As Walmart changed the way customers and manufacturers bought and produced respectively, social media has heightened the expectations of what a consumer can expect. Today, we expect that we can access information and get anything we want, when we want it. And every business is strategically watching their quality assurance and fulfillment requirements like never before because of the limitlessness and power of the possibilities of social media. There are countless manufacturers that know the power of what one review can do to make or break their business. It can turn into 10,000 reviews within a day and 1 million in a few more days.

> "In two hours, Paul Revere covered thirteen miles. In every town he passed through along the way – Charlestown, Medford, North Cambridge, Menotomy – he knocked on doors and spread the word, telling local colonial leaders of the oncoming British, and telling them to spread the word to others. Church bells started ringing. Drums started beating. The news spread like a virus as those informed by Paul Revere sent out riders of their own, until alarms were going off throughout the entire region. Paul Revere's ride is perhaps the most famous historical example of a word-to mouth epidemic. It is safe to say that word-of-mouth is even the age of mass communications and multimillion dollar advertising campaigns-still the most important form of human communication."
>
> **-Malcolm Gladwell**, *The Tipping Point*

"On November 29, 2010, QVC achieved its highest volume in its 14-year history attracting 2 million sessions from more than 1.4 million unique visitors. On average, the website generates approximately 1/3 of OVC orders. On Cyber Monday, it accounted for nearly half of the company's total U.S. sales for the day."[15]

"Recently, AdAge looked into how content was really shared by users and how it goes viral. What they found was that its users sharing links with their social networks that really drive traffic. With their research, they found that for every Facebook share, there were nine clicks to the story. They also found that different types of content lead to different clicking behaviors. The longer a video is when posted, the more likely it is to be shared. From their research, AdAge believes that content truly goes viral when many people share the same link with their networks, not one or two people with huge networks sharing. What AdAge focuses on is that it's the content that drives people to share. With longer video, the more inspiring and engaging the content is. Content driven articles that create and stimulate conversation are what gets shared and goes viral." [16]

On July 18, 2013, history was made at the Emmy nominations where Internet based shows (the political drama *House of Cards* and the comedy *Arrested Development*) were nominated for multiple awards. On September 23, 2013, history was made once again when David Fincher won best director for *House of Cards*. The unusual side to this is these shows had never been broadcasted over the traditional television stations but still made it into the nominations because of the vast use of Netflix - (a subscription based on-demand Internet streaming media site). This type of Internet programming represents the future of broadcasting. How exciting!

Convenience, choice and comfort are huge selling features to the world now more than ever. With rapid innovations, world-wide access to every product and entertainment program, pushed by the ability to research and be entertained anywhere while you ride the bus or take the dog for a walk, social media has changed the way we do business and live our lives. No longer are we saying, "I wonder…" Answers and conventional programming from newspaper to television to documentaries are now at our fingertips playing on more platforms than ever before. It's a wonderful and liberating advantage that has affected and altered the way we all work and play.

The recent influx of devastating storms like Hurricane Sandy hitting New Jersey in late 2012 and carrying on through the better part of 2013 to most of North America has been unprecedented. What has been a significant difference is that many of the people affected by these natural disasters relied on social media to ask for help, inform and find loved ones and have provided up close and personal live eye reports for many of the news programs. Recently, Toronto, Canada experienced torrential downpours that flooded the infrastructure within minutes of the storm arriving. People were stranded in their cars, on buses, on the subways and their homes because of the heavy flow of water that accumulated in record time. So many people were calling for help that cell service was down. A stranded passenger along with thousands of others sitting on a commuter train flooded almost all the way to the second level of the train. She used her Facebook and Twitter pages to get the word out to the authorities for help.

In a report done by reporter Janet Shamlian for NBC on October 12, 2012, online retail shopping is a $200 billion business. The leaders at the time of printing were Amazon.com and Wal-Mart. In 2012 as the holiday shopping approached, both conglomerates were competing for same day delivery. Wal-Mart had well over 4,000 distribution points where Amazon.com had just over 60 and yet Amazon was still in the lead with consumers. Size sometimes doesn't matter.

TV and Web retailing, namely HSN, QVC, ShopHQ and TSC, are the leaders in direct response. Although all four home shopping retailers have built their business driving coast to coast television sales, as of 2011, Internet sales have increased 7 % for

"With the Olympic Games now available in more formats than in any other time in history, smartphones, tablets and websites are as prevalent as television, radios and newspapers, the old model is breaking down. NBC lost $250 million on the 2010 Vancouver Winter Olympics."
-**Rachel Brady**, *Globe and Mail Reporter* [17]

ShopHQ to a high of 31% for QVC, according to *Internet Retailer Top 500*. TSC Internet business has jumped to almost 40% online traffic and transactions. Where in the past each website drove most purchasers to the TV and telephone for sales, the balance has completely flipped, and as we speak, the TV portion of home shopping is becoming the occasional store window and is driving most business to the web for final transactions. In the summer of 2013, HSN did a complete overhaul of their website to increase ease and flexibility for their customers and in the fall of 2013, after almost thirty years, TSC rebranded itself with the new launch of its website, logo and on-air look and feel.

What Is Special about Home Shopping?

It is the original reality television without the curious plots and manufactured drama. One of the many unique aspects of the home shopping business is that we as guest experts and hosts are invited into the homes of our customers. We have the opportunity to create neighbourly, friendly and trusted relationships with our customers just by being on-air, relating to one another. One quick sentence made by the guest expert or host can spark memories and bring joy and fun to our customers. It is the sense of familiarity and even company that many of our customers look for as they enjoy their first cup of coffee in the morning or their last sip of hot chocolate before they retire to bed. As viewers, it makes us feel like we are all in this together. It comforts and entertains us. The guest experts who know those details are also the best in the business and they understand that building a trusting relationship is a huge part of their job.

The live aspect of the home shopping world brings many people into real-time excitement. In one of her last interviews before her sudden passing in 2013, soap opera actress Jeanne Cooper shared, "This is what entertainment is all about. To get you involved. I know a lot of people who have spent their life-times right along with me."

(Jeanne Cooper originated the role of Kathryn Chancellor in the long-standing soap opera *The Young and the Restless* and masterfully played that role for forty years).

CHAPTER 1 — The Home Shopping Experience

Used with Chad's permission

Chad Telfer (above) is one of the most successful, comical and highly relatable pitchmen and guest experts in Canada and the US today. He was my first interview when I started writing this book and shares, "A bonus to us has been the demise of the soap opera. We're getting some of those people who were sitting at home watching the soaps and are now looking for that void to be filled. I think they gravitate to the live, familiar aspect that we (home shopping) can provide. Part of my proof of that is following the comments on Facebook. When you read the comments on Facebook, you see that there are forty or fifty people who review the products and talk and gossip about the hosts and guest experts as if it was a soap opera. They review their favourite *characters* and their favourite products."

Transparency Is a Key Marketing Tactic

To be transparent in how you market and sell your product is one of the best sales tactics you can have. There are so many choices out there for consumers to go anywhere in the world to purchase therefore every business transaction must be held in high regard. No one wants to feel they are being taken for a ride or not getting the full story of what can be expected when we take the plunge to buy. When a family is researching a great vacation spot, most go online now to figure out what the options are. Do you believe the corporate descriptions of the resort site or the customers who have taken the time to write a review? Don't we all look at the customer reviews now to get the real scoop on what they experienced? Customer reviews work on so many levels and it has improved the level of quality delivered from any service provider, retailer and business. This is the new wave of social media. Let us be heard!

On a day to day basis, we are being blasted from all sides with information and opinions. The home shopping business is no different. As a regular part of business to maintain the trust factor, shopping networks also rely on customer reviews and ratings, good or bad. This type of communication has become a normal marketing initiative as it leaves an open door policy for each consumer to ultimately make his or her own choice.

Home Shopping Website Reviews

There is a fine balance of what people should be able to post online. Truthful opinions good or bad is our right to share and can be very helpful to other consumers. However, when people just want to use their keyboards as fists, this is when transparency may not be as necessary. This issue will continue to be a challenge for all businesses moving forward.

Here are two completely opposite reviews recently posted about the exact same product on a home shopping website: [18]

1. Posted by anonymous
Love my Pillows!
Overall Rating ***

"Thank God I am not having the same problem that some of the other writers are talking about. I love my pillows. I put 2 in my room and gave the other two to my children and they haven't made a complaint yet. When I first took them out of the box, I wondered how a pillow this soft could offer you any support. Well they do offer me the support I need. So I am very thankful to *name brand* for offering these pillows at such a great buy."

Would you recommend this product as a gift?
Yes
Who would this be a perfect gift for?
Families

2. Posted by Anonymous
Cannot Stand This Weird Puffy Hard Pillow!
Overall Rating *
"I tried to like this pillow but finally tossed it from my bed and returned to my old pillows. My husband said this pillow is only tolerable under his original pillow to watch TV with. What a waste of money. We sure were sold a fairytale story on how great this pillow would be to rest your head on. When I put my head on it I sank into it so much that the sides covered my ears and blocked my hearing - very weird! I wanted to ship them back but my husband said just give them away to someone who has no pillows at all rather than pay shipping cost for such a disappointing product. The cording around the gussets also hurt my ears & face. I guess because the pillow stuffing is so firm it's hard and creases your skin. It is very difficult to describe how weird this pillow is."
Would you recommend this product as a gift?
No

Predictable Show Structure

Television daytime infotainment shows (as they are often referred to), like ABC's *Good Morning America*, CBS' *This Morning* and the most successful morning shows of all, NBC's *The Today Show*, have long since relied upon predictable programming, taking the lead from the wheel format structure from the radio. The clock face is divided into pie pieces where each small section of time in that hour is dedicated to a specific item of business. A typical show structure might be news every 15 minutes on the quarter hour, sports and entertainment on the half hour and traffic on the 1's every 10 minutes. This predictability works around most morning routines in almost every home in North America and provides information at certain times that considers daily family household schedules. Similarly, home shopping also uses a time structure that caters to busy schedules, one that their customers can rely upon to get the information they want. Each shopping network loyalist knows when a new GVS will be announced and recapped and they're always ready to receive email and Twitter teases of upcoming shows and celebrities.

Matching Time Slots to Customers' Buying Patterns

There is an art to matching up time of day with customers and with the variety of products offered. Shows and programming are created based on who is buying when. For instance, beauty, around the home and jewelry is sold more predominantly within the weekdays. The technology, collecting and sporting categories tend to show up more predominantly on the weekends. (More in Chapter 10, The Three P's).

Need for Speed

We all want things when we want them in exactly the way we expect them. And why wouldn't we? In the world of YouTube and twenty-four hour news networks, speed is a normal component of everyday life now. The more information that can be crammed into the same amount of time is a kind of badge of honour. One of the most important aspects to consumerism is speed. Speed of response, speed of delivery, speed of fulfillment and turnaround. Heck, our lives as we know them are based on *how fast we can get it*. You only have to look at the success of Amazon.com that has worked out a way for their customers to only have to click once to get what they want. These smart marketers know that they have a very short window of opportunity to close the sale with their customers. They recognize that without the option of speed, they may lose the impulse of the customer. With that one click of my cursor at my desk in my house while I water the garden and plan for what we're going to cook for dinner that night, I have paid for a book on horticulture, I have purchased a set of 1000 thread count blue spruce king sheets and a beautiful dress that I'm going to wear to my best friend's wedding, and I also clarified my shipping preference. Now I can get on with the rest of my day knowing that I will be receiving presents later in the week.

Currently in Europe, there is a test market that has added a *buy* button right on the TV converter itself. All you have to do is press that button and because the address is tied to the cable bill, they know who and where to send the packages to.

In a recent statistic on attention spans of the average adult movie watcher, eight minutes is all we have to spare until we get bored with a movie. That seems like a lifetime! In past, the shopping channel market sales loop for the guest expert was somewhere between six or seven minutes: open, hook, entertain, demonstrate and ask for business. That was the approximate turn-over standard both host and guest expert would take to do a full pitch. Now the loop is less than three minutes. You can't take away any of the quality of information, you just have to get to the point a whole lot faster.

Brand Theatre

Just a little while ago, I was shopping…oh, I mean researching… and came across a line of home décor bedding branded by a reality star. Now, I'm not necessarily intimating that the brand and employees haven't researched the merits of top-of-bed, but I would venture to guess that this affordable line is yet another avenue to extend brand reach. This type of category might perhaps reach a new demographic and for that, I tip my hat to the marketing and business development team. Name brands are perhaps not more important, but certainly as important to the consumer (and therefore the marketer/distributor) than ever before. As a result, no longer is the home retail network gambling on new, never seen before products. There has to be a lead-in familiarity, proven desirability and sustainability with the products gathering on shelves, and mostly that involves national brands.

Our sales agency recently had the pleasure of pitching a new brand to arguably one of the most successful retailers in Canada. It took our sales director six months of perseverance to find meaningful ways to stay in touch in order to get an appointment. With this retailer, it is extremely common to have to wait two years to finally meet with them. Many times, wonderful vendors never get even one chance. We were the lucky ones this past spring and we knew it. As I clicked in with my power high heel boots and walked the hallowed halls of nearly one hundred years of history with my show-and-tell suitcase in tow, it hit me:

"You are now playing with the big boys. This is your one shot, kiddo," I whispered to myself.

Our team was well rehearsed and knew our overall customer very well as each of us in our lifetime had grown up shopping at their nationwide stores. We were led back into one of the meeting rooms and after initial introductions, we got right to the business at hand as the buyer had communicated she was on a very tight timeline. Sitting face to face opposite the 16-foot table, our team of three highlighted the individual products which our colleagues seemed very interested in. If one had walked by to see us all in action, it would have represented a textbook tableau of proud ambassadors representing their side of the story. Then, the question that seems to be of ever-increasing frequency in boardrooms today came: "Do many people know this brand? If I put it on the shelves right now, would anyone recognize it as something they would trust and therefore buy?" A valid question, and unfortunately one we could not answer with an unequivocal YES!

The buyer went on to say, "Here's my concern. Unlike most times when we have a lead-time of 12 or 18 months, we want these products delivered in two months. We are working on small quantities to start in order to test whether this new category will *go* or not. If we see some quick turnovers, our plan is to roll it out across the country within twelve months. We love your product and actually see a great fit with what we are currently carrying. My hesitancy lies with the fact that no one knows your brand. Are you doing any grassroots, social media marketing, perhaps conversations with young moms and other marketing initiatives to quickly increase awareness?"

Well, we didn't get in and that was the big reason why. We were invited back once we had done our own marketing. Large or small, multi-level marketing is a must whether you are the retailer, home shopper or vendor. The manufacturer has to play a part in a stirring up excitement, preference and ultimately brand insistence. When traditional retail markets are not turning their products over fast enough, retailers are pointing fingers back at the manufacturers wondering what they're doing about promoting *their* product. The same is true with home shopping except many times, unsold items will be shipped back to the manufacturer with an invoice.

How to Get Products on the Air

When my buyers give me a new product to sell on-air, I go through a quick checklist of what I will do to differentiate my sales style and marry that with the product. I try to quickly identify how many ways I can:

- Sell dreams, hope and beauty that are tangible for the customers to see and get
- Demonstrate and show its value and how it solves problems
- Prove it's a time saver and will truly benefit our customers
- Prove that it makes life more beautiful, longer, youthful, and easier for them

In a recent magazine interview, Kevin Harrington (Infomercial Guru and entrepreneur) sited several points critical to the success of getting products on the air. This is Kevin's checklist:

"**1. Is it a mass-market problem solver?** If the product doesn't solve a problem, people aren't going to be willing to buy it. Although many of the shopping channels are more interested in products and guests who already are recognizable – (there is huge value in market familiarization and pre-selling power), uniqueness and *never seen before in this configuration* is still one paramount ingredient. You will have to prove that in your meeting with competitive comparisons all the way through to the presentation.

2. **Does it have unique features and benefits?** Is it different enough from what is already out there? Is there already a "good enough" solution for this problem?
3. **Does it have good stage presence?** Harrington looks for products that have the 'magical demo.' Immediate, visible results sell.
4. **Can you explain it?** People don't buy fluff; there has to be a viable explanation of how and why the product works. Be prepared to back up your claims.
5. **How does it compare?** You must be able to prove how it works by comparison. Before and after pictures or side-by-side demos remove doubt from the buyer's mind.
6. **Can someone else back up the claims?** Establish credibility through documented third-party studies or recommendations and quotes from associations, doctors, engineers or experts who can testify that the product works.
7. **Can you defend it?** Raise and answer obvious questions. Ask questions that the consumer is likely to ask about the product, and then answer them.
8. **Does it offer big results?** Harrington says he likes products that offer a *magical transformation*.
9. **Is it multifunctional?** Adding extra features to a product can double the perceived value.
10. **Does it come with an incredible offer?** Think of the *But wait! There's more!* approach used in infomercials. Can you present a powerful offer at an incredible price?

When you consider an idea for a new product, put it to the test by asking the questions that have made the Ginsu Knife and the Ab Isolator household names. Then you can confidently ask people to 'Act now!'"[19]

Massive Access

The chance to get on-air with your product is beyond exciting and potentially very lucrative but you have to eliminate as much perceived and real risk as possible. At minimum, the Canadian shopping channel reaches more than 1.5 million viewers per week, and at the most, QVC reaches over 250 million households worldwide per day. Many companies therefore want access to shopping channel markets to get in front of the high volume potential of business. It is about making money, after all. It's similar to why traditional retailers want to rent space within the largest malls in the country. Let's take The Mall of America for instance, in Bloomington, Minnesota. It attracts over 40 million visitors annually. (That is approximately the combined populations of North Dakota, and Iowa...or more than the entire population of Canada as of 2013). Who wouldn't want that kind of traffic?

Home Shopping channels are always on the lookout for new innovative products, particularly from entrepreneurs and inventors, but as we said earlier, the risk is great if there is no former brand awareness. For this reason, buyers have been known to use the popular entrepreneurial TV shows such as *Shark's Tank* in the US or *Dragon's Den* in Canada. These shows act as their audition rooms to source new products because there already is a certain amount of familiarity which can be used to their advantage.

Recently, I became aware of a prospective vendor who drove a 45-foot pink bus from Florida up I-95 to Toronto, Canada to sell their products to the buyer of that category. They invited the buyers to come into their world (on the bus) where the models and the guest expert put on a full 3-minute show/pitch to sell the experience, and the product line. At first you think, it sounds like a huge undertaking and is this all worth it? It is and the right products can do exceptionally well on-air.

You just have to be sure to do ample due diligence on how to approach the respective shopping network you are interested in approaching. Each website will tell you exactly how they work. It is a fairly simple operation no matter who you target. If you're already accustomed to pitching products as a new vendor to other distributors, this process is much the same. There are options to start the process as web-only to see how your product does. It's generally a lower risk way to go about it and can often work well for the smaller manufacturer. Buying trends everywhere continue to change and evolve. Take a chance if you believe your product has potential to be sold on-air and if you have the infrastructure to support the potential of big business. Most of the shopping networks have their own online vendor portals and hotlines that you can glean valuable information from.

Vendors' Eyes Wide Open

The best buyers align themselves with great vendors who deliver what they ask for the first time. Most buyers are juggling many different products and vendors within their category and the pressure is always on them to make fast decisions with products that will sell. When presenting your ideas whether you are new or a returning vendor, make the buyers decisions simple and easy by being a turnkey service provider. Become an avid fan of this type of medium and do all the due diligence you require in order to determine whether your product may be a good fit. Not all products suit the home shopping format or audience.

People often send me products or promos saying, "This is the perfect product for a shopping channel." Really? Not necessarily. To find that out on your own one should take note of competitors that may be currently selling on-air. Watch how it is presented, sold and produced. Ask yourself, would your product fit into the model? All the big four shopping channels have at least fifteen to well over twenty-eight years (and counting) of business history and they know, to the second, what works and what doesn't sell to their customers. Use their current shows to educate yourself on what will work, and what won't and don't try to re-invent the wheel. If you feel there is merit to your product, go in with a similar success product with a differentiating spin.

Be real about your expectations. As an example - Who provides the LC (letter of credit)? It is usually the vendor. If that is the case, you in essence bankroll the entire project and are forced to wait until show day to see how the sales go. That is why I encourage you to be very careful with how you approach selling to a shopping channel and do your thorough due diligence. What is most alluring and why the risk is often worth it, is the access to a huge swath of customers you might never be able to hit in a decade of strong business. There is certainly high risk but the potential for high reward is often what keeps all vendors looking for that one shot.

It's vitally important to have a strong and seasoned on-air guest as part of the vendor's success plan. Vendors may think that selling on-air is just like training employees or holding a marketing seminar. It is not. Many vendors try to cut costs by hiring an in-house person either from the marketing department or the front desk person who is an extravert even though they may have no TV selling experience. It is almost always a mistake because the pressure to entertain, sell with style, perform under pressure and make it all seem effortless is a skill and something very few can just pick up. Invest in the sales people who specialize in this art-form of selling.

I remember speaking with the fashion celebrity Steven Cojocaru who regularly appeared on *Entertainment Tonight* and the *Today Show* (among many others). He was selling his beautiful fashion line and I asked him if the skills were transferable from his vast experience on the red carpets and entertainment shows to the arena of home shopping. He shared that he was shocked how different the experience was. He had to make very different adjustments to his style and he had to speed up his pace considerably in order to be a successful on-air seller.

Guaranteed sales (meaning the networks will only pay for what sold regardless of original purchase order size), is, for the most part the usual course of business with most shop-at-home networks, particularly if the vendor is new. Anything that doesn't sell that day is shipped directly back to the manufacturer. This can present all kinds of problems as any vendor will know and is often where the biggest risk lies. For instance, the network intentionally or unintentionally may sit on the inventory for a long while before returning the goods. This delay decreases the vendors' ability to resell it to an after-market or secondary retailer. Most of the other pitfalls are similar to working with any other retail partner. As long as the vendor has a good handle on the risks and rewards of doing business with shopping channels, the relationship can be lasting and greatly rewarding.

Pitching Your Product to Buyers

First point: Never cut out the infrastructure within the company. Go through the right channels if you want to make fast friends and not fast enemies. Even if you know the president of the company, initiate conversations with the appropriate buyers just the same and copy him or her with relevant communications.

Remember who your customer is. They are busy, overworked, price, customer and product knowledgeable, budget obsessed and always looking to be the hero to earn a better and bigger bonus at the end of the year. Buyers meet with suppliers and vendors all day so they really have seen it all before. They have to be wowed when you come in. You only get the first minute to make a winning impact and you only get one shot to get it right. Does this pressure to perform sound familiar?

This selling game is all about momentum and speed of turnaround. Take the straightest route to get where you want to go. Brand names, as we've said before, have a perceived *safer currency* and there is obvious historical data to back that up. One reason again is because customers already recognize it and on some level have a relationship with it. A brand name is an asset and resonates with decision makers. Use it to your advantage. Be sure you are 200% confident in your ability to sell the product, concept, the company and most importantly that you can be trusted to fulfill the orders on time in exactly the way the samples were designed and fabricated. The product has to be beyond extraordinary in quality, affordability and uniqueness. You have to have all financing and operational logistics including shipping on time and ready to go. This includes all testing results and documentation proving its validity, longevity, trademarks, patents etc.

Leave Your Porsche at Home

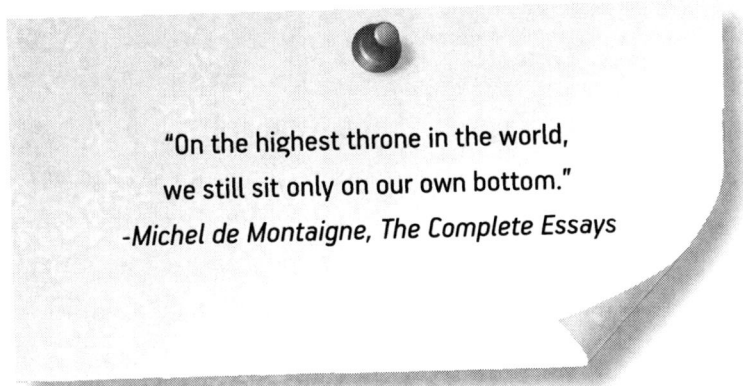

"On the highest throne in the world, we still sit only on our own bottom."
-Michel de Montaigne, *The Complete Essays*

If you are the prospective vendor (for the first time especially), and you're pitching your product to most any retail buyer, leave the Porsche at home. I mean that both literally and figuratively. Particularly if most of the parking lot is full of more working-class vehicles. You have to know your customers and the culture of the corporation. Yes, walk in confidently with your pinstripe suit and shiny cufflinks and fabulous shoes. Yes, nail your pitch with all the pizzazz and showmanship you have to bring. Leave nothing behind in the meeting room, but know who you are talking to. Buyers work their tails off and may or may not be making as much coin as you are. If a buyer sees you are doing extremely well, you might have a harder time getting the margins you need to make the deal happen. There are many factors that play a part in overall decision making. Best advice, keep your profile low-key. Be aware of who your customers are and what your expectation of the meeting is.

On the flipside, there are many circumstances to give the Porsche a wash and to drive it. For instance, if I am selling my house and if the real estate agent representing me shows up in a grimy looking ten-year old car, I'm concerned I haven't made the right choice because I don't know how successful this person will be at selling high ticket items. This is the world of showbiz, after all, and the timing to press the image of success is appropriate for some circumstances. As stated earlier, consider who your audience is and the type of impression you want to convey to get what you want.

The Importance of Face-to-Face Meetings

Winning any buyer's time and attention comes down to meeting with them in person. Emails and phone calls work well to confirm meetings and provide follow up thank-you messages...etc. Just like the real estate agent who is negotiating bids with three other couples, you have to be there ready to make decisions and adjustments to meet the needs of your customers at that moment.

In your presentation to the buyers, be sure to include these three solutions:

Eliminate the Risk   Show Me   Prove It

ELIMINATE THE RISK	SHOW ME	PROVE IT
• Answer what's in it for them • Neutralize the perceived risk on every level	• Provide competitive comparisons	• Prove that you and your manufacturing operations have what it takes to fulfill orders on time without delay or any quality issues
• Include customer testimonials and other proof of brand recognition	• Answer why should they care about your product	• Prove that there are buying customers ready to purchase
• Answer what kinds of guarantees, safety and quality assurance, warranties, exclusivity and patents are offered	• Build an atmosphere of partnership	• Be extremely transparent and upfront with your approach

The Trifecta of Marketing - Brand Awareness, Recognition and Insistence

The business of building a brand is insurmountable for many companies. As we mentioned earlier, in the direct response world of marketing, the average media buy per week can easily be $2 million just to launch the brand. If sales don't work that first week, there's only so much time and money any company is willing to invest.

If you as the vendor can't prove your pre-sales strength, most shopping channels won't consider taking a risk on even a small order. Margins are tighter than ever before and no business has the time or resources to waste on possibilities. They need virtually guaranteed throughput. With that strength, shopping channels can provide a *unique offer* by configuring exclusive packages that can't be duplicated anywhere else in the world. (For instance, 100 exclusive recipes of the best restaurant cuisine in the world or one price for any sized mattress.)

Here are two examples that show how marketers and manufacturers push brand recognition to brand insistence. They both have opposite target markets and both have executed extraordinary business results. The first product is targeted to women - The Genie™ Bra - and the second product is the popular workout videos - PX90, Insanity and Asylum Video workouts from Team Beach Body. Who could believe that such general targets vs. such micro targets could do as well as these producers do?

1. Genie™ Bra:

Target – All Women:

This was their key promotion posted on Facebook and their website when they launched in 2011:

"The revolutionary new Genie™ Bra should be gracing the drawer of every woman's lingerie collection. There's no spillage, no back fat, wires, hooks or adjusting straps in sight. It's basically what a dream bra is made of, only this is reality and it still provides you plenty of support. There is a waiting list of over 15,796 prior to its retail launch and has sold over one million in the USA in under four weeks. It's simple sizing, just match it to your dress size, is perfect for those who find it a hassle to find and try-on hundreds of bras." [20]

This company is a great example of how they used all possible media angles to reach every woman on the planet to move through the perfect triad of brand awareness to brand recognition to brand insistence. Their sophisticated multi-social media marketing programs including reviews of support on the *Dr. Oz* show and others, the use of top direct response marketer *Guthy Renker* and launching on QVC followed by TSC July 2011. They also started appearing on traditional store shelves. And their product does what it says it's going to do. This is the dream scenario and what every manufacturer should be taking notice of. Besides their website, Genie™ Bra invites their customers to include conversation on their own personal blogs. This strategy works both ways to heighten awareness, show the newcomer to their site what other people are saying about their product and as a personal strategy to each blogger to increase their hits, moving higher in the world of SEO's (search engine optimizations).

The Genie™ Bra is a unique example of how, by tweaking the design offer incrementally, a crescendo of excitement and *gotta have* mentality is built. In the beginning, customers would receive six bras in total: two flesh colour, two white and two black. The price didn't change, the configuration didn't change for months, and yet, they kept selling. As of the summer 2012, they had added bright pastel colours and sales continued to soar. They have capitalized on retaining their current customers and continue to attract more and more every day because of the increased options to women's wardrobes while maintaining overall comfort and options. Now, there are copycats as you'd expect to take away some of the market share. The cycle continues to push lead manufacturers to constantly differentiate the offers.

2. **Target** – Weekend Warriors

Team Beachbody™ is a master direct response marketer who has reinvented their niche marketing by producing boot camp style intense workout programs. *PX90, Body Beast, Insanity* and *Asylum* among others. The company has a combination of a compelling infomercial campaign and shopping channel presence, raw gritty viral testimonial videos, nutrition, free coaching, celebrating before and after shots including receiving a t-shirt after you can prove you did the workout and more. These highly intense workouts are targeted only to serious athletes looking for intense cross training. They are extremely good at building a club atmosphere where you are assigned a personal coach who will keep you feeling included and excited about your progress. You can track your workouts, compete against other athletes who are posting their results and you get rewarded for your efforts. They have built on their team atmosphere to deepen retention and brand insistence.

Quality Assurance

31-page test report for one product

If I'm out in my everyday life and someone knows that I work in this industry, inevitably the question comes up about believability. People will ask, "Are those products as good as they say they are?"

Quality assurance (QA) is what our business is built on for the exact concerns these people above shared. No business can afford to either have their brand reputation spoiled nor can the manufacture afford to take poor quality products back. All QA departments follow stringent legal parameters, often requiring third party testing and no one, even the guest expert, is allowed to oversell products. Guest experts can actually be held liable if they make false claims without the proper back up and credible support.

Shopping channel networks have extremely high quality assurance programs. Stringent test results and clinical testing is a mandatory portion of the scrutiny required before it gets past the buyer's office door. All categories have to provide documented 3rd party testing from reputable companies and provide as many quality classifications as possible. It's a practice as regular as assigning a purchase order number to an invoice. There are obvious reasons for this requirement, but now when one bad Twitter review can affect the success or failure of a product, it is pushing the quality of workmanship and raw materials to a new level. And one of the many reasons why 'made in Canada' and 'product of the USA' is bringing buyers from all over the world back to our shores to take notice. In fact, on January 15, 2012, ABC news aired a story that Walmart USA will be spending $50 billion dollars over the next twenty years to promote 'Made in America' products. As of 2014, their domestic commitment has increased even more. The largest retailer in the world changed the way business is done today thereby affecting us all. It will be interesting to see how this new domestic pledge will *rollback within the retail industry.

*Rollback is a Walmart term used when there is a change within the price of a product.

SOURCES

1. http://www.celticthunder.ie/node/101228
2. http://www.youtube.com/watch?v=qKjr_uTfY30
3. http://www.youtube.com/watch?v=ydfjSbieBg4
4. http://en.wikipedia.org/wiki/Joy_Mangano
5. http://www.qvc.com/AboutQVCMiles.content.html
6. http://www.youtube.com/watch?v=ElqZms_SUjg
7. From the article "Why we spend" Globe Life (July 24, 2012 section L, written by Andrea Woo, Vancouver).
8. http://en.wikipedia.org/wiki/Levi's_Stadium
9. http://www.hsni.com/about.cfm
10. www.reuters.com/finance/stocks/companyProfile?symbol=HSNI.O and http://www.top500guide.com/top-500/the-top-500-list/
11. http://www.asm.qvc.com/at_a_glance.html
12. http://www.internetretailer.com/shop/2013-mobile-commerce-400.html Internet Retailer Top 500 Guide as of 2012
13. Internet Retailer Top 500 Guide as of 2013 and http://shophq.mwnewsroom.com/
14. July 2012 TSC Vendor Communication and their website: www.theshoppingchannel.com
15. http://www.qvc.com/AboutQVCMiles.content.html
16. http://www.themarketresearcheventblog.com/2012/03/how-do
17. Globe and Mail newspaper, Monday, July 30, 2012.
18. QVC website – 2012
19. Article in the January 2011 edition of SUCCESS http://www.success.com/articles/1235--more-1-on-1-kevin-harrington-on-top-10-qualities-of-a-hot-seller
20. http://www.geniebra.com/press/pr-2012-01a.php

Here are the direct links to access vendor information or you can always go to their home page to access the information you require:

QVC: *http://vendorportal.qvc.com/SitePages/Home.aspx*

HSN: *https://view.hsn.net/ProductSubmittal/default.aspx*

ShopHQ: *https://www.shophq.com/pom2k.aspx?category=cc/vendor&page=vendor_steps&title=vendor_steps&displaytype=5&ft=0&icid=BN-_-VENDORS-_-N&cm_re=BN-_-VENDORS-_-N*

TSC: *http://www.theshoppingchannel.com/go/aboutus#4*

CHAPTER 1
The Home Shopping Experience

1. Home Shopping on every social media platform is here to stay and is ever growing. There will be more focus on creating a one-on-one experience for the consumer which will both enlighten and educate even more.

2. Transparency is the key on all levels of communication and selling.

3. To sell out on any shopping channel, be thorough with your due diligence regarding every aspect of your product, the industry, your competitors, who's purchasing and who's not and the reasons why.

4. Brand insistence is the ultimate goal. How you get there depends on how well you perform the above three points.

CHAPTER 2

THE GUEST EXPERT

"To do things well, you'll need to cultivate a deep understanding of yourself—not only what your strengths and weaknesses are but also how you learn, how you work with others, what your values are, and where you can make the greatest contribution. Because only when you operate from strengths can you achieve true excellence."
-Peter F. Drucker

One of the most important qualities a pitch person has to have is to know who they are. It's one of the most important and salable skills you can have because no matter what challenges arise during the sales day, you are grounded and confident enough to get through whatever challenges or surprises may develop. If you love performing without a net, entertaining and exuding intense amounts of excitement and energy, have the ability to connect with people quickly, change your actions and alter your message on a dime and you don't sweat the small stuff, the role of the on-air guest expert may be for you!

CHAPTER 2 — THE GUEST EXPERT

Why do we do it? We do it for that one chance. To have that one moment where everything that got you to that studio comes together and you have that perfect show. You sell out! You have worked for months, and most likely years for this first chance. You've been here before but you've never had that perfect night. Is this the one? People say that getting to this point is hard. What is even harder is staying there. Every show is potentially your last show, so no matter how out-of-gas you feel, you've got to be able to step into another realm. That's what it's all about.

No matter what your expertise, you will learn how to deliver your best performance on command and be able to repeat it time and time again! As a guest expert you make your living by excelling in the moment. One needs to be consistent and one needs to stay in the game with a keen belief in your abilities to not only deliver when it counts, but also attract the best brand of products and categories to give you a trend cycle that is lasting. On the studio floor, you have to be able to manage and compartmentalize massive amounts of pressure. It takes a unique type of personality and skillset to sell on live television, but this kind of pressure is what we're wired for. If targets aren't met, depending on the life cycle of the product line and the on-air guest's track record, that one poor showing may end the opportunity to sell that product or to ever be asked back.

A guest expert needs to have some winning qualities and a myriad of skills in order to be successful. Following is a list of the most important skills and qualities. They are essential for the success of a guest expert:

- Ambitious and consistent
- An extraordinary ability to sell anything
- Compelling personality and relatable
- Empathetic thinker
- Entertaining and engaging
- Excellent memory and a quick study

- Exceptional communicator and storyteller
- Extreme versatility
- Extremely well organized, disciplined and prepared for any eventuality
- High energy levels
- Highly aware of his/her own strengths and weaknesses and knowing how to manage them
- Highly likeable and approachable
- Humourous and able to laugh at one's self
- Intensely curious
- Looks good and in good physical and mental shape
- On-air experience and very much at home in front of the camera
- Passionate for what you are selling
- Persistent, tenacious and highly focused
- Quick witted and fast on his/her feet
- Strong vocabulary and diction
- Thick skinned – one needs to be able to take criticism and utilize it positively
- Ultimate multi-tasker and can stay on track regardless of distractions

Effectively utilizing the skills and qualities relayed while on-camera without a safety net is another matter entirely. Following is a random list of just a few experiences, scenarios and circumstances that a guest expert may encounter where some of the above qualities and skills will be necessary in order to succeed. It does not take a rocket scientist to appreciate how and why all of the skills and qualities are so important, and:

- It is obvious that a successful guest expert must possess **an extraordinary ability to sell anything** no matter what the circumstances.
- Being highly **likeable, approachable** and **relatable** is so important in this public medium. You may remember the early days' of ABC's *Good Morning America* with the host David Hartman. He wasn't the crisply

dressed, perfect looking anchor we are more accustomed to seeing today. Some would even have said he was funny looking, and most importantly - he wasn't a journalist. He was an actor and knew nothing about interviewing hard news stories. When he started in 1975, journalists in the booth would cringe as he posed questions to some of the most important political figures of that time, but the viewership continued to grow stronger. Hartman's contention was always the same. I'm not interested in asking questions to impress my guests with how smart I am, I'm asking questions our viewers would want to know. He had it right and enjoyed a career of more than twelve years, which at the time was one of the longest runs for any host.

- The more **versatility** you have as a professional, the more opportunity you'll have at any given time. When there is so much on the line every time you work, when one door shuts on your face, you have to be able to react quickly without any time lost to open the next window. Hugh Jackman (Tony award winner for *Boy from Oz*, Oscar nominee for *Les Miserables*, and Wolverine of *X-Men* movie fame) said it best in an interview with anchor Chris Cuomo on CNN: "Versatility for me growing up in Australia was my survival."

- Part of your job is that you have got to be available. Programming changes happen all the time for various reasons. For this and other reasons, the guest expert often needs to be available and 'at the ready' to fill-in with very short notice. If you are not ready, someone else will be and that would likely reduce future offers for your services. Being **extremely well organized, disciplined and prepared for anything** is obviously important to be ready and available when called upon.

- GVS's and other daily blockbusters are set up differently on all of the big four networks. Regardless of the configuration or time slots, rest assured, there can be a lot of shows all crammed into a short time period. The expectation is to sell out for every program time slot. Is it any wonder why tremendously **high energy levels** and **ambition** are a must for any successful guest expert?

- A regular scenario on and around the set will find you talking live on-air with an IFB (interruptible foldback earpiece) in your ear, with the producer and/or sound people giving you messages and directions in your ear. Some of those messages may be helpful, others may not be. There will likely be three or more TV monitors in front of you, and still many others above you, the cameras will surround you; the show coming up next may be doing preparatory work right next to your set that might consist of a lighting crew climbing up and down ladders, cutting or hammering, dropping and opening boxes of inventory and the upcoming guest expert may be coming and going. An example scenario like this makes it clear why it is necessary for the guest expert to have **on-air experience and be very much at home on camera.** In addition, among other things, it can be clearly seen why one must be an **ultimate multi-tasker who can keep things on track regardless of the distractions.**

- If sales are not going well, you will be offered suggestions to alter your pitch and/or your style by the buyer, the producer, the director. Although these come across as suggestions, they could be construed to be criticisms of you and your work. You therefore need to be **thick skinned to accept the criticism and utilize it positively**.

- You need to know how to share the **passion, excitement and pride** of every detail of the products you sell.

Rules and Regulations

Prior to your show arrival, you will receive a guest package outlining all of the rules and regulations specific to that particular network. If you are new to the network, you will be asked to come to the studio for an orientation and/or on-air training before your actual show date. Each network has their own version of training and some are gratis, not including travel and lodging (if applicable) and others the vendor has to pay for. At QVC as a matter of interest, they have what's called QVC University. It is meant only for the guest expert to attend. No other partner or vendor representative is included in the invitation or the tutorial. They have a designated department of professionals who have you run through your entire pitch, demonstrations, any primary and secondary film footage or any other enhancements you have planned for your show. The team of experts will coach you on how to augment your style and presentation to suit their customers and the QVC culture. This approach is similar with all of the networks.

According to Chad Telfer (quoted earlier) who has been working at QVC for many years, "QVC training is awesome. They help you to establish parameters and limits on what you can or cannot do and say. It helps to alleviate some of the pressures you're feeling by being crystal clear on what your role is and isn't. Their strong direction helps to affirm all you are doing right and guides you out of possible pitfalls, completely taking away the mystery as much as possible."

Directives such as, the guest expert never mentions the item number of a product are provided for in the rules and regulations. Every network has their trademark *feel* and the guidelines provided are for the most part, non-negotiable. Just follow their guidelines and all will be well. These networks do know what works for their customers; the corporate culture and the clarity of expectations make for a smoothly produced show. By the way, if you're doing your job, you won't have time to talk about item numbers anyway.

The Chosen Ones

What do a tradeshow seller, a police officer and an actor have in common? They all have potential transferable skills to sell on TV.

The Tradeshow Seller

As a tradeshow pitch person, you have some of the greatest transferable sales skills to suit TV selling. You have the thick skin and have the ability to multi-task with fluidity. You know how to walk the aisles to drum up more business and you are ultra-aware of the connection you are making - listening for when you need to speed up your speech, slow it down, make people laugh, to engage, be silly and outrageous or whisper to get their attention. It's a joy to watch the best in this business and is a real art form.

If you've ever sold at tradeshows, you know it is difficult work. The tradeshow seller is often exposed to more products, people and pitch styles within the trade show circuit than most anyone else. They are accustomed to learning about multiple products and know how to use a variety of pitch levels, pace and attention-getting tactics. It takes a certain type of person to be able to sell and talk about their products for ten hours per day, day after day. You have to be excited about standing in the middle of your 10 x 10 royal blue draped booth trying to grab the attention of hundreds of people (or few people) that may or may not care. If they are not in need of your product or the tradeshow itself doesn't fit into the demographics of your target, there's nothing you can do to get them interested. If you get some action into your booth - you hope they'll stick with you long enough for you to get to the 'good stuff' of the presentation. You learn very quickly that if you can't say the good stuff in less than ten seconds, you'll lose them.

All of these skills work well for the on-air selling discipline. Keep the intensity, keep the content, keep the need for speed delivery, but be ready to perhaps adapt your pitch style. The typical tradeshow spiel can often come across as talking *at* people and can be interpreted as too artificial, almost appearing like the snake oil salesman of yesteryear if out of context. Keep all the content and excitement you share for your product, but consider adjusting how you package it to suit the listener and the intimate environment of the TV and Internet medium. Sometimes pitch people can also be too product, information or *spectacle* focused. Here's a simple way to check if you need to augment your performance: Call a friend or whomever you have a good relationship with and invite them over for a coffee. Talk to them (just talk) about why they would need the product. Let go of your pitch style for that moment and see if your message still gets across. You'll soon know if you're delivery needs to be augmented, especially if it sounds either fake or canned in some way. Make the adjustments accordingly and layer that knowledge into your performance as you build your pitch. If you are able to do this, your time on-air will connect to your audience.

The Police Officer

Used with Simon Fraser's permission

One of the most engaging on-air guest experts I have seen is this gentleman (seen above), who worked as a full time police sergeant for over twenty-five years. Part of the police training is to perfect how to be a successful communicator with many different types of people at the same time. You have to be able to deal with tremendous amounts of urgent pressure, be fully engaged with not only what you are saying and not saying, but know exactly where your audience is and how they are receiving your message. It has trained him to know how to get people's attention, gain people's trust quickly and he knows how to throw his weight around when needed.

The Actor

At the 64th Prime Time Emmy Awards, the illustrious career of the late Andy Griffith was publicly honoured by long-time friend and fellow actor/

director Ron Howard. He described him as an actor who had "…an unwavering respect for the audience."

Great actors have tremendous respect for their audiences, the script, the writer's intent, and they know how to access the best of themselves to fly within the structure of a play. The number one job as an actor is to entertain, thrill, connect, excite and empathize with the audience. They understand the tremendous range of possibilities to tell a story without saying a word and they use their instrument, their heart, body, intellect, humour, life insights and professional experience to convey all they can to their customers.

The actor has an inherent skill of knowing at all times who he/she is talking to because that is a big part of connecting to the words and other actors on stage. It is their job to bridge the

> "In theatre and in live performances, the audience has to believe that there's no place else you'd rather be."
>
> **-Alec Baldwin,** in an interview for a tribute on Sept. 12, 2007 for American Masters on PBS' *The Tony Bennett Story, The Music Never Ends.*

connection between the written word and the audience. They are also masters at the 'new world approach' (learn more in Chapter 10) by making the same line they have been saying for 500 consecutive performances sound like it's the first time they had thought about saying it. They keep the audience guessing as to what will come out of their mouths next. Will it be song, soliloquy, or sonnet? The best ones keep you guessing and keep you interested until the curtain goes down and the stage manager says over the intercom, "Good show everyone, call time tomorrow is 1:30 pm."

Actors go to school for years to understand how to access their imagination and to prepare their instrument. Sometimes the amount of invented backstory work and intricate history of each character they play can cover pages and pages of written work. For them, it is a paramount ingredient to being believable on screen or on stage. (Refer to Chapter 7, Anchor Seven™ for how this in-depth understanding can be applied to intimately understanding who your customers are.)

CHAPTER 2 — THE GUEST EXPERT

One of the best examples of the connection from page to actor to audience is from the "1997 drama film directed by Gus Van Sant and starring Matt Damon, Robin Williams, Ben Affleck, Minnie Driver, and Stellan Skarsgård. Written by Affleck and Damon, *Good Will Hunting* was both a critical and financial success. It was nominated for nine Academy Awards, winning two: Best Supporting Actor for Williams and Best Original Screenplay for Affleck and Damon."[1]

This scene is the conversation between Robin Williams and Matt Damon's character (Will) sitting on a park bench outside. Robin's delivery was raw and jumped through the screen. In case you are a movie buff, here is the excerpt:

"You've never looked at a woman and been totally vulnerable or known someone who could level you with her eyes. Feeling like God put an angel on earth just for you and could rescue you from the depths of hell. And you wouldn't know what it's like to be her angel, to have that love for her, to be there forever, through anything, through cancer. And you wouldn't know about sleeping sitting up in a hospital room for months holding her hand because the doctors could see in your eyes the term visiting hours don't apply to you. You don't know about real loss, 'cause that only occurs when you love something more than you love yourself."

If you have seen this movie, I am confident you are either tearing up or pausing for a moment after reading the above excerpt. The words, the scene, the performance all come together in glorious harmony stirring us up in ways we normally wouldn't be. This is the type of brilliance that we as on-air sellers have access to if we can learn how to combine it all together. (Refer to Chapter 10, The Three P's, to learn more.)

The gap between acting and selling is that the on-air world of shopping is a selling business. Telling stories, connecting and entertaining are all mandatory skills but if you can't sell and convert people from shaking their heads no to nodding and clicking to order, you are just another actor working a gig. The other important distinction is that there are no real scripts to follow word for word.

Notable Actor Turned Electrifying Guest Expert and Host

Image used with Forbes permission

Arguably one of the most successful and dynamic on-air sales experts once made her living on Broadway as an actress and dancer among many other career high points. She is known as the *billion dollar woman* with her seemingly effortless ability to turn water into wine. She is none other than Forbes Riley and sells predominantly on HSN and TSC. Do yourself a huge favour and watch her in action. "Forbes Riley is one of today's most accomplished entrepreneurs, a highly sought-after spokesperson, motivational key note speaker and life coach to celebrities and CEOs. She's known worldwide for promoting the Jack Lalanne Juicer and other products."[2]

Do Great Products Find You or Do You Seek Out Great Products to Sell?

Yes to both questions. Many pitch people will walk the tradeshow aisles of Las Vegas and New York to find new and exciting products to bring to the shopping channels they have relationships with. If the guest expert has a following and has created a trusting relationship with the viewing audience and the networks, the better for everyone involved! There are two exceptional women entrepreneurs who are at the top of their profession. They are none other than Lori Greiner and Joy Mangano.

"Lori Greiner is now regarded as one of the most prolific inventors of retail products, having created over 400 products, and holds 115 U.S.

and international patents. A well-known celebrity personality on QVC-TV, Greiner has hosted her own show, *Clever & Unique Creations by Lori Greiner*, for over fifteen years. She is also starring as a "Shark" on the *ABC* hit show *Shark Tank*."[3]

We talked about Joy Mangano earlier in this book highlighting some of her outstanding sell out performances. Although Joy started selling on OVC (in 1992), she has made HSN her permanent home and is easily considered to be HSN's most successful purveyor, with annual sales of more than $150 million. She holds more than one hundred patents for her inventions. I think my products have been successful because they have mass appeal, she has said. I'm just like everybody else out there. I'm a mom, I work, I have a house to clean, things to organize. We all have certain similar needs, and I address them. An executive at HSN has written, "HSN fans, the media, and viewers alike can't get enough of Joy. [She] shares the passion, excitement and pride of every detail with her viewers."[4]

Category Expertise

Success as a guest expert is in how you choose to differentiate yourself. On QVC alone, there are more than 1500 new items introduced any given week. Those items are all catalogued within categories such as: Beauty, Electronics, Fashion, Health and Fitness, Home and Garden, Jewelry, Shoes and Handbags. This is true for the rest of the big four home shopping channels. Within these larger categories, there are many more sub-categories. For example, you may be a home décor expert selling only soft goods, bedroom and bathroom items. The outdoor décor items will often be assigned to another guest expert even though you may have all the skills to handle it. The next few sections address this issue.

Crossing Categories

You will most likely become a category expert. (For example, home décor expert, kitchen authority, fitness guru, etc.) Whether you're hired because you are the expert or you walk in with the product, it will quickly pigeonhole you, which is a good thing in this business. Consistency and brand identification are what you want. For instance, if you're selling wonderful vacuum cleaners, 'around the home' will be considered your category of expertise. The issue arises when the guest expert thinks they can cross categories, which is not as common within the same network. It's like turning a ship around at sea. It takes some time to make it work. In this business, the time is generally six months to cross into another category and the guest needs to be off the air before she can re-start selling under the new category. There are obviously exceptions to every rule, but this is fairly common practice. The reasons for the time delay between category changes are many. If people saw you running the vacuum over Smarties and other fragments to illustrate the efficiency of a vacuum cleaner, and then the next day saw you sitting in a fabulous v-neck dress looking runway ready selling jewelry, what do they believe? The viewing audience as a whole have a hard time switching with what they're used to and somehow short circuits the believability of the guest expert's expertise. In essence, your *perceived* credibility is diluted if you cross without a break. This can be a short term work stoppage for a longer term commitment from the network you work with. If you are a solid guest expert, shopping channels jump at a chance to work with a known guest because they come with audience familiarity and experience, which is worth a lot.

Overexposure

In home shopping retail, the good news is there is no such thing as being overexposed. The decision to book you or not is driven by the success and demand of the products and the category you sell. If you are good at what you do, you look good and you sell the product well, you may be working all the time! The minute the viewers see you, they will instantly know what kind of category is being sold. You in essence become part of the brand. (Of course, if it's your own product and brand, this goes without saying.) They might say, "Oh good, he's on! He always makes me laugh. What crazy demos will he be doing today?" That bond between viewer and familiar guest expert can be sacred and has the potential to lead to higher sales simply because they feel they know you, they trust your word and expertise. (More in Chapter 8, D.I.E.T Your Way to Sales Success™). And remember, you may have many other opportunities to sell within other direct TV venues, including infomercials, industrials and even being a celebrity guest at trade shows and morning television. If you build your recognizability by being associated with one category, there are many avenues open to you. The more the better!

Actors on the flipside know all about the concern of being overexposed in the market. Networks claim that it has the potential to water down the excitement and the marketability of your image and the product you are affiliated with. For example, if the actor is lucky enough to have four or five national commercials running at the same time, you and your agent pretty much know that you won't be asked to audition for a long while after that. It's part of managing overexposure in that particular business.

Networks

If, for instance, if you're hired by QVC US, the chances are pretty high you most likely won't be hired to sell on any of the other big US TV shopping networks like ShopHQ or HSN for the same category. The simple reason is that they are all fierce competitors. However, there are exceptions to every rule, so be open to the possibilities. If you sell different categories at different networks, that may work. You may also have the opportunity to sell products in other countries. For instance, you may be selling a great electronics product in Canada at their shopping network, TSC. This same product may be selling at ShopHQ in Minneapolis, and at QVC UK and you may have the chance to sell in all of those destinations. Keep focused on what your brand and expertise is.

Time Management

Depending on the size of the network you are working for, you may not have enough days in the week to handle all of the home & garden shows and the bedroom & bathroom shows. You may also not have the time to understand all you need to know about your category and the items within them. If you've marketed yourself successfully and have a solid database of vendors that you are currently working with, this is a full time commitment. Every time there is a new show, there are samples sent to you, new products and information to be learned and memorized and new demonstrations to work up. It is an ever-changing business and your sales acumen needs to be fresh in order to be properly prepared.

Know Your Entertainment Style

There are many different entertainment styles. If I were to name fourteen famous people not necessarily related to home shopping, I bet you would be able to identify their individual styles if not with a word, certainly with an image of their style, image, pace, and vocal range: Ivana Trump, Tony Little, Tony Robbins, Oprah Winfrey, Larry King, Andy Rooney, Martha Stewart, Matt Lauer, Kathy Lee Gifford, Regis Philbin, Rosie O'Donnell, Ellen DeGeneres, Johnny Carson, Ryan Seacrest.

Your job is to show off the product you are selling with as much entertainment, candour, specifics and professionalism as possible and combine that with a delivery system that connects to your audience.

As a guest expert, you have to be able to adapt your personal style to the product. For instance, if I am selling knives one day and décor products on a completely different network the next day, my style will alter slightly to complement the product and the customer who is watching. Knives are a black and white product – they work or they don't. Everyone is familiar with the basics of the product, so you have to work at a quick pace to keep the attention of your viewers. There is a certain intensity and quick pace required to sell this type of product. On the flip side, if you're selling a glamorous red carpet style gown, all the intensity still remains but the main anchor is that you're selling hopes and dreams, fashion and beauty. It is a more one-on-one approach and requires a slightly altered pitch style that may allow you to swing a little wider instead of keeping it tight and structured.

The late, great pitchman Billy Mays, known for promoting 'around the house' items like OxiClean and Orange Glo could also have sold fashion if he wanted to because he would figure out a way to adapt his hard-hitting delivery to suit his audience. This ability to be a chameleon made him exceptional at his job.

If you're just beginning and you're not sure what style will work for you, watch your favourite television personalities and take note of what you like about their style and model it. We're often attracted to the style we would also like to emulate.

Modeling with Etiquette

The choices we make to demonstrate our own brand and products is in essence part of our trademark and intellectual property. Having said that, I consistently watch about fifteen or twenty guest experts and celebrities to get inspiration on how they handle certain aspects. I take something from everyone and weave it in to creating my own unique performance. Watching helps you to confirm what really works and what doesn't. Will I ever be Ms. Rivers or Ms. Mangano? No. Nor would I want to be. I watch them to see how they handle the success and excitement of a great selling day, how they get out of jams, or how they quickly switch tactics or steer the host in the direction they want to go. Modeling is about finding ways to inspire your best performance, not copy theirs.

Be careful not to become a blatant copycat in dialogue, demos or style. There is a silent gentleman's agreement that is never mentioned but always honoured by the pros in the business. In the tradeshow circuit, certain aspects to a person's pitch, for instance how they craft their close, are sacred. Not unlike the magician who holds his tricks close to the vest. Other pitch people have to ask permission to watch the pitch of other professionals. It is the gray area of intellectual property that shouldn't be messed with. This is not a book on liturgy, so I will keep this point short and sweet. For you to last in this business, ensure that you find your own voice and techniques and demonstrations that work for you. Be inspired by other great pitch people by all means, but do not copy them. It's in bad taste and is a transparent rookie move that is looked down upon.

Finding Your Own Unique Voice

Near the beginning of this chapter, we spoke extensively about what qualities make an exceptional guest expert. As a contract worker we are often pushed and pulled in many directions from our buyers, vendors and customers. It is difficult to stay on course with so many voices offering their opinions and points of view. This next section provides an exercise that will help you to identify what your entertainment style and vision for executing excellence is. At the end of this section, you will have created your own vision statement. It provides a framework of expectation, behaviour and level of execution. I assure you if you have a strong knowledge of your entertainment style, it will help you to react like a young cat to any possible changes and adjustments that need to be dealt with quickly. This statement will release your creativity and drive you to excel like never before. Companies create vision statements as a public commitment to excellence. Why shouldn't we as guest experts establish our own vision statements?

Over the years, I have facilitated this one simple exercise with many people, from CEO's, to new moms, to students looking for direction and people changing careers. It has proven to be a great exercise to identify the heart of your belief systems and establishes your foundational voice. What I love about it is you can't outline how it will develop. If you answer the questions in order with honesty and commit to believing in the outcome of the process, you will arrive with a strong vision statement specifically designed for you alone.

My Two Favourite Books

I first stumbled onto creating this exercise many years ago when I was struggling to find my own voice within the fluid reality of the acting profession. I found that through understanding the true meaning and the synonyms of certain words, it often woke me up to a reality or interpretation of a circumstance I hadn't seen before. Admittedly, it also acted like a cup of icy cold water poured over my head like a parent or mentor when I needed it. To this day, when I'm grappling with a concept and I suspect my ego is getting in the way of good judgment, whether it is a personal or business issue, or I'm just curious about how best to approach a situation, I go to my *Webster's Encyclopedic Unabridged Dictionary of the English Language* and *The Synonym Finder* by J. I. Rodale as seen in the photo below. (As you can see by the dog-eared quality of them, they have been well used).

When I started working as an on-air guest, I felt I needed to identify my entertainment selling style. After some work with my dictionary and synonym finder, I developed my vision statement just as you will do next. What you will get in return for working to identify your own vision statement is quantifiable clarity on the value you bring to vendors and your customers. Like the mission statement does for many corporations, you will find that this statement will elevate your inspiration and keep you focused on your job to deliver results. It will also provide a strong marketing foundation when you have to pitch yourself to prospective buyers through websites, social media and other promotional platforms. As a matter of reference, my vision statement is the **Best Friend Seller.** My personal vision statement helped to simplify my pitch down to three actions. I'll share it, as well as a portion of my step-by-step process at the end of this chapter. It has helped me to become strategic in the alliances I continue to develop and has never allowed me to burn a bridge because of what the Best Friend Seller stands for in my mind. It keeps me sharp and up to date on all technical minutia and quality issues of products I sell because people count on best friends to share both the dirt and the truth about everything.

Toolbox to Create Your Vision Statement

Through this process, the goal is to start to build a foundation of behaviour and conduct on how to create a style of selling that works best for you.

Time constraints provide pressure to create results. Therefore, before we continue, get a stopwatch or use the microwave timer and get it ready to start:

Plan to work for 40 maximum minutes. 20 – 25 for the first section and 15 for the written section.

- Have access to an unabridged dictionary and synonym finder (or thesaurus).
- Work with a blank sheet of paper (yes, old school it), pencil and eraser.
- Please set a timer (use the microwave, egg-timer or your phone if you don't have a stopwatch).

What to do:

First 20 – 25 minutes

List as many words (20 – 30 at least) that you feel represents the heart of who you are. Use your dictionary and synonym finder to help expand the list to exhaust all possibilities.

- Look at the list and take note of 10 to 15 words that jump out at you and best represent your vision of life.
- Circle them.

Last 15 minutes
- Re-set your timer for 15 minutes.
- Out of the 10 to 15 words you identified as the best representatives of the heart of you (as above), write your mission statement. This can be a story that strings the words together. It can be an anecdote or you can create your own inaugural speech if that suits your style. This is your expression to find your voice so do whatever you need to do to gain inspiration and a sense of occasion and importance.
- Once the timer goes off, pencil down.
- Read it aloud and listen to the overall message of what you just wrote. There will be a living and predominant theme that will be evident to you once you hear it.
- Capture it in one clear statement. This is your Vision Statement.

Example for Your Reference

As a review, I shared that my entertainment style and vision statement came out as the Best Friend Seller. Here is some of the extra work that confirmed the vision statement for me. As I was gathering the ten to fifteen words, both *best* and *friend* were words that stood out to me the most. The meanings and synonyms of best and friend are highlighted next for your reference. I used the publications cited in the picture a few pages ago, *Webster's Unabridged Dictionary* and J. I. Rodale's *Synonym Finder*.

Best: (definition):
1. of the highest quality, excellence, or standing
2. most advantageous, suitable or desirable
3. most excellently or suitably; with most advantage or success;
4. one's highest degree of competence, inspiration, etc.
5. the highest quality to be found in a given activity or category
6. to manage as well as one can under unfavourable or adverse circumstances

* I chose #4, **one's highest degree of competence, inspiration, etc.** It doesn't mean that the other definitions didn't apply, but to me, competence and inspiration apply wholeheartedly to my vision of what best friend selling is all about.

Best (synonyms):
Excellent, unexcelled, unsurpassed, first class, first rate, preeminent, peerless, wholesome, best suited, genuine, fitting, most desirable, most happily.

*I chose the following words: **wholesome, best suited,** and **genuine.**

Again, it doesn't mean that the other words are disregarded. I chose the words that best suited the on-air selling work and what words meant the most to me. I then looked up the definition of each of those words to understand them more fully, dissecting them down as far as I needed to in order to gain the clarity required.

At times, delving further into the meaning of the words solidifies in your mind that you have chosen the right word, or tells you very quickly to find a better one. In the case of the word 'genuine', it solidified further my conviction that it had to be included. As a reference, let's look up the definition of 'genuine' before we move on.

Genuine (definition):
1. Free from pretense, affectation, or hypocrisy
2. Sincere

Genuine (synonyms):
Authentic, honest to goodness, heartfelt, earnest, natural, up front, frank, candid, straightforward, thorough

Let's move on to the meaning of "friend":

Friend (definition):
1. a person attached to another by feelings of affection or personal regard

2. a person who gives assistance; a patron or supporter
3. one who is on good terms with another; one not hostile; to identify oneself as friend (not foe)

* I chose definition #1: **a person attached to another by feelings of affection or personal regard.**

Friend (synonyms):

Companion, sidekick, other self, dinner companion, confidant, familiar, intimate, soul mate, ally, collaborator, cohort, helper, teammate, co-worker, colleague, peer, supporter, backer, assister, advocate, encourager.

* I chose the following words: **companion, confidant, ally, collaborator, teammate, colleague, supporter, backer, advocate,** and **encourager**.

My personal vision statement (see below) is frequently consulted before and after shows to remind me where I need to be in thought and action. There is great comfort knowing that these words will never fail by helping me to stay consistent with my approach at all times. I also include it in my pre-game preparations. (Refer to Chapter 12, 10-Point Checklist). It focuses and confirms what I'm doing today is still on track or quickly tells me if I need to re-align my approach:

Through behaving at my highest degree of competence and inspiration, acting first class and talking about products and services that I am best suited for with a wholesome and genuine delivery, I will achieve a winning outcome! I understand in order to be a winning connector to my customers I need to always approach my work as if I am the familiar companion, sidekick, entertainer, confidant, intimate, soul mate, ally, collaborator, cohort, helper, teammate, co-worker, colleague, peer, supporter, backer, assister, advocate and encourager.

Clarifying what my vision statement meant to me, helped to simplify the value proposition to three actions: Focused. Straight-Forward. Results

SOURCES

1. http://en.wikipedia.org/wiki/Good_Will_Hunting
2. http://www.forbesriley.com
3. http://www.lorigreiner.com/
4. http://en.wikipedia.org/wiki/Joy_Mangano

CHAPTER 2
The Guest Expert

1. There are many people who can become exceptional guest experts if they possess the right core qualities. It is, however, a selling and closing role. You have to know how to use the urgency of the home shopping model to motivate your customers to buy.

2. There are rules and regulations that are exclusive to each network which must be followed by all guest experts. They exist based on what has worked historically and most are tried and true principles.

3. Becoming highly aware of your skill set and selling style will help you achieve top performance at a quicker pace. See the exercise Know Your Entertainment Style.

CHAPTER 3

TO WEAR OR NOT TO WEAR, THAT IS THE QUESTION

Your wardrobe choices should be the highest extension of your personality and overall message. This profession is a visual medium and the picture you paint is as important as knowing every technical aspect of your product. Ask yourself this question: If the sound were muted, would you still be able to communicate that you are a credible and likeable person who can be trusted? Dressing to look your best on television is one of the most important opening statements you can make. That is why I have gone to the extreme in explaining as much as possible about the importance of choosing a winning wardrobe, so stick around!

CHAPTER 3 — TO WEAR OR NOT TO WEAR, THAT IS THE QUESTION

"I simply believe that when a man is well dressed you don't notice his clothes. I want to wear my suits and don't want my suits wearing me."
-Johnny Carson

An illuminating quote from the 2006 film, *The Devil Wears Prada* performed by the actress Meryl Streep:

"This... stuff? Oh... ok. I see, you think this has nothing to do with you. You go to your closet and you select out, oh I don't know, that lumpy blue sweater, for instance, because you're trying to tell the world that you don't take yourself too seriously to care about what you put on your back. But what you don't know is that sweater is not just blue, it's not turquoise, it's not lapis, and it's actually cerulean. You're also blindly unaware of the fact that in 2002, Oscar de la Renta did a collection of cerulean gowns. And then, I think it was Yves St. Laurent, wasn't it, who showed cerulean military jackets? And then, cerulean quickly showed up in the collections of eight different designers. Then it filtered down through the department stores and then trickled on down into some tragic Casual Corner where you, no doubt, fished it out of some clearance bin. However, that blue represents millions of dollars and countless jobs and so it's sort of comical how you think that you've made a choice that exempts you from the fashion industry when, in fact, you're wearing the sweater that was selected for you by the people in this room. From a pile of stuff."

Attention to detail and carefully focusing on what you choose to wear is one of the only actions you have 100% control over on show day. What you look like plays a defining role on your sales success because customers pay as much attention to body language as they do to verbal communication.

In the theatre, the wardrobe of the actors on stage play a major part in creating the illusion and setting the scene for the audience. The director knows that in conjunction with other important production values, the wardrobe of the actor is irreplaceable in setting the scene for the audience long before the actor utters a word.

According to Mr. Bradley Dalcourt, Assistant Head Wardrobe at the Stratford Shakespeare Festival in Ontario, Canada (sister to the Guthrie Theatre in Minneapolis, MN):

"Costumes can range in price from as low as $350.00 to as high as $25,000 per costume. In one show there can be as many as 300 costumes and some appear for only minutes on stage. Our team spends thousands of hours cutting and sewing fabric and applying sequins, beads and embellishments only the front row of the audience would ever see. Multiple fittings and restructuring on the fly as well as testing the costumes under the stage lights before they are finalized are all a part of making every image as perfect as possible."

Change It Up

One of the things that I love to do is to change my wardrobe every show. It is part of my style and is a deliberate selling tactic. It keeps each show fresh and provides another layer to the overall message. One of my pitches as a designer is that small changes and playing with opposites in colour and fabric weight creates a big impact, so that is what I do with my wardrobe. I'll make subtle changes throughout the day to complement my message. Customers have told me that they find it entertaining to see what my next outfit will be. They tend to return later in the day to see what else I'm wearing. I tend to dress in colours that complement the show and the products I'm selling. This is a subliminal way of creating a pleasing picture on the screen. It's a beauty and dream medium after all, and dressing well is part of creating the success prescription.

If you are currently selling a wearable product (jewelry, clothing etc.), be sure to wear it! Again, this gives you one more chance to position your product in the minds and imagination of your viewers.

CHAPTER 3 — TO WEAR OR NOT TO WEAR, THAT IS THE QUESTION

Photo used with Sandie's permission

Sandie Savelli, fashion designer and long-time guest expert on TSC, goes a step further and matches the colours, weight of fabric and overall style to whatever the host is wearing. She has identified the best 'sitting' and 'standing' outfits, and will often match her heel height to the height of the host as the camera can frame the whole look more evenly and elegantly. For the good of the network, she will also try to wear jewelry or other complimentary products that are also being sold that day to provide some subliminal continuity. This synergistic approach is masterful and has contributed to her success and high popularity with her customers. She believes that by painting a pleasing picture for her customers to look at, it makes for a visually enjoyable experience and establishes her as the expert in fashion. This is clear the moment you tune-in regardless of whether the sound is turned on or not.

Body Language

Confidence is the best dress code. Your wardrobe is an extension of your personality and should reflect you on your best day. What wardrobe choices make you feel overwhelmingly confident? If you feel confident, you will exude that energy. The reverse is true as well. If you are uncomfortable, you will appear uncomfortable, and that can be misinterpreted in many ways like an ill prepared guest, scared guest or egotistical guest. Don't give your audience another reason to be distracted from your message or your product.

If you personally have a lot on the line with the success of a show, you can't appear to be struggling with the way you handle yourself. The desperation you may be feeling inside can read on camera. How you position your body when you speak communicates its own set of visual messages. More than anything, it reflects your attitude, telling your listeners whether you're confident, alert, and in command of yourself and the situation. Planting yourself balanced on two feet will always be your strongest position: your voice and body will consequently be more energized. Slouching or leaning into one hip from the point of view of the camera can create too casual an image which may not always work for your category or for your audience. (I do however use this *casual position* deliberately when I want to change the pace or direction of the message.) If your category has you sitting or standing behind a counter where you can hide, be sure to still keep that energy in your body. It makes a difference in getting your message across.

In Chapter 2, The Guest Expert, we talk about the quality of having empathy to make you a strong sales personality. The ability to understand and share in another person's emotions and feelings is an important quality and can be reflected in your body language. When you speak, your audience unconsciously feels what you feel and responds accordingly. Therefore it's vital that your body faithfully portrays your true feelings. If the audience is convinced you are sincere and trustworthy, they will pay attention to what you say and evaluate it on its own merits.

Two-Dimensions of the TV Screen I

The two-dimensions of the TV set will magnify certain things you would never guess unless you were familiar with the medium. We do look bigger than we really are on TV because of the *flat* look (think Gingerbread Man) or 2D effect. Think about when you try to buy a piece of clothing for a loved one. You hold it up in front of you by the shoulder seams. It looks overly large and like a flat blob of textile. You wonder if your nephew will fit it, as it looks just way too big. That's the 2D effect. With no sense of dimension, we can all look like flat blobs. There are many ways to accentuate shape and definition of body which we'll go through in this section.

The 'techies' may be wondering about high definition and 3D within this medium. High definition is fairly common now on most shopping channels, but 3D will be a long while off but no doubt will be the future.

(See Chapter 9, The Lily Pad Strategy™, for the second part of this section).

Categories Home Retail Networks **Do Not** Sell

At times, it is helpful to identify what is not acceptable in an environment. Miss Manners and dear Ms. Emily Post prescribed a few rules when dining with guests: Never talk about politics, sex or insult the host's cooking! Well, there are a few topics of conversation while on-air that are strictly prohibited. The list below quite clearly identifies what discretion and taste have to do with your wardrobe choices as well as topics, references and conversation in general. Your guest expert handbook will no doubt include these. For your reference, they include:

- Feminine/personal hygiene
- Firearms
- Fuel additives
- Gambling-related products
- Genuine furs
- Sexual aids
- Spirits and alcohol
- Tobacco-related products

 **EMERGENCY WARDROBE TOOL-KIT**
Here's a Quick Checklist of things to consider bringing to the studio

- ✓ Band-Aids
- ✓ Belt for IFB and microphone
- ✓ Bobby Pins (for IFB cord to secure in your hair)
- ✓ Bottle of water
- ✓ Clear nail polish
- ✓ Dress shields
- ✓ Dry shampoo (to help freshen your hair)
- ✓ Elastics
- ✓ Emergency sewing kit
- ✓ Extension cord
- ✓ Extra pair of black socks
- ✓ Extra pair of nude hosiery
- ✓ Extra set of 'flat' shoes (to wear to and from set)
- ✓ Hair spray
- ✓ Hand sanitizer
- ✓ Hair straightener and curler (as required)
- ✓ Heel and toe grippers
- ✓ Hemming tape or two-way tape
- ✓ Lint roller
- ✓ Makeup powder and concealer (for unexpected blemishes or bruises)
- ✓ Safety pins
- ✓ Scissors
- ✓ Shoe polishing cloth

CHAPTER 3 — TO WEAR OR NOT TO WEAR, THAT IS THE QUESTION

STYLE THAT COMPLEMENTS YOUR CATEGORY

CATEGORY	STYLE AND FASHION GUIDELINE
• Beauty and Skincare • Bath and Body • Fragrance • Hair and Nail Care • *Healthy Living Products	**Simplistic:** Most of the best beauty and makeup guests keep their wardrobe and makeup very simple to show off their products easily. Think in terms of an exclusive salon and spa owner. (Remember to not get lost within your set or the other models if you wear all black). **Elegant:** News Anchor Professional **Authoritative:** Lab coat or scrubs or a variation of. Some guests choose to wear lab coats – Dr. Perricone of Dr. Perricone MD Skincare often wears a lab coat which suits his pitch and style. Some chiropractors from the *Healthy Living category may also wear lab coats.
• Camcorders and Cameras • Collectibles and Memorabilia • Computers • Tablets and E-readers • Consumer and Car Electronics • Home Audio and Theatre • Home Office • Weight Management	**News Anchor and Daytime Talk Show Host:** Many of the home retail networks suggest watching respected anchors like Anderson Cooper or Matt Lauer or Katie Couric as a great guideline for identifying the level of refinement and style required. You can range from - pinstriped suits to pressed khakis and golf shirts depending on your category.
• Apparel & Accessories • Handbags • Travel and Luggage • Home Décor • Jewelry • Shape-Wear and Intimates • Weight Management	**Fashion Forward Professional:** There is a tremendous amount of leeway within this category depending on what your personality is and what you feel you can pull off from a fashion perspective. Match your wardrobe to your product and consider how much moving you'll be doing. Careful to be not be too trendy in any of your fashion and grooming choices and use discretion with hemlines and necklines.

STYLE THAT COMPLEMENTS YOUR CATEGORY	
• Cleaning and Laundry • Floor Care & Vacuums • Heating and Cooling • *Healthy Living • Hobbies and Crafting • Collectibles and Memorabilia • Home Improvement • Storage and Organization • Seasonal, Outdoor Living • Pet Supplies	**Sunday Garden Barbeque:** Match your wardrobe to your product and consider how much moving you'll be doing. Range of outfits can include: Trousers and a blazer to a pique golf shirt and khakis. Keep it casual and simple but still professional.
• Health and Fitness • Fitness Equipment and Workout Regimes	**Fitness, Pilates and Dance Instructor:** Wear a cleaned-up version of what you would wear to the gym or studio to teach or coach. Make sure that shoes and laces are clean, including the soles. If you're selling in bare feet be sure that your feet are nicely pedicured with no extra jewelry.
• In the Kitchen	**Chef and Sous Chef:** Most every time a show is done in the kitchen, the host will be wearing a network apron. You as the guest may also wear the network apron or bring your own. Many other kitchen professionals prefer to wear chef's coats and corresponding attire.

Wardrobe Considerations Before You Pack

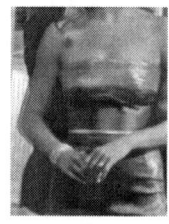

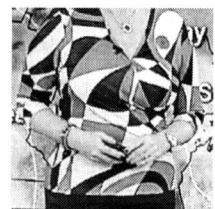

This neckline is too revealing, except for some fashion categories. Watch out though, some networks will not allow bare shoulders.

This skirt is too short, even if you have great legs. It is too revealing and won't allow you to bend over with ease.

This is a great camouflage/colour blocking top. Be sure to keep your accessories simple.

CHAPTER 3 — TO WEAR OR NOT TO WEAR, THAT IS THE QUESTION

Questions to Ask before Final Wardrobe Decisions

1. What kind of overall impact and scene do you want to convey with your wardrobe?

2. What is your product category?

3. What is your sales style and personality? What kind of freedom of movement do you need?

4. Are you a celebrity?

5. What time of day are your shows? Matching your outfits to the time of day, season or celebration is a simple event to take advantage of and capitalize on.

6. Will you be standing or sitting on a chair or on a higher stool for the entire show? Categories that may apply: electronics, collectors, jewelry, fashion.

7. What colour is the chair or stool on the set that you'll be sitting on? Don't let the chair or barstool swallow you up by wearing the same colour as it is.

8. What colour is the set you'll be working in front of? Ensure you stand out within the set. If the set is all white – don't wear all white.

9. Will you be standing or sitting behind a counter with only the top half of your body showing? Categories that may apply: makeup, skincare, jewelry, hobbies.

10. What colours are your products and how will you best show off your product? (Same coaching as in point #14 - if you're selling something that is white that you will be touching and standing next to. Don't wear a white top, the product will disappear.)

11. Do you have models as part of your show?

12. Will you be working beside and/or in behind the models? If all of you are wearing the same colour, make sure that you still stand out. Avoid

the one-colour blob affect. You can work with production beforehand to confirm traffic flow between you and the models.

13. Will you be in the full view of the camera for most of the time or half the time? Categories that may apply: fashion, handbags, luggage, home improvement.

14. Will there be many close-up shots of you handling the product? Categories that may apply: home décor and decor, in the kitchen, collectibles and jewelry.

15. What features of your body will be more frequently shown in close-up shots? (Make sure you dress these areas up.)

- Hands, décolletté, face and hair
- Feet
- Legs and hips

16. Are you tall or short and how does your height compare to the height of the host? This makes a difference when the cameras are doing a two-shot of both you and the host. If you can make adjustments with your heel height, sitting or kneeling more frequently, do so. It makes a difference and is a strong image when both of you are framed well within the shot.

17. Are you working with another colleague to present your line as well? (More details on how to work with multiple guests in Chapter 10, The Three P's.)

On the next number of pages, I have included at-a-glance charts highlighting the most important wardrobe considerations when on camera and online. There is a lot more to say but these guidelines will certainly solve some overall issues and questions you may have:

I. Wardrobe Overall Don'ts (2 pages)

II. POV (Point of View of the camera) Wardrobe Guidelines for Women and Men (6 pages)

CHAPTER 3 — TO WEAR OR NOT TO WEAR, THAT IS THE QUESTION

WARDROBE OVERALL DON'TS	
SELECTIONS	**DON'T**
Accessories	1. Wear anything too chunky or too trendy. (As a rule, no toe rings or anklets as well). 2. Wear distracting pieces that clank and distract or take attention away from your product.
Cell Phone	Wear on your trousers unless it is part of your demo or pitch.

Colours, Fabrics and Textures	1. Wear white on its own. White tends to wash you out and is not great for TV cameras.
	2. Wear bulky, shiny or busy fabrics and textures. Such as:
	• Tweed that is chunky and/or bulky
	• 100% linen that is too wrinkly
	• Taffeta or any shiny finish (unless you pair that with a jacket)
	• Tie-dye or acid washed (too trendy)
	• Fashion-ripped unless you're selling it (including jeans, trousers, tights, shirts)
	• Shear fabrics are not for the camera. It tends to make you look too wispy and thereby weakens your position on camera
	• Wear any pattern less than 1/2 inch in scale. (Fine patterns tend to dance on screen creating an unwanted visual distraction)
	• This includes:
	   • British check • Glen check
	   • Chevron • Paisley
	   • Colour blocking • Pinstripe or horizontal stripes
	   • Herringbone
	   • Houndstooth • Polka-dots

SELECTIONS	WARDROBE OVERALL DON'TS
	DON'T
General Wardrobe and Overall Grooming	1. Look like you just had a nap, ran with the dog or have worked all night. (Even if it's true). ☺ 2. Let your eyebrows, mustache, chin hair, side burns, ear hair, nose hair, etc. get too unruly. Reason: You don't have full knowledge or control of where and what the cameras may focus on at any given moment.
Hair Grooming for Women	1. Let your hair roots enter the room first, before you do. 2. Let your hair bangs shade your eyes. The studio lights create many shadows you wouldn't expect. If you can't see the camera fully, the camera can't see you fully. 3. Over rmanicure your eyebrows. Keep it simple.
Hair Grooming for Men	1. Apply too many products to weight down your hair. 2. Dye your hair on your own. Get it professionally done. Pour dye jobs have a matte finish that can be seen from a mile away! 3. Over rmanicure your eyebrows. Keep it simple.
Makeup for Men and Women	Apply heavy eye makeup and foundation make up.
Rehearse in your wardrobe	Leave anything to chance. The more comfortable and confident you feel, the more successfully you'll be able to perform on camera. *Especially your shoes!
Hemlines	Wear hems that pool on the floor or are too short. This will break the line of your leg and make you look like you are either knock-kneed and/or have bad posture - this sloppy look makes you look weak on camera. Quick Hemline Guideline: • Slacks – hem should line up with the back of your heel • Cropped Pants – Hem should line up with the ankle bones • Skirts and dresses - General rule on hem height: Just below your knees. If you are sitting or kneeling frequently, your skirt should not ride higher than the top of the knee.

CHAPTER 3 — TO WEAR OR NOT TO WEAR, THAT IS THE QUESTION

POV WARDROBE GUIDELINES FOR WOMEN

POV	CLOTHING	COLOUR OR DESCRIPTION	BE AWARE OF YOUR CHOICE	SPECIFIC INFORMATION
FLOOR TO KNEE	Shoes and Boots	Black or Natural pumps	1. Sandals are great choices ensure they are not 'around the home' or 'edgy nightclub' style 2. Mules – not a strong choice (particularly if you're moving around a lot) 3. Boots are a very strong choice and are always welcomed *Be careful of the distraction caused by over-done embellishments, too trendy heel sizes, finishes and styles*	1. Basic pump style with a solid no-slip heel are your best choices 2. Choose from the range of patent leather through to matte/suede finishes 3. Pointed toe-styled shoes often create a longer leg look rather than a rounded-toe *Current fashion trends may play a part with this choice*
	Hosiery, Leggings, Jeggings & Bare Legs	Nude and black hosiery are wardrobe staples	1. Unless you can fully pull off the fashion responsibility of wearing dark and/or animal print leggings/jeggings, do not do it. This look has to be crafted properly otherwise it will work against you and/or look too casual thereby inappropriate on TV 2. Bare Legs * Watch out for visual distractions such as tattoos, varicose veins, scars, cellulite, paper-white skin, etc.	1. No patterns or ultra-shiny finishes seam down the back of the leg. *All above examples can be distracting on camera* 2. Black leggings and jeggings on their own are not recommended at all (unless you are selling fitness or fashion or your legs are not seen on camera) * *Wear more as a layering piece that is worn with a jacket or a tunic that covers the derriere* 3. Bare legs *If the outfit, your category, your taste, your age and/or the season warrants this choice, go for it
	Lower Body Accesories		Anklets and toe rings	Be prepared to remove certain embellishments if asked to by the network

POV WARDROBE GUIDELINES FOR WOMEN

POV	CLOTHING	COLOUR OR DESCRIPTION	BE AWARE OF YOUR CHOICE	SPECIFIC INFORMATION
KNEE TO MID SECTION	**Skirts, Dresses**	Solid and/or designer colour blocking	1. No denim skirts 2. No wearing only onecolour - The 'Big Blob' look – wearing one colour without creating shape with a belt or jacket. Exceptions may include chef's coat 3. Be aware of fine patterns (Refer to the don'ts list earlier) 4. Stay away from the following styles: • Schoolgirl – (includes mini and pleated kilt) • Bubble skirt • Fishtail • Hi-Lo Skirt (too trendy) • Peasant hobo style (too trendy)	1. Choose whatever style works best for your body shape including: • A-line • Pencil skirt • Flip skirt • Wrap-around (with discretion) • Sheath dress 2. Safe choice is to pair skirts/dresses with slightly opaque hosiery/tights
	Trousers, Denim, Shorts or Cropped Pants	Dark solid and suiting	1. Denim - Wearing jeans is a distinct fashion choice and not appropriate for most categories (Fashion or Beauty may be exceptions). They have to be well fitting and cannot be baggy or sloppy 2. Only dark trouser styled jeans. (No weird washes, tears or embellishments)	1. Cropped pants – the best option is a pair made of suiting fabric 2. A nice black pair of slacks is always a great choice 3. No shorts unless you can pull this look off with a tailored knee-length pair. (Very few people or body types can)

CHAPTER 3 — TO WEAR OR NOT TO WEAR, THAT IS THE QUESTION

POV WARDROBE GUIDELINES FOR WOMEN

POV	CLOTHING	COLOUR OR DESCRIPTION	BE AWARE OF YOUR CHOICE	SPECIFIC INFORMATION
MID SECTION TO HEAD	Belt	Slim, medium or wide. Use any colour that suits your outfit	Be aware of being too trendy	1. Belts finish the look of any outfit 2. Ensure it tightly fits around your waist as it will be used to clip your microphone pack and IFB pack to *There are other ways to secure your packs, but the belt is the most reliable and the simplest choice*
	Blouses, Tank Tops and T-shirts	Solid, strong colours and fabrics	1. Be aware of the 'Big Blob' look – wearing one colour without creating shape with a belt or jacket. *Exceptions may be chef jackets 2. If the set or your product is white, don't wear white. (Refer to wardrobe questions above) 3. If your arms are exposed, ensure they are in shape – out of shape arms can be a visual distraction	1. This outer layer is your 'money shot' so ensure the colours and weight of material are the best choice you can make for yourself 2. Add a jacket, vest, sweater or accessory like a scarf, to define style, dimension and definition 3. No Cleavage. Use discretion at all times. Most networks have stringent rules disallowing lower cut necklines. Check before you choose your wardrobe 4. Tank tops. Never wear straps so thin that you look like you'll have a wardrobe malfunction

113

POV WARDROBE GUIDELINES FOR WOMEN

POV	CLOTHING	COLOUR OR DESCRIPTION	BE AWARE OF YOUR CHOICE	SPECIFIC INFORMATION
	Jackets, Cardigans, Sweaters and Vests	Solid, strong colours and fabrics	1. Larger scale patterns and textures add nice dimension 2. Ensure to avoid the 'Big Blob' look – choose a jacket or sweater that can still define your shape and/or use a belt	1. This layer may also act as your 'money shot' so ensure the colours and weight of the material is the best choice you can make for yourself 2. Well cut and fabricated sweaters and jackets add attractive movement and layering interest to your overall look
	Glasses		Hot studio lights and the angles of the cameras can cause major glare and distractions on TV	If you have to wear glasses, spend the money to get non-glare prescription glass (or wear contact lenses)
	Accessories	Scarves, Chokers, Jeweled Collars, Necklaces, Broaches, Earrings Bracelets, Time pieces, Jeweled cuffs and Rings	Choose wisely! Also refer to accessories section in the Don'ts list (earlier in this chapter)	Don't allow yourself to overdo the accessories. Less is more, in almost every case with accessories

CHAPTER 3 — TO WEAR OR NOT TO WEAR, THAT IS THE QUESTION

POV WARDROBE GUIDELINES FOR MEN

POV	CLOTHING	COLOUR OR DESCRIPTION	BE AWARE OF YOUR CHOICE	SPECIFIC INFORMATION
FLOOR TO KNEE	Shoes and Boots	Black or Chestnut Brown	1. Be careful of the distraction caused by over-done embellishments, too trendy heel sizes, finishes and styles 2. Running Shoes: make sure they are clean and scuff free	If your shoes are going to be seen, be sure they are clean and shined up
KNEE TO MID SECTION	Trousers, Denim or Shorts	Dark solid and suiting materials.	1. Denim: Wearing jeans is a distinct fashion choice and not appropriate for most categories (Fashion or Beauty may be exceptions). They have to be well fitting and cannot be baggy or sloppy 2. Only dark trouser styled jeans. (No trendy dyes, washes, tears or embellishments on TV)	1. Ensure all hems are proportioned to suit your heel height 2. For trousers - no hems sweeping and pooling on the floor. 3. No shorts – unless your category is fitness or seasonal home
	Belt	To suit your style and your shoes.	1. Not too trendy in your choice of belt. Anything that distracts from your overall message or the product is never a good choice	1. Belts finish the look of any outfit 2. Ensure it tightly fits around your waist as it will be used to clip your microphone pack and IFB pack to *There are other ways to secure your packs – but the belt is the most reliable and the simplest choice

POV WARDROBE GUIDELINES FOR MEN

POV	CLOTHING	COLOUR OR DESCRIPTION	BE AWARE OF YOUR CHOICE	SPECIFIC INFORMATION
	Socks	Match colour to your trousers	1. This is always a fashion debate but for this medium, is the best choice for continuity 2. If you're wearing lighter trousers or khakis, then match your shoes	You can match your socks to your shirt, tie and even a pocket square. (This is not for the fashion timid. It may suit certain personalities who can pull off that look)
MID SECTION TO HEAD	Shirts, Jackets, Vests, Sweater	Solid strong colours and weight of material	1. Be aware of the 'Big Blob' look – wearing only one colour (black being the most common) without creating dimension with a belt or jacket. *Exceptions may include chef coats 2. Refer to fabrics in don'ts list (earlier) 3. In fitness - if your arms are exposed, ensure they are in shape. Out of shape arms can be a visual distraction	1. This outer layer is your 'money shot'. Ensure the colours and weight of material is the best choice you can make for yourself 2. The best colours to wear on TV are usually the ones that you feel the most comfortable and strong in. (White is one colour that fights with the cameras and washes you out. If you wear a white shirt, be sure to wear a contrasting coloured sweater, vest or jacket) 3. Adding a jacket, vest or sweater defines personal style, dimension and definition
	Glasses		Hot studio lights and the angles of the cameras can cause major glare and distractions on TV	If you have to wear glasses, spend the money to get non-glare prescription glass (or wear contact lenses)
	Jewelry and Accessories	Necklaces, earrings, bracelets, time pieces, cuffs- links, tie clips and rings	1. Beware of pulling focus away from your product by being too trendy 2. Refer to Accessories in the don'ts list earlier in this chapter	Less is more, in almost every case with accessories

116

CHAPTER 3
To Wear or Not to Wear, That Is the Question

1. Your wardrobe choices are the highest extension of your personality, professionalism and overall message. What are you wanting to convey to your audience and are your clothes reflective of that?

2. At-a-Glance Charts to refer to quickly:
   a. Wardrobe Emergency Tool Kit
   b. Style Options that Complement Your Category
   c. Wardrobe Considerations Before You Pack
   d. Wardrobe Overall Don'ts Chart
   e. POV Wardrobe Guidelines for Women Chart
   f. POV Wardrobe Guidelines for Men Chart

CHAPTER 4

THE JOB OF GETTING THE JOB

The Job of Auditioning

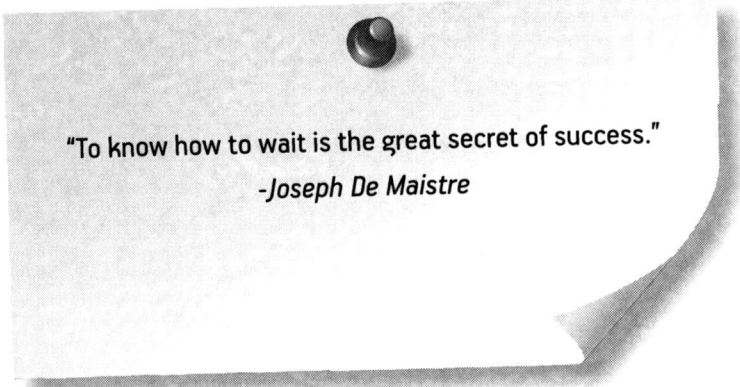

"To know how to wait is the great secret of success."
-Joseph De Maistre

Become an expert at interviewing and auditioning and you will never be without opportunities to work. Auditioning and interviewing are skills that are essential to moving through your career with growth and excellence.

CHAPTER 4 — THE JOB OF GETTING THE JOB

Setting the Scene:

You arrive 15 minutes early. It was impossible to park so you had to walk much further than you planned. "I'm glad I left early," you murmur to yourself."

You check in with the young man with the potbelly who takes your name and asks for your photo and resume.

"Have a seat. We're running a few minutes behind," he says.

There are rows of hard grey chairs set up against the wall of the community centre. A few other auditionees are already sitting cradling their water bottles. Other employees of the community centre saunter in past you smelling of fresh air and their newly poured coffee that wafts through the hallway. The world continues to go around.

"I've had a cold all week. I hope my voice doesn't crack in there," one woman shares.

"This is my third audition this week. It's been crazy busy for me. How has work been going for you lately?" another woman says.

The positioning and nervous chatter continues as you sit wondering if you brought the right material. Under your breath you utter, "Why am I so nervous. Calm down! Will they hire me? What do they need? Oh that's great, I've got a run in my stocking. Is that mustard on my sleeve? What will I get out of today? Am I putting too much into this one audition? I need the work. How much longer is this going to take?"

> "Reveal yourself. Talk. Take a chance. What have you got to lose? You'll lose out on the interview anyhow if you sit there like a mummy. Better to take the chance of communicating to the person sitting on the other side of that desk. Treat him like a prospective friend instead of a hangman."
>
> -**Michael Shurtleff**, author of *Audition*

We all have to interview to get work whether you are a performer, manager or CFO. Rarely do we ever get a free pass. Well known actress Sally Field (a veteran screen actor for well over forty years) with all of her past credentials still had to convince Steven Spielberg that she really was right for the part of Lincoln's wife in the 2012 award-winning movie. Only after arriving looking exactly the part of Mary Todd Lincoln in period costume and makeup and then performing the daylights out of her screen test did she prove to Spielberg that there was no one else better to play the part. There are countless stories of famous actors who have enough money to purchase the entire production who still audition for every part they get. The same is certainly true for most every other profession.

My first talent agent said my job as a performer was to audition. I really didn't understand the magnitude of what that meant until much later because I thought the job only started when I was hired. What I realized is that the audition is the tradeshow for performers and the panel sitting behind the desk are the buyers (and not necessarily for just this audition). It is as simple as that. Booking and doing the job is merely an extension of executing a strong audition/interview and being right for the part/job. The skills and techniques gleaned from auditioning multiple times, prepares one to deal with a lot of pressure to perform on-call and that is the skill that needs to become second nature to you. It's a combination of aligning your thought into the right mindset in order to be ready for your two minutes of putting on a show and then just do it. Oftentimes, that involves getting out of your own way so that you have room to do your best work.

I know of one director friend of mine who will literally stop someone during their weak audition to ask if he (the performer) would spend $5000 of their own hard earned money to buy what he is selling with the quality of work he just provided. It is a question that generally stops the auditionee in his tracks. This is the way we must think. Whether you are interviewing for a temp job, negotiating a guest expert fee or in the final decision stages of landing a full time high paying job, we have to know that we can deliver the true value of what we say we can deliver to our buyers. Therefore, the job of every professional is to present the best of what we can offer at the audition and interview. Walk in that room fearlessly because that is the confidence the panel has to see with the person they will ultimately hire. I've sat on both sides of the audition desk, and from the buyers' perspective we want to see you (not your interpretation of what you think the buyers want). Most times we know, but sometimes we really don't know what we're looking for. That shouldn't affect your performance level one bit. If they want to buy Diet Coke and you're selling Orange Crush, they will appreciate the different options but will not buy your Orange Crush this time. Make their job easy by being prepared and blowing their minds away with your ability to nail a solid performance – regardless of whether you are *right* for this particular season or show. Remember, buyers have many projects on the go and every business is a tight knit community (no matter the industry). Buyers talk. If you wowed them and they didn't hire you this time, you may well be filed in the *yes* pile for the future.

The prize is the work you do, the subtleties you learn about yourself and the reputation you build. These experiences teach you everything you need to know about performing with winning results. It also teaches you how to recover, how to rejuvenate and how to focus on building your portfolio of best performances.

I have auditioned hundreds and hundreds of times in my career and have learned vast amounts from each experience. Whether it's auditioning in front of a panel of twelve decision makers in huge theatres and soundstages or literally having to set up a toppling rickety old light stand in a tiny, dank studio pouring my heart out to my long-lost son who is actually the messy haired camera guy and his coffee stained, rolled-up Tim Horton's cup. It's all part of developing your craft as an artist and professional.

Used with David's permission

According to David Hogan, Veteran Artistic Director, Producer and Performer (in the corresponding picture), "The worst thing an actor can do is to play small and wishy-washy, unsure of what they should be doing to get the part. When performers come in and take charge of the space and entertain me, that's what I'm looking for. It's impossible for them to guess what my vision of the best 'Mama Rose' or 'Anna Karenina' is. Wardrobe, set and lighting will clarify a large portion of that anyway. What they need to do is to concentrate on delivering their vision and how they choose to show up. What I need to see is that person on their best day."[1]

You learn how to command that room as soon as the door opens. You are being watched and listened to and your energy is being felt very carefully by the panel. The panel is full of experts at assessing dynamics, potential and charisma. They are looking for people who will light up the studio in that first moment. Therefore, make the right impression the first time. Walk in confidently knowing that your job is to communicate in an instant that you can thrill, that you can take charge, have character and integrity, charisma and strength to handle the pressure of this moment to deliver your best.

A colleague friend of mine in New York has well over twenty Broadway credits to her name. She is a lady of stature with arguably one of the best coloratura soprano voices in the business. Since she started auditioning years ago, she has only ever auditioned with one song, the beautiful aria, "Summertime," from *Porgy and Bess* music by George Gershwin, libretto by DuBose Heyward, and lyrics by Ira Gershwin. Her reason for only ever doing one song is because this is her song. She *owns* it. She performs the daylights out of it. As soon as she opens her mouth to sing, the panel knows instantly that she is capable of playing any coloratura soprano part because if she nails this difficult song, she can deliver anything a musical director can throw at her. She doesn't concern herself with guessing what they want; she focuses on what she does best. In this business, like most every other business, if the panel puts you on the short list of candidates to play the part, the director will ask you to sing directly from the show to narrow the decision down in the call-back or the second interview.

Control what you can control. Show up being your best and the right jobs and desired outcomes will attach themselves to you.

Let's take this same principle and apply it to a completely different environment:

Scenario – Selling a House

If you've ever gone through the stress of this event, you know that you do everything you can to make the house 'show ready'. You accessorize and clean it within an inch of its life. You banish all guests from visiting for fear of dirtying up the house. You decide on a price and declare pertinent information about the house to attract the right buyers, (just like your resume). You keep the house available for showings at the convenience of the potential buyer. What you can't do is add another bedroom or widen the rooms to suit the customers who say it's too small. You have to manage your own expectations and do what needs to be done within the confines of the space to the best of your ability. You can't be all things to all people.

The Audition Starts at the Front Door of the Building

Never underestimate the powerful influence the front desk and other assistants have with the decision makers. It takes one quick thumbs-down from the assistant and your chance to move on is shot. Arrive at least fifteen minutes prior to your audition to breathe in the space. A friend of our family would always say about punctuality, "If you've arrived on time, you're late!"

Remember, there are generally forms to fill out and other administrative tasks to complete. Give yourself the time you need. I can't tell you how many times people walk in half dressed, with animal hair stuck to their skirt, smelling of a cigarette put out moments before, to then be dismissive to the receptionist. Believe me, it is noticed. Keep in mind that your ticket into that audition/interview room was the resume and forms you sent in (or your agent sent) online to get to this next step. Once you're facing your panel, the resume has little importance. Show them how your resume of work has shaped who you are and your professional capabilities. They are curious about knowing who you are.

In the business world, the same principles apply. If you are interviewing for a computer programming position for instance, they will talk to you first to see what kind of person you are and the resume will answer what kind of experience you have had. Then, oftentimes, they too will ask you to perform and prove that you can actually do the job. They'll often give you a project to code within a short span of time. You think that isn't on-the-spot pressure to perform?

Due Diligence

Be sensitive to the reactions of your interviewer and if you start talking about something that seems inappropriate, change it up quickly. Remember, they are looking for the right person for the job. Do your homework on the company, the type of role you will be doing and audience you are meeting with.

A corporate director colleague of mine shared a recent experience while he was interviewing potential CFO's for their public company. Although he was a promising candidate on paper, he obviously didn't perform his due diligence on the corporate culture of this particular company. He shares:

"We were interviewing a short list candidate for our CFO position. This gentleman with a resume as impressive as anything we had seen to date walked in with an open collar. No tie. I couldn't believe it and couldn't shake the image during the interview. He was an excellent candidate for the job but his choice to arrive casual when we clearly do not have that type of culture said to us that he did things his way, that he wasn't a team player and that he didn't care what people thought of him. (In one way, he did us a favour by dressing that way.) We didn't hire him not because he didn't button up but because we noted the choice he made was consistent with the interview."

Recently I was invited by the artistic directors of a regional theatre to be a part of their audition panel. This was a general audition and we were casting for their next three seasons which included both musicals and plays. A man walked in and performed his audition pieces. He was a decent performer and had a good look for one of our shows. Since we had some extra time, we invited him to pull up a chair to talk with us. We asked him what parts he had played recently that he found to be challenging to play. He answered quickly and proudly sharing, "Recently I had to play a gay guy. To make me believable, I had to change the way I walked and I raised my voice to sound *more gay*."

We all looked at each other and were in awe of what this *boy* just said.

Audition Perspective

You are not the only one being auditioned. You are also auditioning them. Check in with yourself to assess whether this is a job you want to be doing. Can you relate to working in this environment? This puts your mindset in a focused frame of mind. It is an important component to building your level of confidence. Notice I said confidence, not *cockiness*. This approach makes you think of questions you may have for the panel. It also propels you to research the panel, which prepares you for the audition even more.

With online search engines available for researching the people and the companies we will be interviewing with, there is no excuse for generalized, uninformed communication anymore. Whether you are being interviewed for a job or closing a deal to get your first purchase order, it is your job to know who your customer is.

Principles to Live by

As we learned in Chapter 3, To Wear or Not to Wear, That is the Question, painting the picture of success is part of your job. More times than not, we'll get stronger buy-in if we look and act the part. No matter whether you are a performer or corporate businessperson, creating a strong image is vital. In a corporate situation, no doubt you will have spoken to someone within the firm to confirm the appropriate dress attire, and will have done your research and due diligence of the company and the people you will be meeting with for the meeting/interview/audition. The *costume* for men may include a nicely pressed suit, shined up shoes, freshly cut hair and clean shaven appearance. They may choose to show their personality through their timepiece, tie clip or cuff links and women often provide a personal touch through their choice of purse and jewelry. Women too will ensure hair is tidy, hose (preferred over bare legs), dresses and skirts will not sit too high on the thigh when standing or sitting. The briefcase or portfolio of work brought will be tidy and ready to be pulled out with practiced ease and grace.

One may argue, I'm not a wardrobe or hair department, I shouldn't have to do all of this to get a job. Well, why risk it? Paint the picture to the best of your ability and then perform the daylights out of your script or your pitch or the interview. Then you can rest assured that you did all you could. Decision makers don't have the time to envision and imagine as much as we think. If you really want to be a working professional in whatever profession you choose, do as much filling in the blanks for them as you possibly can. If you set the scene clearly, you'll have a much greater chance of getting the job. That should be your motto always. Put everything you can into positioning yourself strongly. If you don't get that particular job, you've learned tons, you haven't let your guard down and you bring all of the work and knowledge from that interview and carry it into the next. And this advice bears repeating - the world is so, so small.

You might be surprised of how the news of a strong audition or interview can spread quickly throughout your industry and may very well open a few more doors the next time for you. A chance you may not have had, prior to the impressive audition or interview you just did.

The Power of a Strong Image in an Audition or Interview

If an actor is auditioning for a part that calls for him to be a 'down and out' rubby dub type character with absolutely no prospects, etc., the smart actor will appear to have not washed in a day or two, come with dirty-looking clothes, smudged makeup and arrive looking the part. It's the full impact package that needs to be considered and is an important part of your pitch. Audition panels can tell almost immediately by the attention to detail and the way the actor carries himself whether they will provide a strong, penetrating performance. You can quickly spot the individuals who are dedicated to bringing their A-game to any experience.

Another tactic actors use is to wear the exact same outfit every time they are asked back for the same project. Why? Because auditors frequently make mental notes of what you are wearing to help identify you later when they sort out their *yes/no* piles. If you change outfits frequently, you can easily confuse them and potentially lose the job because you looked and dressed differently.

There's a famous story of one of the most influential directors and minds in the theatre business. His name is Michael Shurtleff and he wrote the critically acclaimed book every actor should read: *Audition* (cited earlier in a quote). On page 31, he talks about when a famous director asked him about a certain girl in the orange sweater and why she hadn't been brought back. Michael answers, "I had, [brought her back]: she was wearing a purple dress." He continues…"You can help the auditors by wearing the same thing every time you audition."

Anything that helps the audition panel remember you in one image (for the right reasons) is a strong choice to make.

The Power of One Image in the Boardroom

A very high profile advertising team walked into an important pitch meeting with a huge hotel chain with this sign above in hand. The first image the buyers saw was the red and white NO VACANCY sign. It was the only image the client needed to see and all the ad team needed to show. That sign bought five more minutes of time and the slick presentation they presented answered how *no vacancy* would become expected in their hotels. The ad company got the contract and the hotel chain increased their no vacancy frequency immediately, never looking back.

My First Shopping Network On-Air Audition

When I walked into one of the many meeting rooms in the building, there was a panel of six people sitting behind a desk. They each introduced themselves and were all very pleasant but you could tell they were thinking about the next forty people that were waiting outside to do exactly what I was just about to do. It is big business finding the right guest expert to represent any line. It is a world that is built around dollars per minute and every minute they spend has to be well worth their time. The first thing that was said to me was "And what brings you here today?"

Be intuitive and know what the panel is *really* asking you to answer and why. This is your *one* chance to set yourself up for more minutes on-air or in this case, more minutes in the audition room.

A quick aside: That question is similar to what the host will ask you the very first time you meet with him/her, "Tell me about your product." This is one chance to let the host know that the upcoming show will be a good

CHAPTER 4 — THE JOB OF GETTING THE JOB

tennis game and will be successful. It seems like a simple question with a simple answer but it is not. Don't allow yourself to be fooled.

The panel gave me the floor for thirty seconds to establish that I was knowledgeable, trustworthy, personable, a best friend, entertaining, in charge, a team player, flexible, buoyant, assertive, funny, quick on my feet and can deal with distractions and the unexpected. My future ten minutes in that room solely depended on how I handled the next thirty seconds:

"I am here because I know you are looking for a design representative to launch your new private label line. I have owned and operated my own sportswear line and have always felt that the products we made needed to make people's lives easier, more luxurious and help to solve the fitness clothing dilemmas for my customers. I think of them as my best friends and frame my selling style around that assumption. I know where they live and what their home life is like, their ages, their hobbies and how many kids they have. I consider my products to be my co-star and make sure that I equally *show* the benefits of the product as much as I *talk* about them. I am confident on camera and know how to work with angles to show off the products well."

There was no comment from any of the panel. There was no fanfare. I kept my mouth shut and kept my thoughts up. I have heard that in an important negotiation, once the *final ask* has been made, the first one to speak loses. I've taught myself to shut up and let the silence build even if it's heart wrenching— *which it was...*

"You pitch a good pitch, now show us!" One of the panel members finally said. "Please pick up the pencil and sell it to us. Don't stop until we ask you to stop."

A quick aside: Remember the panel wants you to succeed as much as you want you to succeed. That's one of the things that many of us forget in the heat of the battle. You have to click into an abundant mindset as part of your preparation.

HB Pencil

The product they gave me happened to be a brand new orange HB pencil so immediately I talked about why brand-new is so important (the panel laughed of course). I talked about the strength and diameter of both the pencil and the lead itself, the actual construction of the pencil including a whole dissertation on the eraser and how convenient it was to be part of the construction of the pencil. I was running out of things to say so realized very quickly that I had to flip into a more right-brain approach. I then ventured into the imagination of all the possibilities a pencil could provide. I included all the effects and possibilities you can create with a pencil from math homework to writing your first letters and words, to artwork to hanging pictures to marking up the walls with your new renovation ideas in the family room to how mom measured the heights of your siblings on the kitchen doorway year after year. I also highlighted the benefit that, unlike a pen, a pencil will never freeze in the car in an emergency whether you're living in Marquis, Saskatchewan or Embarrass, Minnesota. Or if you're just jotting a quick grocery list down while running into the store before you have to pick-up your son from kung-fu classes. You write your SAT's with a pencil, vote and take notations and, out of all the writing utensils in the world, the pencil is the universal connector that has an infinite amount of uses.

I would have gone back to the beginning of my loop, but luckily, they stopped me.

Glass of Water

We went on to a glass of water. Now this particular glass was a true-to-form goblet glass and was filled halfway with a clear liquid (I decided it was water). I immediately started with the theory about glass-half-full thinking and how that attitude can often brighten your day. I knew that line was going nowhere but it was my anchor to start. I changed gears quickly and launched into how you can pour anything you feel like into a glass – it can create an instant sense of occasion, you can decorate it to honour your event, it can take a cold or hot liquid and you can even apply a line of sugar or salt around the top of the rim which adds to the overall effect and flavour of the drink you choose to fill it with. The weight of the glass is also an important component. This particular glass weighs less than two grams (I, of course made that up), which suits most everyone including your child who has perhaps just graduated from the plastic 'sippy cup' to an adult glass. It's also useful for someone who may have dexterity issues, or arthritis or is somehow weak perhaps from recovering from surgery or sickness. The circumference fits nicely in your hand and the distribution of the weight of the glass is nicely balanced. Before I knew it the quiet panel burst out laughing – all six of them. They stopped me before I went into the whole 'saving the planet/green push' I was about to launch into. It was hilarious and I had a ball!

The one thing you realize is that if you are having fun and are truly committed to your work, that spirit of energy will read on camera or whatever platform you are communicating from. People feel your genuine sincerity and react positively to it.

Remember, your job is to *entertain* as well as to *sell*.

Quiet Before the Storm

Not a lot of books talk about what it's like to manage the stress, noise and the *quiet* of not working, and the sound of the phone *not* ringing once you've done all you could to get a job. You left it all out on the field and now you wait and wonder if you could have done better. The wave of insecurity and anticipation is as strong as the feeling you have after your 5th fabulous date with the greatest person you've ever met. Will he call? Does he feel the same way? Did he *get it* when I said that? Why am I not hearing from him – no Facebook, no texts, and no phone call? Do I need to refresh my page? Is it working? Most of us rush to the *do* because we get scared of being still. Doing something, *anything* is better than doing nothing at all. Right?

If you haven't auditioned or interviewed for a while, the waiting game and wondering how it went in their eyes may take you down unexpectedly like a tidal wave. You have to learn how to protect the work you did at that audition or interview and trust that the higher plan for you is intact and let it go with confidence. Wrap up the experience with a nice bow and take all you learned about yourself and the experience and move on. After an audition or interview I often schedule something to do directly after that involves emotional connection. You want to find something that mirrors the heightened state you've just tapped into to perform your best. Go for lunch, see a show, meet a friend for tea, or whatever makes you feel alive. Honour the strength and work it took to get you prepared by mirroring something just as satisfying. Don't allow yourself to sit at home and wait. Instead of approaching your interviews as beginning and end, think of them as part of your day – just like checking emails, sautéing onions for spaghetti dinner tonight and pressing your suit for the next day.

By the way... four weeks later I got the call from head of casting at the network and they told me **I got the job!** One of my all-time favourite sentences!

Stay Calm and Carry On

Let's face it. You will not get every job you audition for. That is the reality. There is a lot of great work to go around and if one door slams in your face, another window is available to be opened. Your job is to build on all of your experiences in a positive way so you are ready to tackle the next assignment. The pros thrive in this crazy business because they know the secret. The secret is to stay full, keep the opportunities flowing and the conversations humming. Keep the balls bouncing and don't allow the mind to outline how the outcome will shake down. Our job is to remain calm and carry on with our life.

To follow is a three question strategy that may help you cope better when times seem tough and/or you feel stuck in some way.

3 Questions in Life

There can be certain times in our lives when we wonder what *is* happening (particularly if work is sporadic and/or slow)? We may be out of work or we're just not satisfied with the speed or direction things are moving. Ask yourself, how are you participating (or not participating) to rustle up new business? Times have changed and will continue to do so. It is tough to get work and almost tougher to keep it. Although it may suggest a doom and gloom predicament, this is the time to thoroughly 'spec-out' your situation by thinking your way through the challenge.

Your best, most reliable currency is the relationships you have garnered both professionally and personally throughout your life and career. Get busy making sure you are staying in touch with your circle and find ways you can be helpful and valuable to them. Become a memorable ally that others can rely on as well. It's a two-way long-term street. This is a time for due diligence and strategic thought. Call up your colleagues, perhaps to find out what's going on within the industry. Try to get the pulse of the industry and business itself.

We can all sit within our four walls becoming discouraged that no one is calling. Can they find you? Are you hiding or moving forward to get in the game. It's extraordinary how, by pragmatically moving forward with this disciplined and informed thought process, plans and events begin to positively unfold before your eyes but you have to ignite and instigate the forward energy. To begin the thinking process, give some serious thought to become fully aware of **what is really happening** out there. After getting a good handle on **what's happening,** you are in a more informed and better position to decide on **what all of this means to you.** Will you have to seek out more vendors, become a better marketer, should you go to a tradeshow to see what is out on the market to bring back to your buyer? Once you know **what it means**, based on your assessment of **what is happening**, then you are in a much stronger position to take educated and pragmatic steps forward to **do something** about the situation.

To review, when you are in a situation that puts you in a *seemingly* unstable and/or precarious position of great concern or insecurity, use the simple **3 Questions in Life** process to strategically think your way through the challenge. It is meant to be quick and uncomplicated to light the way pragmatically.

Ask yourself and answer each question in this order:
1. What's happening?

2. What does it mean to me?

3. What do I do about it?

I Got the Job, Now What?

Congratulations! Enjoy this moment, as there's a lot of new business to take care of now. In negotiations, there are two distinctions between the entertainment world and home shopping world. Most on-air talent in the entertainment world is usually represented by an agent or manager to handle business transactions whereas in the home shopping world, the on-air talent generally represents him or herself.

In the entertainment arena, whether you are an actor, speaker, musician, celebrity or broadcaster your agent or manager will have already arrived at a competitive rate for you, whether it's a per hour, per show, per day or per appearance rate. If you're a member of a union, rates are most times already pre-determined. Agents and managers make a commission ranging from 10% - 25% of your gross revenue depending on the services they provide. It may sound like a lot, but like the insurance agent they are there for you in good times and bad. For the bad times, the good agents and managers earn every dime you pay them.

In home shopping, the guest expert usually does his or her own negotiations. Most times (particularly if the guest expert is new), you'll get the job without knowing exactly what the guest expert rate is. You'll audition because it's a chance to work. If you get the job, the negotiating generally consists of agreeing to the terms provided by the vendor or the shopping network who hired you thank you very much.

This next section is to help the brand new and the more seasoned guest expert to think like an agent during the negotiation process. My best advice as always is to do your homework before you walk into the negotiating room. Whether you are new or re-negotiating your contract, the next set of details and negotiation guidelines (at the end of the chapter) will arm you with the knowledge to be able to represent yourself with confidence. Being an entrepreneur, most of these notes may very well be reminders but the hope is that it will provide some extra clarity. There are many variations of pay methods. Fee standards vary greatly depending on your experience, sales success, recognizability and celebrity status as a guest expert. Regardless of whether you are new or seasoned, be informed on what is happening relative to compensation and agreements of other guest experts in the current market.

It's Not Where You Start, It's Where You Finish

You may remember in Chapter 2, The Guest Expert, where I talk about the validity of being *available* to work. Changes and cancellations can happen at a moment's notice where all of a sudden a buyer will call you to work that day. If your answer continues to be "No, I'm not available," consistent unavailability may ultimately contribute to decreased hours. Being available to work is part of your job. Therefore, if you don't set your working rate high enough in the initial negotiations, it won't be feasible for you to be available when they do call.

Reputation, past sales results and audience familiarity does play a part in the position you can take while negotiating. The leverage of experience you have today will only grow with every success you build upon. Be sure to keep records of the sell outs, the live on-air hours you've logged, favourable reviews, popularity, number of *likes* and followers and the surpassed sales targets you have accumulated. At the same time, remember that times are tough in every line of business. Margins are getting tighter at all levels of business and there's always another younger guest expert biting at your heels to take your job. As important as negotiating a good rate is, you are also building a relationship with a client that could be a part of your professional life for a long time to come.

Basic Business and Negotiation Principles

In simple terms, to generate a profit you need more revenue coming in than cost being put out. (Costs may include hair care, skin and nail care, clothing, travel, samples, demo set-ups, rehearsal time, research time, script writing, etc.) This is your business and the purpose and goal of the business is to make money and for your brand to become more recognizable and trusted. Be sure to get everything in writing to confirm what both parties mutually agreed to, plus any other noteworthy discussions, even before the final contract has been written. Prior to signing your final contract, you may wish to consult with an entertainment or intellectual property lawyer, as the guidelines provided are just that - guidelines.

There are two basic key principles in any negotiation: **Leverage** and **Win Win.**

Leverage is the ability to influence the other side (vendor/network) to move towards your terms based on your ability, experience and potential to provide them with what they want, to sell out their product thereby generating income and profit. To the new guest expert your leverage starts with the fact that they hired you and believed you would do a great job at selling their product. That is a good start. For the experienced guest expert, reputation, past sales results and audience familiarity does play a part in the position you can take while negotiating.

Know your category and the specific line it falls into within the network. Try to understand how important the product line you are selling is relative to the percentage of appearances within the year. Ask yourself are there any other competitors that would be compared to you or your product on the network? If so, learn what the sales are and how many shows are being aired per month and per year. Try to understand the frequency of airings for the category during each month and year. For instance in most networks, jewelry and beauty hold the highest percentage of air-time followed by home and décor. What category do you fall into? Is your line a specialty line? What are the projected sales per quarter, per year and what are the sales projections you feel you'll be able to generate for them? What kind of buzz can you generate via social media and other grassroots initiatives? Do you have a strong fan following already? If you don't know the answers to some or any of these questions, ask whoever you can until you have a clear idea of how strong your position has the *potential* to be.

Win Win is where you as the guest expert and the vendor/network are both satisfied with the deal achieved. In this process, there is usually give and take between both parties but the outcome is positive for both. You need to protect your business interest in your negotiations. This is your time to communicate what you need in order to do your job well and give them what they want, which involves more than just dollars. Many factors need to also be considered including: receiving show line-ups, scripts and script changes and all other pertinent information well in advance of your show airing. Knowing when to communicate all set and demo requirements, specialty videos and other presentation requirements well in advance for the network to fulfill your requests. You have to settle on appropriate payment terms to suit both parties. There may be a network guest expert liaison to help bridge any communication gaps and the guest expert handbook will most likely have some helpful information as well.

Here is a true story to illustrate the importance of protecting yourself and the profession of the guest expert.

There was this guest expert who wanted to be on TV to sell what she felt she was an expert in. The guest expert had the credentials and the experience to talk about the product assigned to her, but she was not a trained sales expert. The product was a high ticket item that was not pre-promoted well and as such high volume sales weren't expected. This guest expert thought she would *help out the buyer* by negotiating an enormously discounted rate of $20 per product sold. So, if she sold ten products during the entire 24-hour day, the network would only have to pay her $200. From the buyer's standpoint this was a great deal. This however, was not the best deal for the guest expert nor good for the profession, as it set a low ball pay precedent in that category. It didn't honour the profession of the business or the highly specialized skill of being a strong guest expert. When negotiating, consider what is best for you at the time, but also consider how your actions may affect others in the future. We want to continue to build a strong alliance of professionals!

Stick to Your Numbers

Let's assume for a minute that you have now negotiated a rate that you are happy with. Your job is to stick to your numbers. There may be some exceptions where a discounted rate is appropriate to offer. It could be a new vendor or a new product that may have potential to add to your sales and work portfolio. If you feel that discounting your rate for a finite amount of time is good business, consider doing it. If you feel you can afford a reduction, call it a one-time discounted fee. Thinking long term is admirable and is one way of showing goodwill. It will build your reputation of being a team player but remember that both parties agreed upon the initial compensation package. The bottom line is any reductions makes you deplete your net gains as you still have expenses to pay. Time does equal money. The time you spend researching, creating and learning scripts, rehearsing, overall grooming, travel (even locally), demo development and all the other preparations do not change regardless of your time on-air. You must consider the behind the scenes time and money spent as part of your daily or show rate.

It is the buyer's responsibility to make money every hour, and if what you are selling isn't meeting budget, the rest of your shows may be cancelled or shortened. If you work on a show rate (which is one of the more common arrangements), you are only paid for the time you work. (The exception would be if you negotiated a daily flat fee or appearance fee regardless of any cancellations). You may have started the day knowing you would be working for six shows, making 'x' amount of dollars. All of a sudden, you are taken off air after two shows. With one quick word from your buyer, your take home pay gets reduced by 60%. There is a certain amount of risk inherent in this line of work and that is why I urge you to stick to your numbers! On the next number of pages you will find the **Negotiation Guidelines Chart**. As stated earlier, this is only a guideline and not meant to replace any professional legal advice you may seek out. It is only meant to provide a big picture idea of important elements to consider. This does not replace the licensed advice of a professional lawyer, manager or accountant.

COMPENSATION	COACHING NOTES	FOR YOUR CONSIDERATION
FLAT PAY RATE		
Per Show	• This is the most common compensation format	• Is this a proven or new product or category? • If you have confidence in the product and have long term interest to work with the vendor, you might consider for the first airing a 'one-time' discounted fee to show your commitment. 'One time' is the important distinction. • Selling product on-air is an exceptional marketing initiative for you and the product line. This is important to take note of when negotiating. • In the event of an unforeseeable emergency where you cannot fulfill your work on the day of the booking, do you have a contingency in place? Is there someone who can take your place? How will this exchange occur? This should be a talking point with you and the vendor.
Per Day or Days	• Most veterans prefer daily flat rates. This guarantees the income. It is also a great idea for bigger-ticket items and/or unproven items/brands.	
Per Piece	• If you are a seasoned and experienced guest expert, consider being paid per piece you sell. There is obviously some risk with this choice and should be considered carefully.	
Per Minute on-air	• This occurs more commonly with the jewelry and fashion categories where you may be selling for many different vendors in one show. (Be prepared to have a good sales record system so you can invoice accurately).	
Appearance Fee	• Some seasoned guest experts, owners and celebrities may receive an appearance fee which may or may not be over and above any other sales income.	

CHAPTER 4 — THE JOB OF GETTING THE JOB

COMPENSATION	COACHING NOTES	FOR YOUR CONSIDERATION
Percentage	• Jewelry and fashion products are predominant categories where you may be selling for many different vendors during your show. • There could be as many as 25 items represented by multiple vendors. This is where per minute pricing may be applicable.	• Commission selling is not new to anyone in sales. You are paid for what you sell – they win and so do you. It is a great choice to include in your negotiation as it motivates and engages the guest expert to do their job to the best of their ability. If the product is well marketed and pre-promoted by the network and vendor, there is high potential to make a lot of money.
Dollars per unit sold	• Some vendors may pay a flat show fee PLUS a defined price (instead of commission) for each unit sold (eg. $0.50 /unit sold).	• This can work well on low priced items where high volume is expected. You wouldn't want to agree to this arrangement if you had a high ticket item with low volume turnover.
Per minute	• Jewelry and fashion products are predominant categories where you may be selling for many different vendors during your show. • There could be as many as 25 items represented by multiple vendors. This is where per minute pricing may be applicable.	• Remember that in a one hour show there are actually only 52 - 54 billable minutes. (There are often promos and breaks scheduled during each one hour show.)

COMPENSATION	COACHING NOTES	FOR YOUR CONSIDERATION
Returns	• If you are paid by commission, the vendor or network will subtract a certain percentage for returns and damaged goods. There are some categories where the percentage of returns are very high. For example in clothing fashion and jewelry, customers may purchase 2 different sizes of the same item and then return the one that doesn't fit. Keep track of the return percentage and take note of any fluctuations within your category and brand.	
Freelance Contracts	• Generally, you will have to sign a freelance contract. This is a straightforward media contract that most every on-camera personality has to sign. It protects the network from any liabilities. • Be informed before you sign.	• Consider having an intellectual property or entertainment lawyer review the contract to ensure there are no loopholes preventing you from working other gigs – either at other shopping channel networks or completely unrelated work for example, commercials, hosting work, industrials training and sales films etc…
Samples from Vendor	• Request a clause in your negotiated contract to receive all samples in a timely fashion at no cost to you. It is imperative to receive all samples in order to understand every aspect of your product. This should be part of the vendor's marketing budget.	• In order to illuminate your product and communicate all the great assets of it, you have to be able to work with what you are selling. • Getting product ahead of time can provide an opportunity to catch any quality issues before going to air. Although stringent quality testing is part of every network, you are still the last line of defense before your customers experience it.

CHAPTER 4 — THE JOB OF GETTING THE JOB

COSTS	COACHING NOTES	FOR YOUR CONSIDERATION
Supportive Products	• Supportive products may include: food when you are selling plastic containers, mixers, storage bags etc… or clothes and home items for when you are selling suitcases, storage bags and hangers etc… These purchases should be a vendor expense as part of the cost of doing business with a shopping network. The guest expert should not have to incur these costs. • Regarding the example of purchasing food for any kitchen show - this product is 100% perishable and will have to be purchased every time a new show day is booked. It can get expensive. • Consider adding an expense reimbursement clause in your agreement for all supportive products. This is especially important if the product you are selling is a one-off products with little or no chance of being repeated.	• Consider adding a reimbursement clause for all supportive products in your agreement. Particularly if the supportive products are perishable, like food products. • Weigh your options on this subject of being reimbursed. There may be times when you consider amortizing the cost of the supportive products (especially if there is a long term commitment to you and the product being sold.) For instance, I built my own custom bathroom set that I bring in every time we sell towels and bathroom accessories. When this set comes in, I know it means higher sales for me. It has cost me a lot of money in shipping, storing and set up time but the risk has paid off on a long term basis. In this case, I own the set and consider it to be part of my demonstration materials. Make the right choices for long term professional reputation.
Air and Surface travel	• For out of town engagements, the vendor/buyer should pay for the essential travel to get you to the country, city, hotel and studio on time. Clarity and understanding the terms are essential.	• Be alert if you are asked to cover any air and surface travel. (Refer to the per diem section on the next page for more information).

143

COSTS	COACHING NOTES	FOR YOUR CONSIDERATION
Lodging	• Vendors will often have a designated hotel and it's usually a minimum three star rating or higher. If you foresee a problem with the standard arrangements, clear up the matter before the booking if possible. • Security, cleanliness and getting a restful sleep contributes positively to your performance. • Be sure you feel comfortable and safe with your accommodations and surrounding area.	• Any upgrades or amenities over and above the standard provisions are your responsibility and expense.
Per diem	• Should be included in your compensation clause in your contract. Most vendors will provide a daily per diem that will cover meals and cab rides, etc. Standard rates can range from $75US - $125US per day. This is only a guide but should at least cover the costs of meals and transportation to and from hotel, the network and the airport.	• Surface travel, lodging, meals etc. is costly and shouldn't be coming out of your show pay rate. It is a separate expense and is essential in getting the product on-air.

CHAPTER 4 — THE JOB OF GETTING THE JOB

COSTS	COACHING NOTES	FOR YOUR CONSIDERATION
Renting a Dressing room	• Some networks provide complimentary dressing rooms and green rooms and others don't due to the volume of programming. • In some cases, dressing rooms are available for a daily rental fee. If you are travelling from long distances and feel you will need a designated dressing room, consider adding this rental into your contract when negotiating.	• The guest orientation booklet you will receive when you first work on the network will inform you of your options.
Renting Lockers or Storage Space	• Some networks offer locker space or storage rental to store products and supportive material only. It is a helpful option if you have demo equipment that is too bulky or costly to ship back and forth. This could be a vendor expense and is a good talking point when discussing the elements within your initial contract agreement.	• The guest orientation booklet you will receive when you first work on the network will inform you of your options.

OTHER	COACHING NOTES	FOR YOUR CONSIDERATION
Cross Border Issues	• Login to the U.S., Canadian and International immigration websites to better understand what kind of documentation you should arrive with at all borders crossings.	
Invoicing and Pay Terms	• As a freelancer, you most likely have or will need to set up a sales record and invoicing system that works best for you. • If direct deposit is an option, sign up for it. It eliminates a lot of paper work and potential headaches.	• Payment terms – every vendor is different. Negotiate mutually agreed upon payment terms.
Mini Accounts Receivable Department	• If you aren't receiving payment within the mutually agreed upon terms laid out in your contract, you may need to take further action to resolve and expedite pay issues. Find out who the contact people in accounts payable are and get to know them. This will help resolve and/or expedite pay issues in the future.	• It is good business to be on top of outstanding invoices!

SOURCES

1. http://www.thevpp.ca/

CHAPTER 4
The Job of Getting the Job

1. Auditioning and interviewing is part of your work and livelihood as an independent professional. Become exceptional at these skills.

2. The panel who is auditioning you wants to see you on your best day. Your job is to show up every time as if it is your best day.

3. Your resume got you the appointment. The audition starts at the front door of the building – not only the audition room itself. There are a lot of people who have influence and pull you may have no idea about.

4. 3 Questions in Life (Exercise) can help you through the trials of not always booking work when you need to.

5. Use your reputation, past sales successes and familiarity with your customers with confidence when negotiating.

6. Negotiating Guidelines Chart – will help you to think like an agent. (This is a guide and does not take the place of a certified professional.)

CHAPTER 5

IT'S SHOWTIME, FOLKS

A Truth About the Business of Performing

Many performers are at their best and most alive when on stage. Performers can be maniacal about control. Good, I said it. The truth is we have to be. No one knows how to make us tick except us.

If you've been in the business of performing of any kind, be it TV, film, theatre, professional speaking, tradeshows, etc., you know that once the show is over, you are out of that space so fast it's as if you've been thrown into the back of the getaway car. We have learned to not linger physically or mentally in an event that has ended. We live in an inconsistent environment of opportunity of highs and lows for large chunks of time and many times left is right and right is upside down. The brilliant highs and dark lows may seem quite striking at times, but this is part of our work. We stay in the moment, and as soon as that moment is over, our light goes out too. It's the way we survive and is a skill that is honed over the years. It also acts as a reset button for us to find our neutral place readying ourselves for the next challenge. We always have to keep our focus up no matter the circumstances.

The reasons brands die, products don't sell, and show runs close generally have nothing to do with us personally. It's just business. There is no step-by-step ladder to climb up the traditional way one expects to in the corporate world. Our ladder is the connections made, the work being created, the merit of our resume and reputation. It is a business that is built on capitalizing on the present moments of life and opportunities for all it's worth for you never know what's around the corner. The successful veterans have learned to never take their work for granted because they know in order to live another day, every minute counts this day!

In the late 90's, *Ragtime* was a musical that was first mounted in Toronto, Canada readying itself for a two-year Broadway run. It was a great success and critically acclaimed being nominated for multiple Tony awards. Shortly after the run closed on Broadway, I bumped into one of the *Ragtime* actors dressed in white and black offering me grilled canapés with my choice of dips. At first, I was taken aback for a quick second by the dichotomy of roles he had played within a few short months but then reminded myself it's just part of the business.

The critically acclaimed Broadway and movie musical *Rent* was written by Mr. Jonathon Larson (seen in the picture). According to David Lipky, "It took seven years to take *Rent* from its idea to its previews." (The show won a Pulitzer Prize and Tony Award among others. The production closed after a twelve-year Broadway run grossing well over $280 million and counting.) "One week before the first preview he (Jonathon) went home, put on some water for tea, and died"... due to an aortic aneurysm. "He was 35 years old." [1]

CHAPTER 5 — IT'S SHOWTIME, FOLKS

You're only as good as your last performance is what all of us say in the business. Life definitely throws us curve balls at times when we least expect it. I share these stories to illustrate the need to always stay focused on your path and working toward realizing your dreams and ideas to become realities for you. Nothing lasting happens overnight, *so get busy*. If you have a burning need to move things along in a different direction or at a faster pace in your career right now, do it and trust your instincts. As my friend Ron Simpson says, "It's never too early – but sometimes it's too late."

If not now, when?

Nerves Are a Good Thing

Public speaking is known to be one of the most difficult endeavours for most people. Exposing yourself in a way that everyone can *see you* is a scary notion. Regardless of whether you are an extrovert who is perhaps wired to want to be seen or more of an introverted person; nerves can do surprising and unexpected things to us. Unfortunately, only in the heat of the moment will you know how your body reacts. Most people expect that as they become more familiar with performing that the nerves and butterflies will dissipate. This is probably true, but in my opinion, you never want to be so calm inside that there is no fire.

Nerves can serve us well as they keep us aware and sharp to what is happening in the moment. Turn nerves into focus. That is really the power behind the importance of preparation. Nerves are a good thing as long as they are managed. You can't be so nervous that your legs or hands are shaking beyond belief or your mouth is so dry that your words don't come out.

The constraint with all of this is, unfortunately, you won't know how your body will express its nervousness until show time. Therefore, prepare your mind and body as much as you can beforehand and ride it out the first few times. Once you know you've survived the first few airings, that experience will help prepare you for your next on-air work. I assure you, if you do enough work, most of these symptoms will vanish.

Up next, is a quick chart identifying some common *nerves-related* issues that many of the experts shared they had experienced at one time or another. I've provided the issues and some suggestions on how to *manage* them.

COMMON SYMPTOMS	SUGGESTIONS ON HOW TO MANAGE YOUR NERVES
Cough and Clearing Your Throat	• If you've ever experienced a tickle in your throat, you know how annoying it can be. Stay hydrated, bring water on set and get it under control. • If you do have a cold, manage it as best you can. Let the sound technician and the producer know that you may have to cough the odd time and ask them how they would like you to handle it. Each network has a contingency for this and the camera crew will be there to help you.
Dry Mouth	• Be hydrated well before you work. Start hydrating three days before your show. (More details to follow).
Giggly	• Figure out why you are giggling – are you ill prepared, bored or just trying to be charming? It interferes with your overall messaging and again, you only have a few minutes to make your pitch don't waste it giggling.
Shortness of Breath	• Arrive early enough to the studio where you can walk around and recite your entire pitch within the space. Breathe in the space, the smell, the feel, and get comfortable. • Keep taking long, slow breaths in and out when the host is speaking and you are not on camera. Time it out well using the monitors to tell you when you can.
Over Perspiration	• Wear dress shields • There are a number of specialized over the counter deodorant products for over perspiration. If you choose to try it out, carefully follow the directions on the bottle. Be aware of certain textiles and blends that either show perspiration more or make you feel self-conscious (silk, and faux silks, linens, etc.). • Be aware of certain colours that show perspiration more (some people can only wear black and white for this reason). • Yes, you can sweat through jackets, so become aware of how you can help yourself if this is an issue for you.
Red Face, Red Neck and Red Arms	• If you find this to be a common issue, wear necklines that may camouflage or soften it a bit. Figure out if you are allergic to certain foundations or makeup when you are performing. Stress can do different things to our chemistry that is not experienced during a normal day. • You may also feel hotter than normal because of the lights or the experience itself. Dressing accordingly, may also help you out with temperature fluctuations.

COMMON SYMPTOMS	SUGGESTIONS ON HOW TO MANAGE YOUR NERVES
Runny Nose	• The studio may be dry or you may have some allergies that the stress of the moment has somehow exacerbated. Have a tissue just off the set to use as required.
Shaking Hands and Legs	• Be as prepared as you possibly can so that everything you do is second nature and drops out of your mouth like reciting your kids names and birthdays or recalling the multiplication table from the past. • It actually takes more energy to stay *quiet* than to move. Shaking hands and legs is adrenaline pumping through your body. It directly impedes your ability to perform and do demos. This is one symptom you **must** eradicate.
Sweaty Hands	• If you are a *sweaty palm person*, you may have the same issue on set as well. Normally this isn't a huge issue unless you are touching fabrics, coins and other material that can be affected by the chemistry and moisture from your hands. There are a number of different things that may or may not work like putting a little baby powder on your hands before you go out or using hand sanitizer that has a cooling effect. These methods are merely quick fixes that may not have lasting effects. Bring a tissue on set and dry them when you are not on camera. • Rehearse all of this before you get on camera to ensure any *customized remedies* run smoothly and strictly unnoticeable.

Stay Hydrated and Well Fed

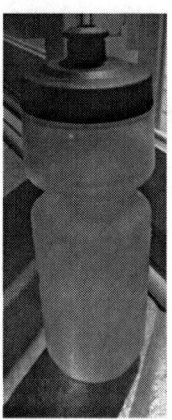

The chart on managing nerves provided some insight into the types of nervous symptoms we can face when under tremendous amounts of stress. By the way, I have experienced almost all of them at one time or another. Although there are perhaps many other symptoms and ways to deal with them, there is only one overall solution that will help alleviate most any symptom: Stay hydrated.

When the stakes are high, our bodies are thrown into a different state often because of the powerful natural hormone we secrete, adrenaline. As it pumps through our bodies, the signs often show up as uncontrollable dry mouth and shaking of hands or legs. You may find you are constantly swallowing, trying to generate any saliva, or perhaps your hands and legs cannot stop moving. Both of these symptoms can make us feel more self-conscious and this nervousness sometimes only builds and gets worse.

Water is essential for regulating body temperature, transporting glucose and other nutrients to your cells. If you are thirsty, that is a fairly clear sign that you are already dehydrated. Never allow yourself to get to that stage. If you are not a very active person, the recommended eight cups of water per day (4 regular sized 250ml water bottles) will be sufficient. However, if you are more active and perhaps are traveling (which can be a huge factor with respect to dehydration), you need to be drinking more than that. To be fair, our bodies are all a little different based on body mass and muscle make up. If you listen to your body and follow the regular guidelines, you will be ahead of the game in your preparations.

Be sure to bring a bottle of water on set (check on individual network rules before you do this). Take care of your instrument. It will make a significant difference to the way your body reacts to a very stressful situation!

One time on-air, I realized how important proper hydration really was:

It had been six weeks since my last show and I had been training for a marathon as well. This particular GVS show-day occurred the day after a long-run training day of more than two hours. When the host introduced me, I launched into my hook and next thing you know, my throat closed down on me like a clamp. The host quickly took over and I grabbed a glass of water. When I came back, simple words were tripping me up like I had cotton balls in my cheeks. I became very self-conscious and couldn't believe what was happening. Luckily, the host I was working with was a good friend of mine and could tell I was struggling. I could only say one-word answers and so that is how the show went. Our sales did well nonetheless, but it was a ridiculous experience. I was so angry with myself. After the show, the host and I spoke and I thanked her for picking up the ball so beautifully. She said she had never seen me like that. "Are you dehydrated?" she asked. I told her I hadn't thought about it. "You are. Get busy and drink water before your next show."

You will notice that most every host always has a container of water set just off camera.

Celebrity Effect

Most everyone is familiar with the game *Trivial Pursuit*. It was conceived and created by two Canadians back in 1979. At the time, Chris Haney was a photo editor and Scott Abbott was a sports journalist for a well-known Montreal newspaper. In 1981, it was first trademarked and commercially released on a limited run. Although they took the game to local trade shows, there wasn't a huge interest to buy at first. The creators knew they had something special and kept on moving forward regardless of the slow start. Soon, sales progress had been made and by 1983, they trademarked and licensed the game to a major US game manufacturer. [2]

The tipping point that catapulted *Trivial Pursuit* into the Games Hall of Fame eight years later was ignited August 22, 1985. (This is the part of the puzzle that is not as well known.) According to a colleague friend with intimate knowledge of this story, the turning point happened on the *Tonight Show with Johnny Carson*. Ed Begley Jr. was the featured guest along with Arnold Schwarzenegger. As Johnny was interviewing Ed Begley Jr., he mentioned *Trivial Pursuit* and said that it was the most exciting and fascinating game he had ever played. His star power and positive endorsement furthered the name and game into the households all across the world. Remember back then, the Internet wasn't accessible by everyday households. There was no such thing as social media and *CNN* was only five years young.

Chuck Norris, (the late) Jack Lalanne and Cindy Crawford are all extremely successful DRTV and home shopping celebrities that bring in millions of dollars per year. They have star power, connection and brand recognition. People believe them because they look like they've been using what they are selling. When you look at Chuck Norris even now, you see his physique at his age and stage in life, and all you want to do is say "I'll have what he's having!" Such an image convinces the consumer that if *he* can look like that, so can *I*.

What does a strong celebrity bring to the network's table? They can attract mass audiences. Stars are ticket sellers, which is why you see many TV and film celebrities starring on Broadway. The theatre producers need the tickets to sell in order for the production to run. They know that if they hire the right stars to draw in crowds, they can virtually guarantee sales. Stars are magnanimous and unpredictable, which makes for an entertaining experience for the audience. They have tremendous charisma and personality and they know how to hold the audience's attention for longer than a minute. It is a skill that can be worth millions.

CHAPTER 5 — IT'S SHOWTIME, FOLKS

In Chapter 1, Future of the Home Shopping Industry, we highlighted the recent influx of ex-soap opera stars selling products on-air as an example of the influence of using star power. They are just one set of celebrities but is a decision that many home shopping businesses are leaning toward because of the elimination (or near elimination) of risk to loss of sales and DPM. They know that if they bring in a celebrity, he/she comes with fans and followers and their chances at solid sales and traffic will be much higher. If their shows are marketed well, and if the celebrity does his or her part at promoting the shows, the chances of a sell out will be even more possible.

I've talked to a lot of guest experts about the celebrity effect and although there are some unsupportive opinions (they perhaps see them as competition), the majority of non-star guest experts see it as a great addition and only serves them better. Celebrity presence almost guarantees customer retention and attracts new traffic to the station and website. And there is an added bonus if you are an ambitious marketer. You may find an opportunity to sell the celebrity's product when they are not able to travel to a certain destination. There's enough work for all but the celebrity effect will always hold an important place.

How can we non-stars learn from our celebrity guest experts? Create a buzz on your own by branding yourself. Pre-promote upcoming shows on your own accounts and the accounts of the shopping channels. Get in conversations on Facebook and send out product teasers on twitter before and during your shows. There is a lot you can do.

Sales Means You Have to Put the Puck in the Net

Not every celebrity knows how to sell or ask for business the way a trained salesperson does. This can be a significant problem. There are many C and D celebrities who are hired to endorse a product they have had nothing to do with. To them it's a two-day gig and tomorrow they'll be shooting a commercial for Cocoa Puffs or denture cream. The $15,000 (approximately) spent flying that celebrity to the station plus room, board and transportation would be better spent on training a professional guest expert who knows how to sell, ask for business and create excitement around a product to get it out the door quickly.

Life Cycle of the Guest Expert

The answer to what the life cycle of a guest expert should be is quite simple. It's up to you. Like the athlete who starts to feel burned out, gets injured more frequently and has a harder time recovering, the guest expert has to know when he or she doesn't have the energy to do it anymore. The traveling, the pace, the preparations, the schlepping can take its toll. Since this is such a personal expression and involves 100% of our effort, you have to know yourself when to step away gracefully.

If you choose to stay in the game, it's important to remain current in both the way you dress and the design of your pitch.

As relayed in Chapter 1, The Home Shopping Industry, we learned that women play a predominant role within the home shopping world of customers. The percentage varies and continually changes, but at least 70% of the customers are women. What's more important is that women like purchasing from other women. Unfortunately, this line of work is often not as kind to female guest experts compared to our male counterparts. Frequently, you will see older gentlemen still selling like gangbusters whereas the older females are somewhat fewer and far between. There are of course the great exceptions like Suzanne Somers, who (at the time of this publication), is well into her 60's, Joan Rivers who is in her 80's and Elizabeth Grant who is over 80, still selling skincare like no one else and still hammering out multi-millions of dollars over two days on a shopping channel in a Canadian market one-tenth the size of the American audience. The identified women are all vibrant professional entertainers who know how to pace themselves in order to be *on* when they need to be.

The smart guest expert can nurture a long and thriving career. There are two women who come to mind that have proven they are lasting forces in this business:

Forbes Riley and Rosalie Brown. Both women sell fitness and wellness products and are among the most dynamic leaders in their industry.

I highlighted Forbes Riley earlier in this book. Her lifetime commitment to health and well-being have made her a true force. She has designed part of her brand and pitch to the fact that she is a normal mother who is raising twin girls and has the same body issues and concerns all women share. She has always been dedicated to helping regular women be the best they can be without having to spend hours in the gym. She has sold millions of dollars of fitness products over the years and all because she is one of the regular women out there helping other regular women.

For well over twenty-five years, Rosalie Brown (seen below), has been one of the most successful personal trainers and fitness on-air guest experts in North America. She regularly sells on TSC and QVC. She has developed a signature brand that is high energy and trustworthy without intimidating the newcomer to fitness. Her style is engaging and highly personable and she plays up the fact that she is a busy mom and grandmother in her fifties.[3]

Used with Rosalie's permission

Never Say Never

If you have reached your limit and feel that you want to step down, even for a while, just do it. The break may re-energize your mind and body. I have worked alongside veteran guest experts who have nothing but complaints to share, from the lack of hours they're getting, to the angle of the lights highlighting wrinkles, to how a certain host should be let go and the buyer has no idea what she is doing. Here's my only advice. If you leave, do it on good terms and don't burn a bridge. You'll leave the door open to have the possibility to come back if you so choose.

Lifecycle of a Product

> "Customers can only be acquired, churned, and reactivated so many times before they tire of your brand. There is a proven marketing equation in which customers willingly share information with you in the expectation of being better served and valued during future transactions."
>
> -Bryan Pearson, *The Loyalty Leap*

Business is moving more quickly than ever. In speaking about the life cycle of business, I consulted my thirty plus year commission sales colleague Donald Lowes who shared, "Every month I count on my business changing in increments. The reasons are many and include, competition doing things less expensively, product lines are dropped due to disinterest in the marketplace or clients bypassing the middlemen (me) and going directly to my suppliers."

We have to be ready to react to the changes and be looking ahead at how to capitalize accordingly.

In DRTV and in home shopping, there are times where a product can last for no more than three or four months before the configuration needs to be changed. Most everyone at one time or another has the option of accessing the newest and the next super trend. (Consider the early adopter craze so common with new technology.) In order to retain customers, many manufacturers have to react quickly with the need to change up the configuration in some way to keep them coming back for more. One has to remain competitive and alluring to the customers.

The Genie™ Bra (highlighted in Chapter 1) is a great example of how to react to the need for change. In order to retain old customers and gain new ones, their winning prescription and designs have to always be re-styled and updated. As manufacturers, there is also the element of competitors nipping at your heels. The copycats come out and there's nothing to stop that from happening. That's just business and is why manufacturers and vendors can never sit back if they want to stay in the game.

There is however the complete other side of the coin where the old adage, *if it ain't broke, don't fix it* applies. In every category, there may always be certain products that are just plain top sellers and remain that way for years.

Alli and Dallas Prince

Long-time jewelry designer and owner of Dallas Prince Designs shares, "For over ten years, there have been a few pieces in my collection that continue to perform well enough to have longevity in my shows. These types of designs can generate multiple purchases by the same customer because they love the styling and versatility so much that they want to gift it to others. I cherish my customers and the relationship I have with them. It is my goal to always make them feel special and excited about my collections!" [4]

The obvious need is to always build our business up with reliable suppliers and manufactures who can be flexible enough to change and re-define our brand when we need to react to the changes in the market.

Ultimately our customers tell us what they want year in and year out. If we're listening, and if we adjust quickly to the ever-changing requirements of the market and still deliver on our word consistently, we'll be in a stronger position to stay in business.

SOURCES

1. http://www.angelfire.com/in2/everythingisrent/jon.htm
   http://en.wikipedia.org/wiki/Rent_(musical)
2. http://en.wikipedia.org/wiki/Trivial_Pursuit
3. http://www.rosaliebrown.ca/
4. https://www.facebook.com/dallasprincejewelry

CHAPTER 5
It's Showtime, Folks

1. Performers are control freaks because we have to be. No one knows how to get us motivated better than ourselves.

2. Learn to manage your nerves. Chart provided.

3. Celebrities invite new business and traffic to the channels for many reasons. Salespeople know how to close, celebrities know how to entertain. The best combination is to have both. If you are not a celebrity, learn from them and create a buzz about your product.

4. You're only as good as your last show. If you have a burning desire to do more, then get busy. If not now, when?

5. There is a life cycle to being a guest expert. Put yourself in the driver's seat and be aware of what is happening around you. Make adjustments as you see fit and know when the time is right to step down.

6. The life cycle of your product depends on who your target market is and what your customers are telling you through their buying trends.

CHAPTER 6

THERE'S NO 'I' IN TEAM

"The leaders who work most effectively, it seems to me, never say I. And that's not because they have trained themselves not to say I. They don't think I. They think we; they think team. They understand their job to be to make the team function. They accept responsibility and don't sidestep it, but we gets the credit. This is what creates trust, what enables you to get the task done."
-Peter F. Drucker

"The world knows he was the greatest management thinker of the last century."
-Jack Welch, former chairman of General Electric Co., said after Drucker's death November 11, 2005.

Relationship Capital I

The relationships you create throughout your life are paramount in helping you to become the person you are today. When things really count and there is urgency about a situation in your life, we count on our network of friends and colleagues to help us get through the challenges we encounter. (Relationship Capital II is found in Chapter 12).

What's the first thing you do if you're told by your family physician that you have a serious illness? You probably call someone you know you can count on who knows someone who can help you get in touch with a specialist they trust or a similar scenario to that.

What do you do when you lose your job or one of your university kids needs a job? You start to go through your list of colleagues and contacts of people who you have maintained a good relationship with over the years. You pick up the phone and ask them for any recommendations on job openings in their immediate circle or within their circle of contacts. They start to work with you and before you know it, you have some names of reliable people to call because of your relationship with that first colleague. You reach out to your network of friends and colleagues to help spread the word and get support and you do the same for them.

It's a pleasure to be able to help your friends and colleagues with the network of people you know and trust. It's one of those quiet moments in life that make you feel proud of the relationships you have nurtured over the years. It's also the one thing that can never be taken from you. Some might say (and I would) that it is more valuable than almost anything in life. There's only one caveat to this sharing process: carefully choose who you are going to share your relationship capital with. If I recommend you to my network, don't make me look bad because my reputation is now involved with your newfound contact.

> "... some people think that I'm some kind of hero or a special person. But it's really the body of people and their mass thinking that caused computers to happen."
> **-Steve Wozniak**

Recently, I attended a professional curling event that highlighted the world's best teams in the sport today.

A quick aside: If you're not familiar with the sport of curling, here's a simple description – It's a 4-person team sport played on ice with forty-pound granite rocks sliding up and down the ice. Opponents gain power and ultimately win by positioning rocks closest to the 'button' (think bull's eye) of each playing surface (depicted in the photo above). The game involves fast twitch muscle power and keen hand eye coordination. It also requires strategy like that of chess with the focus, finesse and understanding of angles and weight like that of golf and billiards.

The featured game highlighted two reigning Olympic gold medal teams. Halfway through the game during the intermission, a young female spectator was selected from the stands to win the chance to throw one rock to the 'button'. She had two choices to make: She could either throw the rock on her own with no guidance from anyone OR she could enlist the expertise and aid from her choice of gold medal team members. The catch was, if she made the shot on her own with no help from the team members, she would win $1 million. If however, she chose to work with the best players in the world to help her succeed, she would *only* win $100,000. Less money for sure but still not bad for thirty seconds of work!

Can you guess what her decision was? Let's put this into perspective: There are thousands of spectators watching, including the eight champions drinking Gatorade on the sidelines, the foreign 'feel' of the arena ice and the pressure to get the right weight and line to hit the button perfectly.

CHAPTER 6 — THERE'S NO 'I' IN TEAM

(Picture a twenty-five foot putt that slopes slightly to the left with high wind. Not an easy shot at the best of times but certainly a makeable shot.) She sat at the opposite end of the ice surface; she lined up her shot, wound back and then pushed off releasing her rock to the other end hoping it would settle right on the button. Amazingly, she actually had the right weight, meaning her rock came to a stop right around the same horizontal line as where the button was. Where she missed was she didn't have the right line and was off by one foot. This simple error could have easily been avoided if she had chosen to use the team expertise as they had the wisdom and experience with that particular playing field. She took a gamble to go it alone where her odds to succeed were in the low single digit percentile as opposed to knowing her team of experts would better her chances by an enormous margin. I remember sitting in the stands thinking how unenlightened we can be when we are too single minded.

On March 10, 2014, famed director Sam Mendes was honoured at an event for New York's Roundabout Theatre Company. The British Academy award winner and director of some of the most prolific and memorable productions include films *Skyfall*, *Road to Perdition* and *American Beauty*, the 1999 Tony award winning revival of Cabaret, and 2014 London productions of *Charlie and the Chocolate Factory* and *King Lear*. In his gracious acceptance speech, Mr. Mendes shared "25 steps towards becoming a happier director."

After I read the steps, I felt that many of the points could easily be applied to all of us as leaders in our industry who want to make a difference in our own careers and in the lives and careers of others. Here are the most poignant steps. To refer to the entire list, I have included the source at the end of this chapter.

"1. Always choose good collaborators. It seems so obvious, but the best collaborators are the ones who disagree with you. It means they're passionate, they have opinions, and they'll only ever say yes if they mean it.

2. Try to learn how to make the familiar strange, and the strange familiar. Direct Shakespeare like it's a new play, and treat every new play as if it's Shakespeare.

4. Learn to say, "I don't know the answer." It could be the beginning of a very good day's rehearsal.

7. If you are doing a play or a film, you have to have a secret way in if you are directing it. Sometimes it's big things. American Beauty, for me, was about my adolescence. Road to Perdition was about my childhood. Skyfall was about middle-age and mortality. Sometimes it's small things. Maybe it's just a simple idea. What if we do the whole thing in the nightclub, for example. But it's not enough just to admire a script, you have to have a way in that is yours, and yours alone.

8. Confidence is essential, but ego is not.

10. Buy a good set of blinkers. Do not read reviews. It's enough to know whether they're good or they're bad. When I started, artists vastly outnumbered commentators, and now, there are a thousand published public opinions for every work of art. However strong you are, confidence is essential to what you do, and confidence is a fragile thing. Protect it. As T.S. Eliot says, teach us to care, and not to care.

11. Run a theater. A play is temporary, a building is permanent. So try to create something that stays behind and will be used and loved by others.

13. There is no right and wrong, there is only interesting, and less interesting.

15. There are no such things as "previews" on Broadway.

18. When you have a cast of 20, this means you have 20 other imaginations in the room with you. Use them.

20. Get on with it. Robert Frost said, "Tell everything a little faster." He wasn't wrong.

22. Learn to accept the blame for everything. If the script was poor, you didn't work hard enough with the writer. If the actors failed, you failed

them. If the sets, the lighting, the poster, the costumes are wrong, you gave them the thumbs-up. So build up your shoulders, they need to be broad.

25. Never, ever, ever forget how lucky you are to do something that you love." [1,2]

The Buyers

Buyers think one year ahead. A month from now is yesterday in their business. The buyer is the centre of influence for almost every logistical part of the retail throughput from the inception and design of the product through to when the customer receives it at home. It's the ultimate corporate entrepreneurial role that comes with more performance pressure than most other jobs. You receive a pat on the back for strong sales outcomes or a shake of the head if sales are soft. The buyer travels frequently, staying on top of market trends, customer trend tendencies and overall trend cycles. She or he has to know their customers intimately and have good taste (particularly if it is a fashion item of any sort). He has to juggle test reports, financial and vendor mandates, concern himself with vendor letters of credit, inventory counts, relationship maintenance, and have the ability to forecast accurately (to name only a few responsibilities). The buyer is also the casting agent deciding on the right guest expert while continually shopping for new and reliable vendors, always pushing current vendors to jump through hoops on margins, latest technological applications, shipping, packaging, unique configurations and designs. He has to be a pitch master to convince his bosses about why the proposed program will sell out, provide purchasing justifications, squeeze out every last dime in order to provide the *and you gets* like free shipping with purchase, TVO (this visit only) or BOGO (buy one, get one) options. Finally, when it's all been decided, and is now on-air, the buyer has to completely give up control of the operation to sit and watch how the buying decisions actually turn out. There is no middle road for the buyer. On the flip side, if you are a good buyer, the chances of you always being employed because of your vast array of skills are extremely high. Therefore, the next time you sell out the product on-air, remember the buyer's winning role. They deserve extremely strong praise for their work too.

Buyers and On-Air Guests

The relationship between the buyer and the on-air guest is of paramount significance. You don't have to be their best friend, but it is a relationship that is most important to you in forwarding your career. Your buyer holds the key to connecting you to the possibility of being employed long term, so in essence, he/she is your #1 customer. He/she also can help you answer some key marketing questions. For instance, I always ask my buyers, "Why did you purchase this product? Out of all the options you have been presented with this quarter, what made it stand out to you? What was the reason for the colour choices, configurations, etc.?" You can also be an important ally to them to provide feedback on the on-air success or ways it can improve.

Their buying decisions have a lot to do with historical sales results, website testimonials and feedback from past customers. If blue, for instance, was the popular selling colour last year, do they bring it back this time as well? If so, what new design tweaks can they add to it in the hopes of WOWING their customers even more? The more insight and pitch alignment you can glean from what the buyer pitched to their bosses, the better for you, and ultimately, your customers.

The Hosts

The job of the host is one of the most intense jobs in live television. You have to have the look and finesse of a CNN reporter, the charisma of a Queen Latifah or Jimmy Fallon, and you also have to have very strong sales skills. You have to be an entertainer, keep the energy of a game show host but still make it personally interesting to the viewers. The past experience of each host involves a wide variety of professional backgrounds including: acting, journalism, TV producers, anchors and weather specialists, radio reporters, teachers and instructors. All the qualities and skills we highlighted earlier in Chapter 2, The Guest Expert, apply to what a host needs in order to be successful. In fact, many times, a successful guest expert is recruited to be a host because the learning curve is a lot less for them and consequently, the network. In speaking to an experienced host from HSN recently, she shared that her teaching background in the inner city of Omaha, Nebraska gave her a sixth sense of tuning into what the customers needed to hear at any given moment during the shows. She felt her job was to let the experts do their thing to sell their products and her job was to be in the ready to jump in to keep the message focused and poignant. Another host shared that each host speaks the same language of their own dialect.

Depending on the structure of the networks, most hosts receive a base salary with year-end bonuses based on overall sales achieved that year. They are often provided with some sort of yearly per diem to help pay for clothing and beauty products. Again, every network is a bit different. Being a home shopping host can be a very lucrative job, and believe me, they earn every penny. They are the face of the network and a lot is expected of them. They have regular host meetings and they meet with buyers daily and weekly to prepare for current and future shows. They also do their own investigation on the merits and selling features of all upcoming products. They are often expected to make personal appearances on behalf of the network as well as attending and hosting many charity and corporate events. After all, they are celebrities. After every show, most networks require them to write a show report reviewing how their sales day went. The report will include good and constructive feedback about the logistics. Perhaps there was a problem with the sound or the staging wasn't up to par, etc. It will also include a review on the guest expert, particularly if they are new. With a review from the host, they can single handedly make or break your chances of being asked back to work on-air. Always strive for your best to ensure that the host only has compliments and high praise about your on-camera abilities, your salesmanship, knowledge and demonstrations.

It's not uncommon for a host to be required to introduce and sell up to thirty or more different products during their multi-hour on-air shifts. They are ultra-competent and often carry entire two and three-hour shows alone. They are exceptional at multitasking and must compartmentalize their attention into six or eight different sections. They are paying attention to the directions shared by the producer talking in their ears, they must work successfully with every guest expert, with the camera crew to get the shots they need, and remember everything about the products they only learned a day or an hour ago; and they have to bob and weave through the inevitable changes that occur minute by minute all the while keeping the transitions and flow of the show moving forward. Be ready!

In a world where youngsters seem to be the only image that matters to ratings, the role of the host (so far) is someone who has had life experience. The best hosts in my opinion are people who have been through it a few times and are cool under pressure, grounded with perhaps a few *earned* wrinkles. The decision makers who hire the hosts look for people who are similar to their customers. As such, as our target demographic changes, we may start seeing younger hosts.

Dances with Hosts

The team of the host and guest expert is a special one. It is meant to make the audience feel warm and safe as well as entertained. In an ideal situation, the show's ultimate success lies with both parties working together at their peak. We both want to connect, to stimulate our customers to purchase and to enjoy a fast paced, entertaining show.

If you are a fan of cycling, you will recognize Phil Liggett and Paul Sherman (respectively) in the photo above. These dynamic gentlemen are the most popular play-by-play cycling colour commentators in the world today. When they work together, their commentary is both personable and infectious. The exchanges are energized, quick and penetrating. They use humour, demonstrations, statistics and facts which interests and educates seasoned sports fans and *their* fresh faced sons and daughters. Phil and Paul feed off each other as if they could finish each other's sentences.

Play-by-play is a precise term to describe the ideal rapport you can share with your host and is by far one of the most important elements to achieving strong sales. When sales are going well, many times your quick interchanges are bouncing high in the air and the excitement continues to build. The best in the business never let the hacky sack drop.

It is your job (not the host's job), to dance around the pace and energy of your host. You are expected to take the lead but not take over. Hosts will push back if they sense you are stepping on their toes. You are a guest in their home. You have to learn how to make subtle adjustments that still honour your style, choreography and messaging while ensuring that your message gets across and penetrates. We all have egos and sometimes certain styles don't mix well. The audience knows the host and may not necessarily know who you are. Remember, the host continues long after you leave the studio, so don't miss this opportunity to make your mark in a positive manner!

I've been within earshot of celebrities and guest experts alike who grumble under their breath about certain hosts they are working with:

"Oh no, I have her. She is so boring and doesn't seem to *get* my sense of humour at all."

"Why doesn't he let me talk? He has me locked in so tightly that he may as well sell the damn product himself. Why the heck am I even here?"

"I can't believe they just saddled me with that new host. She was fumbling with her papers and just repeated everything I said. My show was ruined because of her."

There's no question that sometimes you will have every right to be angry about certain programming and pairings, but your customers don't have a clue about those behind-the-scene details. It doesn't matter anyway. All that matters is that you figure out a way to continue to be professional and keep driving your message in the best possible manner that you can. Trust that the host wants the same things you do, as does the network. If the host is *that* poor, chances are he/she won't be around the next time you return. Don't let yourself get caught up in excuses even if you feel your grievances are legitimate. There's always a way to make the magic happen and many times you find out that the host did you a favour by forcing you to get out of your own head to discover new ways of selling. The term *on the day* applies here and you just have to roll with it. Stay in the moment, react and recover, remain as centered as you can in order to accomplish your goal of staying on message to connect with your customers.

People will ask me, "What host do you have trouble working with?" I can honestly say that I don't have trouble working with anyone. There are hosts that I perhaps click more with than others, but that's more of a personality and chemistry issue but shouldn't have anything to do with how well the job is done. It's easy to blame other people for our missed opportunities but our work is too important to waste time and energy doing that. Go beyond that thought process. You are building your long-term reputation. Your current actions establishes the trail you will be leaving behind.

Show Producer

The show producer can play a key role in your quest to achieving a sell out. They run the show and are generally one of the primary individuals talking in your ear. Apart from their regular role as producer to monitor the show flow and to ensure the host is fully aware of timing, what is coming up next and items left to sell, the good ones can also help push your pitch to the next level of intensity. They can play the part of your sideline coach, sales manager, cheerleader and even statistician. If the sales are kicking high, they have the option to ride on the momentum wave. They can stretch the time originally allotted for that item giving you more time to sell, and thereby more of a chance to sell out.

Multiple Guests on One Show

Working with multiple guests can work incredibly well but it is your responsibility as the guest expert to be extremely clear on your dynamic, flow and structure. This cannot be a winged performance.

Chaos Is Possible

Recently I caught three guest experts selling the same product: One clinician (a female who demonstrated on herself and with the models), one pitch person and one testimonial person. The execution of the three guest experts was spot-on and focused. The dynamic was exciting, as the ball was always being pitched high in the air. It was however, a very confusing experience for the audience because it wasn't well managed on the floor. They were held back by the limitations of the production team and you could tell there was no leadership behind the scenes. Everyone was talking over each other and cameras were missing shots and rushing back and forth trying to capture the guest experts' offerings. The host did her best to keep them in check, but it was like watching a horse in a chuck wagon race that just became unhooked. It ran around with no direction or order. The chaotic show lost the attention of the audience and the low sales numbers confirmed the lack of viewership. Most wouldn't be willing to stick around while they sorted out their confusion. In this case, the team of guests should have brought in *their own* floor manager who was familiar with their timing and flow and had *him* on headset working with the control room and producers. This would have clarified and simplified the camera shots, angles and created more of a balance for the show all around. They needed a conductor and since they didn't have one, they lost out big-time. I suspect if they appear once again, they will have organized this, and then look out. The sales and the show will flow beautifully! In future, I believe we will see more and more of this type of multi-guest packaging with certain categories. If you are preparing for a show with multiple guests on-air, practice working together with your floor manager taking notes and craft a structured plan of triggers for all to know about.

Order Is Also Possible

On the flip-side, there was a brother-duo selling their Holiday CD collection. On-set, they had two pianos where the brothers played, highlighting many of the selections from their CD. The banter and exchanges between them and the host worked really well because it was directed very tightly and was incredibly demonstrative. Because of this organization, the camera crews and director could easily dance around the many aspects of the show. As a result, the sales soared, as did the music!

Your Peers

It is vitally important to stay connected with other guest experts within your network whether they are your direct competition and/or colleagues. I have learned so much from many of the guests I've worked alongside and have proudly highlighted some in this book. As well as being confidantes and great people, they can also be part of your inner circle of influence. There's a lot to be said for the veterans who have been selling on-air for decades. Watch them and learn from them. Take note of how certain GVS's of the day are doing within your category and completely outside of your category. How do their sales and show flow, compared to your last show day or GVS? Up or down? It's important to record what you felt worked and what didn't work and what the overall success of the shows were. (Chapter 11, Assess Your Success, will help you to develop a plan.) For instance, even though cosmetics is not necessarily a direct competitor to décor and design, it is still a fashion and dream sell, so I watch how every guest expert handles their own spin. I also watch out for how they climb out of certain circumstances. For example, if sales are soft or when viewers call in live. Elizabeth Grant (referred to earlier in Chapter 2, The Guest Expert) does extraordinary sales every time she comes to Canada and is one of the strongest sellers and brands! I have noted that she intimately connects to her customers more than anyone else I've seen. She is the age of her audience, she dresses, sounds and talks her age and her viewers absolutely love her. Now, let's be fair, she also has a great product line. You can't have one without the other.

Let's briefly talk about your peers that sell the same category as you do. Your competition is anyone who is selling your category. Get inspired and take note of what they are doing well, differently and even not so well. This should just be part of your work from week to week. Take cues from whose doors the vendors are knocking on. If the vendors and buyers aren't knocking on your door, figure out **what's happening** first before you jump to the need of doing something to solve it without thinking it through first. Refer to Chapter 4, 3 Questions in Life for a quick guide. You may not know the whole story, which in turn might lead to making an incorrect or irreversible move.

The Viewers

Your viewers are your *fourth wall*, a term used more frequently in theatre to insure the actor gives equal performance weight to the audience. They are as much a part of your performance as your product. When you receive your on-air guest package from the network you'll be working on, they will clearly state what their on-air expectations are, including whether you can refer to the camera or only the host. Whether your head turns to face the camera or not shouldn't have any impact on how you connect to the audience. Your technique in developing your pitch will keep the customers' point of view always in the forefront of your mind. (Refer to Chapter 7, Your Customers, for more details.)

Product Competition

Our viewers know our competition as well *if not* better than we do! Consumers know dollar-for-dollar what kind of value they are receiving. Knowing your customers' buying habits is paramount to your overall success in positioning your expertise and assuring them that you know what options are available in the market too. When talking about the competition, use broad strokes. One should refer to the competition rather globally and generically. Identify them as the *big box stores* or the *majors*, for instance. That quickly tells all of us what you are talking about without a law firm knocking on the doors of the network president. Remember that your viewers also shop at some, if not all of the *major* stores you are referring to. Therefore, never speak negatively about the competition. (I realize this is as elementary as it gets in sales. However, I have witnessed this faux pas more times than I can count so felt it needed to be said.) By insulting your competition, it indirectly insults your customers too. Use the comparison as a tactic and positioning point. This way, if they're looking for this product anyway, it will sell itself.

Internal Customers

We may be fixed on our customers *only* being the buying public forgetting sometimes that our customers include the *internal* team members we work with every day. I call them our internal customers and many times, they are the most important customers in order for us to do our job. (This applies to any profession.) They include the marketing and social media departments, the front desk assistants, planners, sound and camera technicians, producers, stagers and the manufacturers themselves. The manner in which we manage these relationships will contribute to continued growth and may further your reach and competencies. In this day and age when employees are being fired and frequently changing roles and jobs, these team members from one company today can easily become part of your very valuable network of colleagues for a lifetime.

CHAPTER 6 — THERE'S NO 'I' IN TEAM

SOURCES

1. http://www.vanityfair.com/online/daily/2014/03/sam-mendes-rules-for-directors
2. http://www.roundabouttheatre.org/Shows-Events/Events/Roundabout-Galas/Spring-Gala-2014.aspx

CHAPTER 6
There's No 'I' In Team

1. This section highlights all of your key team members that directly affect the work of the guest expert. The host, buyers, your viewers, your peers and all of the crew members (to name only a few). These professionals are *also* your internal customers. The manner in which you manage these relationships can easily become part of your very valuable network of colleagues for a lifetime.

2. The more we can understand the degree of scope and pressure our team members face, the better position we'll be in to become part of a *winning* team.

3. Some have said, "It takes a village to raise a child." I agree with that statement and would like to add that it takes a city to grow and develop a thriving business. There are hundreds of people contributing *their* best efforts toward the success of each brand and product, and ultimately their success is your success.

CHAPTER 7

YOUR CUSTOMERS

If you want to make exceptional connections, take exceptional steps to understanding your customers. The closer you are to understanding them, the closer you will be to enjoying multi sell outs in your career.

"We feel that our customers are our most trusted consultants. They share ideas and let us know when we veer off track. We pay close attention when we receive letters of complaint. We tune in to these letters because they teach us how we can perform better."
-Martha Stewart, The Martha Rules

We as Internet and TV sellers have a running start at getting *buy-in*, as the customer has turned on the channel or logged-on to the site *by choice*. Selling in this arena quickly evolves into providing simple, convenient answers and has the potential to even transform a portion of our customers' lives. Sound too simplistic? Sometimes the simplest answer requires the most specific work, and in this chapter we will delve deeply into identifying exactly who your customers are.

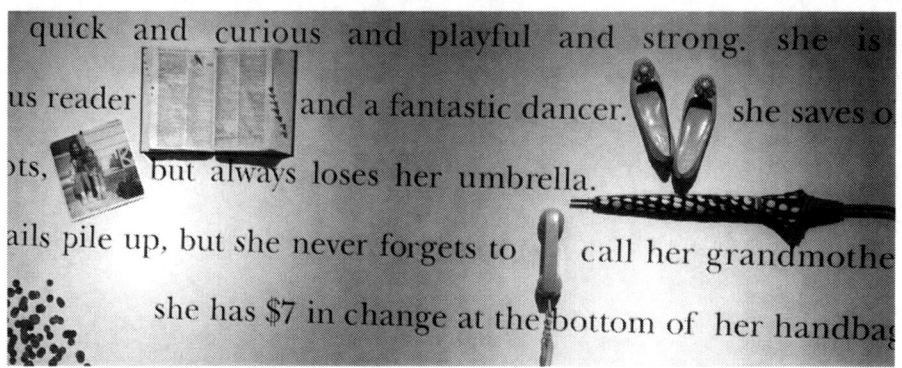

A sampling of what I recently saw at the cashier's desk of a *Kate Spade New York* store. She knows exactly who her customers are!

Sales begin and end with your customers. They tell us what they want, they tell us what they need and our job is to hear them, to understand, deliver and fulfill that need in a manner that suits them. The better you are at knowing who your customer is, the better a salesperson you will be. Ensure the time they choose to spend with you is worth sticking around for. Your goal and your job is to create a personal bond that is lasting and reliable.

When you see a guest expert who is remarkable at on-air selling, you can bet they know exactly who their customers are. They know why their customers are tuning-in, whether they have children, what their taste is and even what their concerns are. This clarity provides a tremendous amount of confidence for the guest expert to push the foot pedal to the floor. Their pace is quick, not pushy and their selling message is creative and crafted extraordinarily well.

Internet sales of any kind share a similar challenge that home shopping does with a few exceptions. Neither platform gets to see the customer, but we as on-air sales guest experts don't even get to know a specific name, an email, a location, an eye colour or anything about our customers that watch and shop. Although some customers will call in live to the studio, this exchange more times than not is handled specifically by the host. The guest expert gets to participate to a degree, but it is a controlled conversation for sure. Therefore, the connection you make with your customers comes from your intuition, your own communication, imagination and your keen understanding of who is buying your product.

A quick aside: You may remember I spoke of the intricate background work an actor does to prepare for a role in Chapter 2, in the section The Actor. This work is similar.

To go at this in a general manner dabbling here and there being satisfied perhaps with vague answers and assumptions is not acceptable if you want to win at this game. That approach is similar to going out on a blind date. You have no frame of reference whatsoever. It may work in dating but it will not work for on-air selling. Until you connect personally, you have no way of knowing who you are really talking to.

How Do You Make a Connection if You Can't Talk to Your Customers?

The dialogue is with the camera, your product and the host, and within that conversation you include your customers. You have to know exactly who is going to buy your product and this will tell you how to differentiate your selling message. In Chapter 10, The Camera and You, we'll talk more about where your focus should lie.

I remember my first corporate marketing job, sitting in an overly air conditioned yellow and red conference room. It was late in the afternoon toward the end of the two-day seminar. The dried up crumbs from the muffins that morning remained scattered on the white tablecloth and all three hundred of us felt equally dried up. We were inspired by the sessions, but we were also tired and were ready to go home. I remember thinking *I can't retain any more information! I'm done!*

The keynote speaker and CEO of our company walked on the platform to close the conference. The usual go-team-go platitudes were shared and although he was a very charming and charismatic man, I couldn't take in anything more. Well, until he shared this: "Determine exactly what your customers look like from the clothes they wear to the books they read. If you don't create that picture for yourself, you'll have no idea if a prospect walks by you or not. You have to be able to recognize the right customers instantly. The more you're able to recognize them, the higher sales turnover you'll have."

The phrase *customer intimacy* was originally coined by Michael Treacy and Fred Wiersema in their book *The Discipline of Market Leaders*. Here are some selected excerpts from their book:

"The message of *The Discipline of Market Leaders* is that no company can succeed today by trying to be all things to all people. It must instead find the unique value that it alone can deliver to a chosen market. Why and how this is done are the two key questions the book addresses." (p. xii)

"…'customer intimacy', involves the selection of one or a few high-value customer niches, followed by an obsessive effort at getting to know these customers in detail. This requires anticipating the target customer's needs as well as (if not better than) they themselves do, and sometimes sharing risks with them when the development of new products or services is required. The operating principles of this value discipline include: A corporate philosophy and resulting business practices that encourage deep customer insight and breakthrough thinking about how to materially improve the client's business are essential…"

What Is Your Customer's Experience?

When you get a new product from your vendor or buyer, one of the first things you should do is to look at it through the eyes of your customer, just as Steve Jobs did with his computer designs. It's a bonus scenario if *you* happen to be one of *your* customers, as you'll be able to use yourself as a *needs* and *wants* quick guide. Remember that this is a two-way conversation that you are building with your customers. The more you know about what they are experiencing the more information and tips you'll be able to supply.

Assume Your Customers Know As Much As You Do

Know that your audience will always know at least as much as you do, if not more. There are certain sellers who have a style that seems to talk down to the audience as if we were preschoolers needing remedial attention. It often happens when the product is perceived to be more technical like most consumer products, but it can happen with any product. Some guests have a habit of inflecting their voices up at the end of their sentences. We talked about what misinterpreted body language can do to change intended messaging in Chapter 3, therefore this point will merely be touched on. Remember, the biggest difference with our selling platform compared to most others in any industry is your audience can *click you off* so easily without any remorse because they know you can't see them refuse you, your message or your product. It's important to put yourself in a position that assures your audience that *you* have *their* best interests in mind.

Used with Elliot's permission

Elliot Smith (seen above) is one the best guest experts in the industry today, making the world of technology seem like anyone can master it. He simplifies his pitch for the layman listener without losing any intricate and technical details that appeals to the highly knowledgeable techie as well. He is the quintessential product specialist for consumer products. Look for him selling on all of the big four networks. He is an exceptional guest expert using all of the levels we talk about in this book.

Used with Kimberley's permission

As well as being one of the top designers in Canada and the U.S., Kimberley Seldon is also an exceptional guest expert. As one of my key mentors, she graciously shared what is important to her when selling on-air:

"When you're in your client's homes there is a lot of information for the designer to use when making decisions. With on-air sales I try to educate the consumer about general rules for design so that they can make an informed decision. If I *oversell* a product, I run the risk of disappointing the very consumers I hope to have a relationship with for many years. For that reason, I do my best to accurately describe the design principle behind a particular choice. I rely on my expertise and training to provide the consumer with practical choices and of course, a good-looking final product."

Kimberley is an interior designer and has more than twenty years of experience in television. She's a guest design expert on City TV's *Cityline* in Canada; and has hosted three of her own series including HGTV's *Design for Living with Kimberley Seldon*. She's also a guest expert on HSN and TSC.[1]

If you know in your heart that you are providing good value, excellent service and are trustworthy, people feel that sincerity and will open the door to you.

Principle of the Anchor

Do you remember when you rented your first apartment? Did you fix it up a bit to make it feel like new? Maybe you painted your living room, or put some potted mums on the balcony to enjoy the southern exposure or perhaps you threw up a few prints on the wall to add that homey feeling. I first discovered the magic of the anchor screw when I rented my first apartment. Although it does make a slightly larger hole in the wall than the conventional plug and screw, this small screw is the only thing that is required and makes your life so much easier particularly if you don't have another set of hands to help you measure. It allows you to mount any item of any weight wherever you choose to on the wall or even ceiling no matter where the studs are. Valuable artwork, heavy marble structures and light fixtures can be hung almost anywhere your heart desires with no restrictions!

The anchor in sales is the glue that holds your pitch and knowledge of who you are directing your message to. As we've said earlier, within the first few seconds of a hot camera lens pointed directly at you, you have to be at top speed, and **anchoring** catapults you there. In the following section, we'll focus on developing seven different customers that you know will purchase. This framework will ensure you consider every aspect of why your customers will be thrilled to buy this product. In Chapter 9, The Lily Pad Strategy™, we'll further develop another side to the power of the principle of the anchor.

Anchor Seven™

Anchor Seven represents seven different key customers. By focusing your delivery and attention (in your mind) to seven of your strongest customers, your pitch and push will be spontaneous, genuine, exciting and engaging because you will have vetted out everything you need to know about each of your seven *key* customers. The more you know about your customers, the better you'll be at relating to them with honesty and sincerity and with a genuine interest in their well-being. Part of what I find fun and highly engaging is talking directly to my seven customers when I'm building my scripts and in the studio. I picture them all hanging out with me doing their own thing. NO, I don't need to be put in a white padded room! This is how I get myself psyched up to the point that I can't wait to show what we have for them when I get in the studio to sell. I know the problems the product solves and the value it adds to each of my **Anchor Seven™** customers because I know what they cherish! This preparation allows me to access similar anticipation that a six year old expresses on Christmas morning. That excitement and childlike spirit is the kind of energy the guest expert needs to cultivate before any show, and by anchoring your message to your friends (customers), you are ready to chat it up with them. You may ask what about the eighth customer or the tenth? If you can catch the attention of your key seven customers, the eighth customer may also be convinced. As this is a creative process, you will always have the option of adjusting the details as you continue to fine tune your pitch and as your category and products broaden. The fact that you make very bold and specific decisions is part of the power of its results. Your audience is far more willing to stick around to listen to you if they feel they are being directly spoken to. One can notice the difference between someone who is talking in generalities and to *everyone* in a large room versus just *you*. The medium of the Internet and television is one of intimacy and therefore needs to be addressed in this specific manner. When we're focused and completely clear on who we are talking to, we're just better at what we do. It's an intangible and powerful element that may be the difference between selling and selling out.

The world famous choreographer Bob Fosse was responsible for choreographing the most memorable Broadway musical blockbusters of our time. Shows like *Cabaret, Chicago* (3rd longest running Broadway musical in history) and *Sweet Charity* were choreographed with every single step, hip pop, head flick and movement having a detailed back-story. There wasn't one step that didn't have specific motivation and a reason for being there at that moment, on that part of the stage, on the down beat of the 4/4 time of music. We can learn immense amounts from the highly detailed genius leaders like choreographer Mr. Fosse and the legendary visionary and marketing guru, Steve Jobs. Although the magic they created was on two very opposite plains, their principles and the intimate detailing of how they intended their art to be experienced by their customers had striking similarities, and why there may never be another Bob Fosse or Steve Jobs.

Anchor Seven™ Discovery

This entire next section is devoted to helping you to create not a 2D cut-out general impression of what you think your customer looks like, but a ffully formed image of seven of your key customers. Many of the networks will have their *ideal* customer and most likely will share *her* with you as part of your guest training. She usually has a name, she has an ideal age range and has a quick back story about her lifestyle. We are left to fill in the blanks of this person. It's great information to have as it's important to understand where the network is targeting their purchasing and marketing predominantly. However, their *ideal* customer may not suit your category one bit. You may be selling an historical coin collection where the *ideal* customer most likely will not even turn the show on, let alone buy it. You may be selling 70-inch surround sound TV's that are credit card thin. Again, the network's *ideal* customer may like the idea but is probably not going to be high on the priority list of her buying needs and wants – therefore, not *your* ideal customer. What's more, you most definitely have more than one customer type.

This is the work of the guest expert. The more specific you can be with your exploration of each Anchor Seven™, the more you will be forced out of your head and into your heart. Knowing exactly who your customers are keeps your message truthful, full of integrity and completely grounded. You won't believe how it unleashes your curiosity on how to solve problems for them and will be more engaging for your viewers. Remember how we talked earlier in the book about people can sense when a guest expert is talking to everyone vs. just you. There's a marked difference in your performance level when you are specific on who exactly you are talking to. At the end of the section, I will gladly introduce you to my Anchor Seven™ and share a story on how I was humbly reminded that there is always more to learn about our customers.

There are no *wrong* answers to this process. This is the creative work that will differentiate you from all other guest experts and will be one of your secret weapons. The intention of this work is not to win at a creative writing contest, but rather to become more able to consider different perspectives as you build your selling messages. It will also steer you away from developing a canned performance as it will free your imagination and inspiration to focus on how best to connect with your key customers and their friends. There are six steps to the process. Each step will build on to the next so resist the urge to jump ahead.

Here's how it works:

1. **Consider your specific category.**

Your customers may change somewhat depending on how many products you are selling within the category. For instance, if your category is outdoor living, which may include furniture, solar planter lights and outdoor fireplaces, each product may interest more males for one product and more females for another. Be flexible enough to make those mental changes.

2. **Identify the general demographic – male/female split**

   Here are two quick examples:

   If the category is kitchen, right away you will know that the general split may predominantly be women – but will of course be further refined depending on the product line you are selling. If it's knives or professional grade saucepans, it may be more evenly split. Conversely, if we deal with the same category but this time the product is slightly more decorative, *from the oven to the table* cookware for instance, the demographic split may be leaning a little heavier into the female demographic.

   If the category is consumer electronics and you are selling large screen television sets, the split balance may lean more to the male demographic.

3. **Take your demographic split and decide how many customers (out of seven) will be male and female.**

   Don't assign ages to your customers yet. Hang on tight, it's coming.

4. **Picture your seven general male and female *no face/no age* customers and think about the geography and socioeconomics of the country they live in.**

   Think rural, think metropolitan, think suburban, think remote areas, etc. Does the area in which they live have a good transit system? What is the soil like? How many days of rain did it get last year? How close is the town hall from where they live? Does the city have a bed bug problem? What is the state flower? Who is the mayor? Are there any big annual summer/winter events the city is known for? Etc...

5. **Decide on the age range of your customers**

   Consider every age range. I have provided a general guide (next) for your reference. You may find that you will have to be more inclusive of certain groups than others. Please consider one important element: who is *actually* purchasing the product? If the product is for Grandma Kate who is 88 – the daughter (in this example) who is purchasing the product is *your* customer – and grandma is your *secondary* customer. Neither individual is less or more important but will influence how you pitch this product.

Here's an example:

If your product is from the category of healthy living and you're selling electric scooters, you might quickly conclude your demographic of customers is a 60/40 male/female split, over the age of sixty-five perhaps and most likely retired. You might be correct to weight your predominant customer in this manner. Be careful not to assume this is your *only* customer however. You may have younger people – daughters, grandsons, etc. who are buying a gift for Grandpa. Or, let's not leave out the younger people who themselves may have chronic issues such as MS, ALS or diabetes where supporting their own weight or walking for long stretches of time could be difficult to impossible.

Age ranges:
20 – 30
30 – 40
40 – 50
50 – 65
65 – 90

Now you are ready to decide who is who in your Anchor Seven™!

6. Name all of your seven customers and picture them as specifically as you can.

With the work you've done in the preceding five steps, images of your customers have most likely started to form. You may even have thought of people in your own life that are your *exact* customers. Perfect! I generally mix a few different people together to round out my Anchor Seven™. Make sure you explore the possibility of every age group before you delete some. Again, your knowledge of your specific product will dictate your selections as will the products you are selling on any particular day.

As promised, at the end of this section, I'll share a few details of my Anchor Seven™.

The questions you can ask yourself are endless. The following lists of questions will spark your imagination and direct you on the right path for you and your category.

QUESTIONS ON THE PATH TO CREATING YOUR ANCHOR SEVEN™ CUSTOMERS

What...

What is their age?
What wonderful surprises have they encountered lately?
What do they like to do more than anything else to relax and unwind?
What keeps them up at night? Are they sound sleepers or do they suffer from chronic ailments?
What do they look like?
What are their favourite colours and fabrics to wear?
What gives them endless pleasure day to day? *List as many as possible
What do they do for a living? Is this shared income or are they the single breadwinner?
What kinds of indulgences do they surround themselves with? Boats, sound systems, shoes, spa days, hair extensions?
What size is their bank account? Do they have money saved or are they burdened by debt?
What are the ages of their children and/or grandchildren?
What kind of challenges have they had to face recently? Are they coping well?
What magazines do they pick up at the grocery store line up? What books do they read to learn more, to relax more?
What Olympic sports would they tune-in to watch? What is their preference.Summer or Winter? Or would they avoid this programming completely?
What one gift would knock their socks off?
What makes them spontaneously laugh?
What is their best vacation destination?
What is their favourite kind of entertainment? Shopping? Going out for dinner? Seeing movies, live theatre, watching television sitcoms or do they choose the golden oldies? Are they ultimate Netflix users, do they have cable, no TV or do they download everything?
What clothes do they tend to purchase?
What types of food do they eat on a regular basis? Relatively healthy or lots of fast food and soda?
If they won a huge amount of money in the lottery, **what** is the first thing they would do with their winnings?

CHAPTER 7 — YOUR CUSTOMERS

QUESTIONS ON THE PATH TO CREATING YOUR ANCHOR SEVEN™ CUSTOMERS

Are They... Do... How... Where... Who...

Are they environmentally conscious? What other environmental causes do they support? **Are** they vegans, raw or macrobiotic eaters or pescatarians?

Are they homebodies or do they like adventure and to travel?

Are they shift-workers or do they work a 9 to 5 job? **Are** they entrepreneurs or work part-time or do they stay-at-home?

Are they pet owners? If so then are they multi pet owners? Cats or dogs, chinchilla's, birds, etc...?

Are they retired? Are they having the time of their lives or is their current situation more difficult to deal with?

Are they single, divorced or married? Gay or straight?

Are they able bodied, ambulatory or unable to transfer their bodies well?

Do they have a cottage or camper? Or would they rather stay in a five star hotel?

Do they have strong faith of some sort? Religious, agnostic or spiritual?

Do they participate in any local charity work? Do they donate family clothing and other household items on a regular basis?

Do they belong to any clubs? **Do** they do any volunteer work?

How many members in their immediate family? At a family event do they take charge or sit back and let it all happen in front of them?

Where do they live – an apartment or condo? In the suburbs, rural town or city? By the lake or in the mountains? What is the demographics, socio-economics as well as location and the size of their home?

Where do they love to shop on a regular basis?

Who are their best friends? If there was no outside pressure to please, who would they choose to spend time with the most?

Example Anchor Seven™

These are my personal Anchor Seven™ customers. I have deliberately been rather general in this sharing as this is the private work that fuels the performer's fire. Like the magician who keeps his secrets close to his heart, I suggest you do the same.

1. **Nancy** – she's seventy-six and is a widow after enjoying a wonderful marriage of forty years. She loves watching QVC on her TV and she loves Joan Rivers. Her home décor is exquisite as she has great taste and ran a boutique Christmas store for ten years. She likes to change colours and décor regularly as she grows tired of the same look, but brags about still owning a twenty-five year old Irish linen sheet set that still looks new to this day. She walks to church and is heavily involved in community support outreach programs and plays bridge every Wednesday night.

2. **Adam and Kristy** – they are both in their mid-forties. They have two adopted girls, one of Asian descent and one of Russian descent. They are both professionals and love to travel when they can bring their kids. They are busy, they cherish great wine, wonderful cuisine and don't have time to care about matching drapes to paint colours, but they are interested in deals that make sense and will last the abuse of two busy kids. She is a long distance runner and has qualified twice for the Boston Marathon. He has breathing issues which have to be regularly checked out by his doctor and he is the devil's advocate customer I adore!

3. **Nigel and Reesa** – They both just turned 50 this year. They have three kids (one that they share). She is a smart shopper and will spend hours and hours online finding the best deal for an oversized Italian down-filled couch. She often uses Groupon where saving even $1 is worth the extra trip for her, as bragging rights are a big part of how she sees her role as a good mom and wife, which she is. The couple loves blowing

off some steam going out with their city friends to enjoy exclusive supper clubs and bars. He's an entrepreneur and owns a gaming company. She has been one of the top pharmaceutical reps for one of the largest firms in the world for more than fifteen years.

4. **Courtney** – She's a university student in her early twenties and shares an apartment just off campus with five other girls. She makes her own money and her parents handle her school expenses. She, unlike most girls her age, isn't too influenced by her peers and takes a while to make decisions on spending her own money. Since she only has a small space to decorate, she loves pretty items that look good now. She doesn't think long term with her clothing or décor purchases, as she knows most of her pieces will be pitched by the time she leaves university.

5. **Michael and Michael** – They are a gay couple in their thirties and have been together for over five years. They met as interior designers and now own their own business designing exquisite accessory furniture for high-end buyers. They are internationally known professionals within their industry and live in an exclusive area in the city. They are both from small towns and still go back home on a regular basis to visit and help out their parents.

6. **Rose** – She was born in a farming community with a population of three hundred. She married her childhood sweetheart. They will soon be celebrating their fifty-fifth wedding anniversary. She and her husband have been wheat and cattle farmers their entire lives. She makes fresh bread for dinner right from the wheat that was harvested that day! She can drive a combine, fix an auger and also scores consistent rounds of golf of around eighty five, still!

7. **Constance** – She is a quiet single lady who works as a cashier at the local supermarket in her suburban town. She knows where every dollar has been spent and can account for every step she has taken for the past fifty-seven years. She does her job and goes home to her large bachelor

apartment and her big orange tomcat. For company she enjoys watching shopping channels but has not bought anything yet. She loves certain fabrics and recipes that remind her of her mom.

A quick aside: My Anchor Six customer, Rose:

Even though I spent a lot of time developing a backstory of who my Rose was, there was still a lot I didn't know about her or her family lifestyle until I had the opportunity to trek and rogue through canola fields in Saskatchewan.

I like making holiday wreaths out of wheat and canola. They add warmth and texture to any décor elevation and can last for years if you store them well. At the local craft store in the city I'm from, purchasing a six-inch round collection of wheat can easily cost you $20. Believing I knew all there was to know about the market value of wheat, I once offered a local Saskatchewan farmer $50 for a healthy armful of his crop that was the perfect shade of goldenrod. He laughed at me and said, "I'll do you one better: I'll give you everything from where you are standing right now to that corner a mile away and twenty feet across for $50!"

In that one moment, I learned that although we think we may have done all of our research on what we think we know, there is always more to learn and be open to it! Settling for mediocre general ideas isn't good enough. My idea of who Rose was and what she looked like deepened on that day.

SOURCES

1. www.kimberleyseldon.com

CHAPTER 7
Your Customers

1. Your customers are your most important allies. In relationship selling, this is a vitally important element to your work. Nurture this relationship on every level of communication.

2. The more specific you can be with each Anchor Seven™ customer you identify, the more you will be forced out of your head and into your heart. It keeps your message truthful and completely rooted in integrity and knowledge. By focusing your delivery and attention to seven of your strongest customers, your pitch and push will be spontaneous, genuine, exciting and engaging because you will have vetted out everything you need to know about each of your seven *key* customers.

3. Identify your Anchor Seven™ – How-to charts included.

SECTION II

SALES

This section takes you through the most important sales principles, techniques and skills and will arm you with the ability to sell anything. This section is designed for any sales professional to use as a reference and tool kit.

CHAPTER 8

DIET YOUR WAY TO SALES SUCCESS™

D	I	E	T
Define	Inspire	Execute	Trust

The acronym D-I-E-T represents four stepping stones to becoming a very powerful and charismatic pitch person/seller. There is a building order to each of the elements and they work together like a slinky, moving independently yet simultaneously.

In any sales environment, discovering how you can **define** your goals, your product, your brand, your company, your values, customers, your pricing, your promotions, your target market, your financials, the more effective you will be at **inspiring** leadership, change and excitement with your employees, your sales people, your customers, suppliers, partners, investors and shareholders. This will allow you to more easily **execute** all that is required in order to perform at your best. Doing all of those things well, you will earn the **trust** from your customers, your buyers, the marketing department, the decision makers, and your colleagues.

ABC's of Sales

Is there a sales professional today that doesn't know the rudimentary training principles of the ABC's -*Always Be Closing?* Whether you're a new recruit at Best Buy or the store manager at La Senza in the new mall, most everyone in sales is made aware of this old chestnut acronym because it focuses the intent of the message and the sales rep. The manner in which this directive is *interpreted* is the key to its success.

"I hate sales guys, they're so pushy and I always feel like I'm being handled."

I hear people say that to me frequently, and frankly I've said it myself describing a desperate, pushy salesperson with no finesse.

This section is going to explore, redefine and teach the techniques of closing and how to enchant your customers in an upfront and trusting manner so that they know you really have their best interests in mind.

Our Bread and Butter

"Here comes our bread and butter just arriving," said the front of house manager of the third largest theatre in Canada. She was referring to the three busloads of men and women enjoying their well-deserved time of leisure. They had just arrived to see the Wednesday matinee show of *Les Miserables*.

Our bread and butter, as sales people and performers, are opportunities. Opportunities for bookings, listings, auditions, go-sees, cold calls, interviews, etc. A tough image is depicted in the empty calendar picture. To be in a position to have no upcoming prospects or bookings is a horrible one. In Joan Rivers' documentary *A Piece of Work*, she said it was the only thing in life that scared her. To have nothing planned or no prospects of work.[1]

Whether you're an entrepreneur or construction contractor, it takes time to get business rolling. Part of our work as sales people and performers is to always put ourselves in a position to turn possibilities into orders and bookings. You have to have multiple fishing rods sitting in different ponds waiting for some bites. They won't all pan out that is for sure, but you have to keep plugging away.

At the same time however, you have to know when to cut your losses and say *no*. According to my friend Rob Hoene, a veteran sales entrepreneur/owner of an industrial automation business, "I always consider three things in order for my business to remain strong: Yeses make me money. No's save me money. Maybes cost me money. I have to know where my prospects and partners fall within these markers; otherwise I'm wasting a lot of time and money."

Salespeople Can Learn from New York Cabbies

Have you ever tried hailing a cab from Midtown Manhattan to JFK Airport in Queens, New York? It is virtually impossible because the cabbie knows the length of the trip probably won't be worth his investment of time versus fare turnover. On a good day it can take roughly forty minutes, but that can easily be doubled if it's midday, and that's just one way! It's true that cabbies are not paid to be charming nor are they necessarily rewarded for getting you there safely, but in their business, it's time/distance/frequency = money. They drive to make money, and high turnover is the success ratio that allows them to feed their families. In this case, there really isn't the extra importance of customer loyalty or retention.

The best sales reps (and cabbies perhaps) know how to say NO as well as they know how to say YES. Now, before you start turning the page and thinking I'm off my rocker, hang in there as I'm sure you will agree with me.

Let's take another quick example: Recently I was talking with a wine representative from Buffalo, New York. Matt's wine portfolio consists of more than 7,000 labels which can be found at eye level on most retail shelves and higher-end restaurants across America. He runs a great business as an outside sales rep and services his customers very well. In turn, they are loyal to him (as well as any restaurateur can be). When a new prospective customer kicks tires by asking him to host a wine tasting at their restaurant with the *possibility* of cases purchased, Matt's first question to them is "What's in it for me?"

You may be saying to yourself, "This guy is crazy. There is another potential customer staring him in the face. Jump at the chance to service him!"

Matt's position is, "I take my job very seriously by servicing my current customers extremely well. If the new client wants to work with me, I'm more than happy to have them come aboard if my products best suit his needs. Hosting a random wine tasting that will take more than half a day of my time plus the cost of gas, will most likely not provide the necessary information I need to service this new customer. So I said, *No.*" The new client was incredulous, Matt told me. Instead of running away in disgust, however, this new customer wanted to work with him even more now because the prospective customer had a glimpse of the level of service he could expect in future.

Think about what we said in Chapter 4, The Job of Getting the Job. We too are interviewing the interviewees. (Of course, this isn't always the case, but is still a good reminder.)

CHAPTER 8 — DIET YOUR WAY TO SALES SUCCESS™

The Perfect Storm Brings Best Practices Together to Become: The Sales Equation DIET Funnel

In the opening chapter, Setting The Scene, I talk about the funnel image and note how well it represents a continuous flow of energy poured with exacting ease in the direction you want it to go without waste or spillage. It seemed to represent a striking image to illustrate the continuous flow of focused energy.

Marathon Training Funnel

- FOUNDATION
- STRENGH
- SPEED
- PERFORM

I also pointed out that each descending field in the funnel **physically mirrors a zeroing-in process.** For this moment here's a quick reminder of the marathon example used earlier but will shortly be developed into the Sales Equation DIET Funnel.

As a review from the first chapter, the **funnel** represents what *Webster's Encyclopedic Unabridged Dictionary defines as*: **To concentrate, channel or focus.**

Sales Success Depends On How Well We *Listen* to Our *Listeners*

In home shopping, if maximizing sales on a short-term basis is the goal, (and it is), then the guest expert has to figure out how to catch the attention of thousands of people and package it in a way that caters to many of their intricate needs and sensibilities. The Anchor Seven™ (from Chapter 7, Your Customers), is a fantastic tool to engage you and your *low hanging fruit* listeners.

The next two examples of noticing who your *listeners* are, illustrates two polar-opposite examples on how a host of a National radio show and a CEO colleague of a large International company assesses how to relate quickly to the customers they do business with.

Example I. Jaymz Bee is one of the most successful national radio hosts on the jazz airwaves today. The station he works at is a not-for-profit arts organization. For this reason, they have a fund drive twice per year where listeners can donate and take an incentive gift. Jaymz explains, "For higher-end donors, I created jazz tours of Toronto called *Jazz Safari*™. We now offer other destinations like New Orleans, Havana, San Francisco/Monterey, etc. We can spend from four days to a week together. Some of these generous donors save up for these adventures while I suspect others are so wealthy they could just shake the couch to pay for it. An International *Jazz Safari*™ bonds people; but as the designated ice-breaker, I try to do as much research on everyone as I can. I'll begin going through the past few years of emails to see if we've had correspondence. If it is someone I have no record of (or can't recall), I turn to search engines or other social media sources. I usually find a few special noteworthy items in common about each of our guests. We already share the love of the same music, but finding topics to encourage a lively conversation is easier when you know the individuals in a group."

Example II. When going into an intense negotiating session where the stakes are very high, my CEO colleague deliberately takes note of the *shape* of the time pieces each individual is wearing or makes note of those who are not wearing one. He often finds that this snapshot of information gives him potential insight as to the personal tendencies and interests that particular person may favour.

By no means is it scientific. It merely provides a first impression that is often useful, helping to know how to craft and package messages. Even if the initial assumption using this watch-shape-guide is dead wrong, it engages you instantly to notice your customers and to understand how you can relate to them quickly. It is the same principle when you apply it to singers singing a song together. If one is singing in B minor while the other is singing in C major, there is instant dis-chord without any chance of resolution. Unless at least one person is tuning-in to what the other is doing, the right key for both voices will never be found.

To further illustrate the idea of noticing who your listeners are, here is a quick analysis: Refer to the watch picture on the left. At first glance this square platinum timepiece gives a clear impression that the male who is wearing it is successful and fairly high up within the financial world where winning is the only name of the game. He is highly meticulous and is a bottom-line thinker. *What you see is what you get* with him and his approach is slightly militaristic. His style might be visually represented by a box, somewhat of an immovable left-brain thinker. (To some, this may sound like a negative description. It is not meant to portray a negative image whatsoever but rather to quickly identify a style preference that you can lock into.)

On the flipside, the gentleman wearing the round black fashionable watch on the right may suggest that he is an athlete of some rank, and is also a highly successful professional. He is most likely a dominant sales and marketing person who thrives in the grey areas of business. His style might be visually represented by a bubble. He is not particularly set in his ways; he is approachable and a relatively unstructured right brain thinker.

For more information on the 'boxes' and 'bubbles' theory authored by Mr. David K. Hurst,[2] refer to this most interesting article from the 1984 Harvard Business Review. [3]

Stage I - The *Define* Listener:

Wants to be shown how things work and be given complete control to decide for themselves whether it's a good product. They react most positively to bottom-line; quick paced straightforward communication, both physically and audibly. Show me, don't just tell me.

He/she is someone who wants the details and demos to be based on pure logic that they can see for themselves. They are incredibly knowledgeable and readily know pricing and competitive comparisons. They would typically be more cautious and conservative and would seldom be an impulse buyer without proper pros and cons determination.

The *Define* customer is more apt to research all options before they make their final choice.

Stage II - The *Inspire* Listener:

Wants to be told a story and wants to be enchanted. They want to be romanced and sincerely entertained. It might be easy to think that the 'inspire' customer would be predominantly female. Men equally want to be romanced and inspired when it comes to automobiles, electronics, home theatres, and audio systems – to mention only a few categories. The inspire listener watches for trends and the latest and the greatest information available. They too are extremely knowledgeable, not unlike the define listener in that way.

The *Inspire* customer is more likely to be turned-on by the possibilities of what it can do for that person. The manner in which the message is packaged is all important.

We all have a healthy blend of both define and inspire tendencies. The dominant trait arises depending on our role that moment, on our history and how our lives are affected by our decision at that time.

Example:
Jess Considers Purchasing a House
Jess may be convinced this is the *right* house because of the beautiful trees and landscaping, the large backyard for the kids to play in, not to mention the gorgeous open concept Scandinavian professional kitchen and the 7.1 surround sound home theatre system with the included 70-inch screen suspended high above the fireplace.

We would identify the partner above as one who has dominant *inspire* tendencies within this scenario.

But wait, not so fast. Jess has also had issues with their current house and wants to avoid these negative issues with the new house purchase. Jess still loves the prospects of the new house for all the above reasons outlined, but the *define* characteristics now dominate the decision. Concerns with the quality of the builder, the age of the roof and furnace, the infrastructure and neighbourhood are all of a sudden the most important deciding factors. Is the neighbourhood safe and is it up and coming or going downhill? Will the school behind them be noisy and potentially problematic and how much will the property taxes rise with that new hospital being built?

This same *inspire* customer named Jess who was a moment ago the blue sky thinker is now the bottom line *define* customer who wants someone to rectify and solve problems.

Embracing both types of listeners in your messaging expands the opportunity potential, to connect with multiple customers in one moment.

Stage III – *Execute* the Plan:

Through my interviews with elite athletes and performers, their insights helped me realize an important part of training, planning and building up to performance level. That is, managing *how* the plan is ***executed***. Therefore, ***execute*** makes up the 3rd element of this acronym. (This important element will be further developed in Chapter 9, The Lily Pad Strategy™ and Chapter 10, The 3 P's.)

Stage IV – *Trust* is the Result of Executing the Plan Successfully:

Trust is the core factor that glues the entire recipe together and is the prize for doing a job well done. In any sales environment, whether it's cars, broadloom, makeup at the drugstore or meat at the butcher, if I don't ***trust*** that the product is as good as the expert says it is, I will reject it. This is where the educated word and knowledge of the expert cannot be replaced. The exceptional sales specialist knows the importance of being trustworthy and truthful and how that factor plays the lead.

Gaining trust *is a consequence of consistently executing* **the tools within the Sales Equation DIET Funnel extremely well.**

Sales Equation DIET Funnel

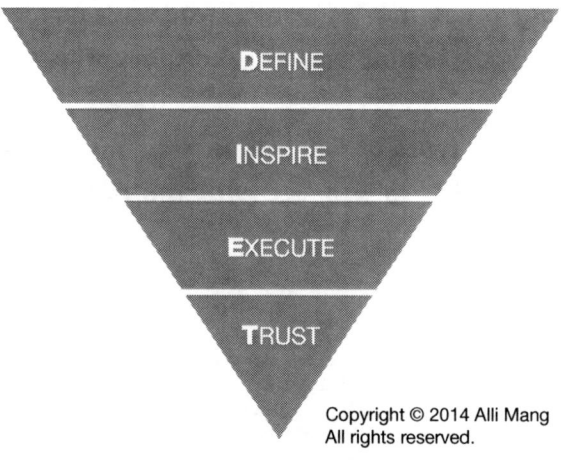

Copyright © 2014 Alli Mang
All rights reserved.

Trust Is Earned

As when we explored the funnel at the beginning of the book, you will again notice that the top portion of the funnel above is the widest, holding the principles and foundations in place so as you move through the funnel, you have the confidence to know you are rooted. Trust is situated at the bottom as it pinpoints your intentions both figuratively and deliberately. Trust is the ultimate target or *light stick* that is directly related to how well the other three levels before it have been developed and executed.

To explain the *trust factor* in a different scenario, let's take it out of a business context for a minute, and apply this principle to an everyday life event:

Suppose you're out for dinner and you ask your waiter what he would suggest for a main course. You play the captive audience (**customer**) and he (**waiter**) plays the role of the expert ready to make his best recommendations for you to buy. He positions his suggestions by detailing the elements of a certain dish (**Define**), perhaps highlighting spices, where it was caught that day or the type of aging process it has gone through; and then will package the message in a manner that will excite and intrigue you (**Inspire**). He may ask, "How would you like that done?" or somehow customize it to your special liking. If he's done his job well, you will have ordered what he recommended in the exact form you chose (**Execute**). Assuming you love it, you'll probably come back to the restaurant and perhaps even sit in his section because now the restaurant and he have earned your **TRUST**. Everyone wins.

"Since trust is the glue that holds free societies together, it follows that lasting success will be attracted to those who can be trusted."

-Samuel Smiles, author of *Self Help*

D I E T Leads to TRUST

According to *Webster's Encyclopedic Unabridged Dictionary of the English Language* and *The Synonym Finder* by J. I. Rodale

To DEFINE	
Definition	**Synonym**
1. To explain the nature or essential qualities of 2. To make clear the boundaries or form of 3. Definite – clearly defined, not vague or general, fixed, precise, exact, bounded with precision, positive, certain	Explain, spellbind, throw light on, interpret, translate, establish, describe, specify, represent, exemplify, illustrate, specific, graphic, precise, accurate, well-founded, valid, decisive, final

To INSPIRE	
Definition	**Synonym**
1. To infuse an animating, quickening, or exciting influence into 2. To affect with the specified feeling or thought 3. To prompt or instigate	Exhilarate, reanimate, rejuvenate, stir, rally, stimulate, thrill, transform, assure, reassure, comfort, restore, suggest, reveal, make aware, explain, instruct, teach, educate, guide, acquaint, impel, spur

To EXECUTE	
Definition	**Synonym**
1. To carry out, accomplish 2. To perform or do 3. To produce in accordance with the plan or design	Perform, fulfill, succeed in, mastermind, make happen, effectuate, achieve, realize, carry through, expedite, complete, finish

To TRUST	
Definition	**Synonym**
1. Reliance on the integrity, strength, ability, surety, etc., of a person or thing 2. Confident expectation of something; hope 3. The obligation or responsibility imposed on one in whom confidence or authority is placed 4. To have trust or confidence in; rely on	Confidence, faith, belief, conviction, reliance, dependence, security, sureness, positiveness, optimism, expectation, credibility, trustworthiness, reliability, dependability, responsibility, commitment, obligation

CHAPTER 8 — DIET YOUR WAY TO SALES SUCCESS™

T-R-U-S-T

On the next page, you'll see the Sales Equation DIET Funnel. This is an at-a-glance picture of 100+ action words that make up the proceeding charts. Each word applies to your pitch and performance level. Read from the top and work down to get an overall understanding of the building process. You will note that each word begins with each letter of the word **TRUST** and incorporates **define, inspire, execute** and **trust** elements.

If you read nothing else in this book, take the time to read the rest of this chapter. It is a sales book in itself and is chock full of real life stories, anecdotes and pure selling illustrations from all walks of life. It is meant to enlighten, engage and entertain you. I'm confident, it will not only make you laugh and drive more creative thought in you but will answer the overall question on how a product can become sold out consistently.

Sales Equation DIET Funnel

Tactic, Tactful, Target, Teach, Technique, Tell, Think, Thorough, Track, Translate, Transparency, Truth, Realistic, Reason to Buy, Referrals, Responsibility, Role, Route, Umpire, Understanding, Update, Scrutinize, Seasonality, Setting the Scene, Show up, Steer, Straight Up, Strategic Thought and Action, Sustainability, SWOT

DEFINE

Talent, Tantalize, Taste, Tease, Tempo, Tempt, Tenacity, Tidbit, Timbre, Timing, Tips, Transition, Transferable, Trend, Triggers, Tune-In, Raise Up, Rally, Rapport, React, Reaffirm, Receive, Receptive, Rely, Relatable, Responsive, Reveal, Risk, Rush, Unify, Uplift, Safe Place, Security, Scarcity, Security, Self-Reliant, Sense of Humour, Sensitive, Silence, Stake, Stories, Surpass, Surprise, Surrender, Understand

INSPIRE

Team Member, Tempo, Testing, Thick-Skinned, Through-put, Time Management, Time Constraints, Time-Limited, Training, Turnover, Raise Your Game, Recall, Record, Recover, Rebound, Re-Energize, Relentless, Reset, Results, Return Policies, Reward, Risk Free, Urgency, Utilize, Sales, Self-Motivated, Sell, Sell Yourself First, Social Media, Speed, Stamina, Success Upon Success, Summarize, Surround, Sustain

EXECUTE

Trust, Trusting, Referrals, Relationships, Reputation, Retention,

TRUST

Sincerity, Thank You!

Copyright © 2014 Alli Mang
All rights reserved.

CHAPTER 8 — DIET YOUR WAY TO SALES SUCCESS™

DEFINE your way with TRUST

ACTION WORD	HOW IT APPLIES TO YOUR PITCH
T	
Tactic and Tactful	Figure out what your top five tactics are for each of your products. This will keep your messaging simple and focused.
Target	Always know your target. Refer to **Chapter 7**, Your Customers.
Teach	A significant part of your role is to teach, particularly if your products have high technical elements. Be aware of how you package your teaching message and assume that your customers are as quick and as sharp as you are. Don't ever *dumb down* your message. Talking down is condescending and can be felt immediately. It will shut down an audience without warning.
Technique	The technique to creating a pitch can be the same every time. This becomes increasingly important when you have been given a new product you know nothing about with 2 days or no days to prepare. DIET (see **Chapter 8**) is a technique anyone can remember and will help you to prepare before and stay on track during a show, pitch or presentation.
Tell	Sometimes we can get bogged down with strategies and the perfect *phraseology* to sell the product and sometimes you just need to tell your customer what the deal is. A friend of mine always says to me when he notices I'm getting overly stressed with my messaging, *"They're just towels. Relax and tell us why you like them."* People love to be told what to do to get great results. HGTV and many of the other DIY shows and networks currently on-air have built a dynasty knowing that. Any opportunity you have to tell your viewers what to do, go for it! There are some fun examples in **Chapter 9**, *The Lily Pad Strategy*™.
Think	Canned messaging can be heard from a mile away. There is a certain negative tone that you feel, when you are spoken *at* instead of *with*. Always be thinking and let people see that you are in the moment by reacting to what is happening now.

DEFINE your way with TRUST

ACTION WORD	HOW IT APPLIES TO YOUR PITCH
Thorough	The more thorough you are with understanding all aspects of the pitch, the product and your customers, the better prepared you will be to deliver performance excellence. Remember that the time you are investing in being thorough will bless your entire line of work done now and in the future.
Track	Maintain your thirst for learning and growing. Track your sales, track your competitors' sales, your progress, experiences, your celebrations, and conversations with peers and colleagues. This will all make you better at what you do.
Translate	The host often takes the role of translating your intricate pitch down to simple sound bites. They are masters at making the message accessible to the mass market of customers. Both functions are important and the host's job is to make it even easier for the customers to make the decision to buy. If you find the host doesn't do that regularly, you can take it as a sign that you are doing a sufficient job of summarizing yourself. Lock that in and remember how you did it for next time.
Transparency	Demonstrations are your greatest tactic to staying transparent. Eliminate objections by showing how the product works with practiced ease and delight. Transparency is a marketing tactic and smart marketers knows its power. *"The more transparent you are, the more engaged your customers will be. They will understand... what you are trying to do, what you're achieving, what's in it for them, and what's not in it for them."* Bryan Pearson, *The Loyalty Leap*

R

Reliable	In **Chapter 9**, *The Lilly Pad Strategy*™ we will talk about anchor statements and other key elements that can be relied upon during any part of your pitch. You will find certain elements that need to be in place in order for you to feel comfortable. Lean on these reliable foundations. I find that if I have all of my demo materials in place and my anchor statement is solid, I know I am show ready.

DEFINE your way with TRUST

ACTION WORD	HOW IT APPLIES TO YOUR PITCH
Realistic	Keep your selling points to a realistic level. As much as we sometimes get carried away (particularly if sales are soft), keep it real. If 36% of the people tested felt their lines and wrinkles on their face lessened, don't blow it up to 45% or 50%. Somehow these little extras backfire on us. In the words of Winston Churchill, *"Men occasionally stumble over the truth, but most pick themselves up and hurry off as if nothing has happened."* Most networks warn the guest expert that overselling a product may put us in the position of being liable for making false claims.
Reason to buy	After all of the preparations and rehearsals, simply declare for yourself why your customers will want to buy today. Simplify it down to one sentence. It will focus you instantly.
Referrals	Personal referrals are not as common as they once were due to privacy issues and even legal ramifications. Getting endorsed by the people you have worked with is an important component, particularly when you are just commencing your career. This must be a part of continuing to build your career portfolio. LinkedIn, professional websites and other business social media sights are great sources to report recommendations and endorsements from your peers, managers and colleagues. The word referral, is the only word that is repeated in this entire chart. You will also find it in TRUST your way to TRUST.
Risk Free	The only time a guest expert should be leaning in the direction of pitching 'risk free' is if the product being sold looks like it might be painful, dramatically altering or concerning in any way. Certain skin or hair removal products and health, fitness and diet regimes may fall under this category. Pay close attention to how your product may be perceived and adjust your pitch accordingly. As for all other products that don't apply, the sentiment of *"Try it, you have nothing to lose"* is not a strong pitch. Don't get lazy.

DEFINE your way with TRUST

ACTION WORD	HOW IT APPLIES TO YOUR PITCH
Responsibility	1. Public eye - when it comes to being in the public eye, you have many responsibilities. Responsibilities to talk about products that you like and that you stand behind. One of the worst things you can do is talk about something and state how great it is when you really don't believe it. At some point, people will see through that. I know many hosts and guest experts who will only sell the product once they've tried it. If they like it enough to use it themselves, great. If they don't, they still figure out a way to sell with integrity. 2. As a public figure on national television and the Internet, be aware that you may be recognized. A host friend of mine shared a very applicable story with me: She was standing in a very long line to purchase some hosiery at a popular national department store. It was a few days before Christmas, and every store was bustling and busy. She stood 10th in line prepared to wait it out as she would be getting 50% off the hosiery she was purchasing. Everyone was in the same boat. However, the lady at the front, who wasn't even purchasing a product, was apparently oblivious to what was going on around her. It was clearly marked everywhere in the store that no returns or exchanges would be accepted until the new year. This lady had the staff running around getting different sizes and it was quite an inconsiderate mess. The entire line up of customers started to band together in their disgust of the woman's selfish behaviour. Well, finally my host friend got up to the cash and our 'returner' was still doing her business. Just before my host friend opened her mouth to give this woman a well-deserved earful, the lady looked at her, greeted her by name and said, *"You are one of the best hosts on TV! I have been watching you for years."* The host acknowledged her compliment and got out of the store as quickly as she could. 3. As a professional representative of brands and yourself, you have the responsibility to not slam other products that may or may not be better than yours. Know how to position your message accordingly.

CHAPTER 8 — DIET YOUR WAY TO SALES SUCCESS™

DEFINE your way with **TRUST**

ACTION WORD	HOW IT APPLIES TO YOUR PITCH
Role	In *Chapter 2*, *The Guest Expert*, we talk all about the roles of each major player within a shopping channel network that affects the guest expert.
Route	1. One of the first things you should do is to figure out your choreography and how you will move from product to demo to host to camera in smooth and seamless serenity. If you appear to not know where you plan to go next, you pull the attention of the audience in a second. Choose your route. 2. In theatre, each cast member has their own *'track'* or route designated specifically to the part they are playing. There's a safety issue so that actors don't bang into each other, but more importantly, each route is specifically choreographed to enhance the overall experience for the audience. A perfectly executed *'track'* involves hitting the right light cues so the actor can be seen passing by on the right side of the actor who is riding a bike or flying in the air without any mishaps.

U

Umpire	During your show, you may be feeling like you're being pushed in all directions. People who have had live television experience know exactly what I'm talking about here. It's part of the game and is truly unlike any other profession. Decide (umpire) quickly what you're able to address and what you're not and keep on moving forward. This is exactly why I encourage you to arrive so well prepared that all of this grey stuff that happens will not push you off your game. No one will know you had trouble dealing with the various directions but everyone will know your performance was shaky.
Understanding	In *Chapter 7*, *Your Customers*, we go into great detail exploring the importance of understanding who your customers are and what inspires them. In relationship selling, this is a vitally important element to consider.

DEFINE your way with TRUST

ACTION WORD	HOW IT APPLIES TO YOUR PITCH
Update	Keep your product knowledge and your look updated. In every category there are always technological advancements and industry changes being made. As far as your look, ensure that when your customers tune-in that they know what decade it is!

S

Scrutinize	Scrutinize your own personal taste when it comes to all of your material, especially when you ask for business. Now is not the time to let them see you sweat or for you to get lazy. We've all seen the closes that can be somewhat cheesy and even laughable: *"You've got to just try this to believe it for yourself."* Or *"This is the only way to get a good night's sleep."* Unless this statement has been proven and you have clinical testing ready to show and prove that what is being stated is 99% true, it is not a viable closing statement. Refer to **Chapter 9**, *The Lily Pad Strategy™*.
Seasonality	Be aware of the seasons and special occasions and use them to your advantage without becoming a cliché. Be sure to keep your slant fresh and inventive.
Setting the Scene	Putting what you are talking about in context is important when you are framing your pitch. If you can get people to anticipate where you're going, it helps the buy-in process when you only have a few short minutes to get it right. In **Chapter 3,** in the section *Body Language*, we explored the importance of wearing the right wardrobe to make a strong first impression. If you look like a bag of hammers or are inappropriately dressed for the occasion, you will have lost many even before you open your mouth.
Show up	Show up with full intensity and readiness. There is not a second to waste when on camera.
Steer	If you don't like the direction the host is taking you, move it in another direction. Unfortunately, sometimes (particularly if they don't know you), you may be boxed in a corner. They may be talking all over your points and not letting you breathe enough to add something. It's a control thing. There's a lot on the line so, do the best steering you can and keep on gaining the host's trust. The host will give you room once they know the ball won't be dropped.

CHAPTER 8 — DIET YOUR WAY TO SALES SUCCESS™

DEFINE your way with TRUST

ACTION WORD	HOW IT APPLIES TO YOUR PITCH
Straight-Up	*"Let's cut the crap and here's the deal..."* This is a great level to hit once in a while to change the timbre in your voice and your energy level. It's just what a good friend would do. I find it grounds you instantly and people react to this no-nonsense approach. Use it sparingly otherwise you'll come across as bossy. You'll know the difference.
Strategic Thought and Action	Most of us rush to the *'do'* because we get scared and doing something, anything, is better than doing nothing at all. Right? Not necessarily. We have to be strategic and aware of how our actions pre-promote us. Refer to ***Chapter 4**, Three Questions in Life*™.
Sustainability	Sustainability is a big industry word used for almost every product and marketing department. As it applies to your pitch, this is in terms of staying ahead in both your current knowledge, but also in how you package yourself including your speech patterns. As we age, we tend to speak slower and more methodically without changing the rhythm (a dead giveaway that you're getting a bit long in the tooth). If you want to have a long TV and online life, you have to stay sharp and not sit back on your own historical success. Make new stories. (Don't become a *Willi Loman* from Arthur Miller's *Death of a Salesman*.)
SWOT	*"**SWOT** Analysis is a useful technique for understanding your **S**trengths and **W**eaknesses, and for identifying both the **O**pportunities open to you and the **T**hreats you face.* ***SWOT** Analysis helps you develop your career in a way that takes best advantage of your talents, abilities and opportunities."* Source: http://www.mindtools.com/pages/article/newTMC_05.htm

INSPIRE your way with TRUST

ACTION WORD	HOW IT APPLIES TO YOUR PITCH
T	
Talent	Plays a significant role in selling on-air. Refer to **Chapter 2**, in the section *Winning Qualities*.
Tantalize	Part of the grand appeal of bringing the products into the living rooms of our customers is we get to show off our products in a way that no other retail environment is able to. The more tantalizing you make the experience, the longer your customers will stay tuned.
Taste	You have to have a strong sense of your parameters – what you can say, how you behave, what you wear. Refer to **Chapter 2**, *Guest Expert*.
Tease	Teases are mainly done by the networks with upcoming promos, coupon redeeming, program guides, mailers, sneak peeks etc. As the guest expert, your tease comes with your opening line directly after you're introduced and every time you reset your message. 1. The best tease, arguably in modern television history commenced after the CBS season finale episode on March 21, 1980 and wasn't resolved until November 21, where 350 million new and old viewers tuned-in to witness first-hand *"Who shot JR?"* The summer leading up to that episode (which was delayed due to a writers' strike) took tease, scarcity, promotion, suspense and intrigue to a whole new level. Now, we give Apple full credit for their brilliant pre-marketing teases. The producers of *Dallas* were the pioneers. 2. In a fantastic book, *The New Rules of Retail: Competition in the World's Toughest Marketplace*, authors Robin Lewis and Michael Dart share on page 99, "... a research team from Emory University found that dripping Kool-Aid into the mouths of volunteers on a regular basis had little increase in brain activity, while those who were given a random "dripping" had a heightened level of activity. This indicates that the anticipation of the reward, whether it is Kool-Aid or a new dress, is what gets consumers' dopamine pumping."

CHAPTER 8 — DIET YOUR WAY TO SALES SUCCESS™

INSPIRE your way with TRUST

ACTION WORD	HOW IT APPLIES TO YOUR PITCH
Tempo	Tempo of communication and vocal range can make a huge difference to gaining people's attention. This is especially important when you are demonstrating and trying to rise above objections. Composers and writers know the power of hitting levels during songs and scripts. The tempo should slow down or quicken to match the moment just as orchestras do in concertos and singers do within a striking ballad.
Tempt	You'll notice strong hosts do this extremely well. They bring the product as close to the cameras as possible. It is something you can do too, as long as it's within the rules of the particular network. It's a great tactic for kitchen products, textiles of any sort, jewelry and the like. It helps the customer to visualize it in their own homes.
Tenacity	If you speak to any successful sales person they all have tenacity. Even though the door is slammed in their face they still keep coming back. This story says it all: Every Tuesday a well-known retailer held open meetings for all sales reps. The meetings were only a few minutes long but no one was ever refused. This one particular rep. that relayed this story had been coming every Tuesday for over a year without any sale. One Tuesday, things changed. The rep. changed his approach. He had brought a similar product already being sold in the store. Before the door slammed in his face for the 100th time, the rep wanted to know why his products were being refused when his products were less expensive with the same quality. He changed his game by actually asking for business and challenging the buyer why he wouldn't give this product line a try. The buyer looked at him and said, *"Ok. I will give you an order."* This product line subsequently did extremely well for the store. ***Never give up. Figure out how to change your game to get different results.***
Tidbit	Sharing tidbits along the way adds spice to any recipe. It differentiates you and endears you to your audience. Chefs often share recipe tips and tricks as they talk about their pans or griddles. It makes you want to tune-in to that particular chef instead of just anyone who is selling the same hardware.

225

INSPIRE your way with TRUST

ACTION WORD	HOW IT APPLIES TO YOUR PITCH
Timbre	Watch your voice and level of anxiety while on-air. If we are anxious, we tend to speak at a higher pitch that sounds exasperated. It makes the listener feel uncomfortable and anxious, therefore less likely to want to listen for another second.
Timing	There is something called a Creative Stall. People who understand the power of good timing understand this as well. If you have an idea that you believe is exceptional, in order for this idea to develop into more than just that, you have to be aware of the right timing to introduce and implement the idea. If the timing is off, even if the idea is truly cutting edge, it will fall on deaf ears. Listen, watch and wait for your green light. It will come and when it is your time to pounce, don't miss your opportunity. The same is true for the goal of selling out. We all want that to happen every time we sell on-air. The reality is it won't happen every time through no fault of anyone or anything in particular. But remember, there is timing for that too. Listen, pitch, watch, wait for that green light and be ready to pounce when it is presented to you. Right product, right price, right time slot, exceptional pre-buzz. Timing.
Tips	Part of keeping the balls bouncing during your pitch may involve adding some industry tips. It's a fun way to throw out your personality, change the pace, connect with your customer and show that you know what you are talking about. It's also a great jump-off point to re-set your pitch to start all over again.
Transition	Transitioning well is a skill that needs to be practiced and felt. Easily changing gears of overcoming indifference to saying something entertaining to bouncing off of some great point the host just made to executing a fast demo is the goal of every person in broadcasting. Think of what the daytime talk shows are made of. From cooking to fashion, to serious news stories, all within a half hour show segment.
Transferable	If you are an entrepreneur who knows how to close a sale, those skills are transferable everywhere in any market. My father used to say, *"If you can sell, you'll never go hungry."* Be grateful that you have the skills to sell and hone this skill for all it's worth.

INSPIRE your way with TRUST

ACTION WORD	HOW IT APPLIES TO YOUR PITCH
Trend	A great positioning point is to talk product trend, customer trends, industry trend, buying trends, particularly if your category has anything to do with fashion. There are many reasons why but here's a simple one: People don't want to be left behind if there is a chance that we could be a part of something special. (Apple and Nike have built and continue to build their success on the excitement of the next great thing.)
Triggers	When you are talking, you have to know where to land and what will trigger your next move. When I rehearse my show on set, I am not merely going over the at-a-glance script; I am working out my choreography of the marks I will be hitting within my time slot. Make a decision on where you are going. It may change for the next show but commit to something. Every visual sparks a different set of selling points and helps one to remember without needing a list in front of them. When I rehearse, I repeat those triggers for that particular show and that particular day. A well known celebrity fitness trainer and inventor on HSN and TSC, uses physical triggers all the time to remember his pitch points and to keep his pace up and energized. It works brilliantly.
Tune-In	Just like turning the dial on your radio, we all have to tune-in to the atmosphere of what is going on in our current environment. This information can help elevate the urgency of why people need our products. Let's take a specific example: There could have been a bed bug scare recently in the news. Use that current news issue that many people are affected by in real time. That gets their attention immediately because they are directly affected by it. The switch from maybe to yes is readily available if you tune-in to what people can currently relate to.

R

Raise Up	You may be the only shining person in the life of some of your customers and that's why they may be tuning-in to see you. Raise up the level of connection and joy you bring. It may make a significant difference in someone's life.
Rally	Rally the troops to take action. As the timer is counting down, this is the time when you re-focus your pitch to access that next gear inside of you. People want to be told what to do. (I don't mean bossed or taught a lesson or scolded.) I mean they want the perfect scenario to be painted so it's an obvious choice to say yes.

INSPIRE your way with TRUST

ACTION WORD	HOW IT APPLIES TO YOUR PITCH
Rapport	Chemistry cannot be manufactured. Either you have it or you don't with the host. Think anchor celebrities Matt Lauer and Katie Couric. Kelly Ripa and Regis Philbin. Rapport is another word for relationship or *"relate to."* Remember, it's your job to come to the host. This is the host's playground. You are merely visiting so figure out how you can relate to them.
React	I remember working with Mr. T years ago on a television series called, *T and T*. He was so charming and a true gentleman. I was the guest star that week and many of my scenes were with him. He told me that what makes an exceptional actor is how well they react to what is going on around them. I have to admit, I was rather surprised at his comment at first but found a new respect for his careful consideration of what the art form of true connection meant to him. *"Good actors stay in the moment,"* he said, *"and are available to react to whatever is thrown at them."* Thanks Mr. T. I have always remembered that piece of wisdom! In **Chapter 10**, in the section *The New World Approach*, we'll talk about keeping your messaging and delivery fresh no matter how many times you describe your product's benefits.
Reaffirm	Reaffirm or recap. You will find that the host is exceptional at doing this. It's part of the job. If you find a host does this a lot every time you make a new point, consider whether or not that they are telling you something about your presentation. Perhaps you need to rethink how you sum up your messaging. Sometimes great public speakers need to adjust their messaging into smaller sound bites. If you can hear what your host is giving you, they will often turn you into a better guest expert.
Receive	Part of the relationship with the host is to truly receive what they are giving you. There are times when they give you all kinds of gems that you both can have a grand time with! There are other times when *they are* too *closed* to work with you. It's life, so go with it. If you feel like you're alone out there, always go back to who your customers are and your demos.

CHAPTER 8 — DIET YOUR WAY TO SALES SUCCESS™

INSPIRE your way with TRUST

ACTION WORD	HOW IT APPLIES TO YOUR PITCH
Receptive	Be receptive to altering your sales approach in a moment. This is one of the more important elements of working in live television as there are a lot of experts watching how your performance and sales are doing. We all have many different customers to satisfy: Your end-use customers, the president of the network, your buyers, their managers, your programmers, your producers and the host you are working with. If one of them comes to you and suggests you make changes, take it in and find a way to satisfy the request. We're in this together and they are the experts in understanding their market just as you are in yours.
Rely	Rely on what you are familiar with first. For example, if you are a fashion model who is changing directions into hosting or being a guest expert, use your strengths of fashion, angles and knowledge of colour, beauty and textiles to ground your work instantly. Those principles can be somehow applied to nearly any product. If you are familiar with working in front of the camera, use this expertise to benefit and build from that. Working from the inside and blossoming out as your confidence grows, is the fastest way to increase your capabilities.
Relatable	When you are looking to connect and switch your customers from 'maybe' to 'yes', The Anchor Seven™ and your Opening Statements (in **Chapter 9**) will help you immeasurably in this very important closing tactic. Being relatable is currency within the TV industry. There is a term known as a 'Q-Score" which is a proprietary metric created in 1963 by Jack Landis "that determines the familiarity of an athlete, celebrity, TV show or brand measuring the appeal of each among those persons familiar with each." Source: http://en.wikipedia.org/wiki/Q_Score
Responsive	The synonym for respond is to answer. Answer the call to whatever is required of you whether it's at your desk, on set, or in the backroom with the buying team. Be present and ready to play.
Reveal	Always connect yourself to your product. The *"reveal"* means there are no hiding spaces. Keep everything open, transparent and available for your customers and the camera to see anytime.

INSPIRE your way with TRUST

ACTION WORD	HOW IT APPLIES TO YOUR PITCH
Risk	When you put yourself out there the only risk you really face is to decide whether you are *ready* to give more of yourself and thereby ready to receive more. Any successful businessperson will tell you that however big the risk, increases your position and potential to develop big rewards. Understand how far and high you are willing to climb and how much you are willing to risk of yourself. Calculated risk is an important skill to nurture. In the brilliant book *The Art of Possibility*, the authors Rosamund Stone Zander and Benjamin Zander provide the following insight on creative risk – "When (Gustav) Mahler wrote difficult passages for particular instruments, like the high-flying 'Frere Jacques' tune for solo bass…he was almost certainly conveying, musically, the sense of vulnerability and risk he saw as an integral part of life. We will not convey the sense of the music if we are in perfect technical control…"
Rush	It's more fun to win than lose. The rush of success keeps us motivated to want to win again and again. Keep finding ways to put yourself in circumstances that increase your odds of winning.

Understand	Understanding and having empathy helps enormously to create your pitch. Anchor Seven™ in **Chapter 7**, *Your Customers,* is worth exploring if you really want to know who your customers are.
Unify	Unify the entire visual and audible experience for the audience from matching your wardrobe to the host and the set. **Chapter 7**, *Your Customers* will again help you feel unified with your customers even more. The synonym of unify, is hook. More in **Chapter 9**, *The Lily Pad Strategy*™
Uplift	Your job as a public figure is to also uplift whoever is watching. Remember that some of your customers may have had a difficult day or are going through a tough time in their life. Although according to the title of this book and many of your professional partners – sales is all there is, it really isn't. If you can help to uplift or help your customers to smile for just a second, this is a win too!

CHAPTER 8 — DIET YOUR WAY TO SALES SUCCESS™

INSPIRE your way with **TRUST**

ACTION WORD	HOW IT APPLIES TO YOUR PITCH
S	
Safe Place	*Safe place* is a term often used in the audition process in theatre and television to remind actors that they are free to fully express who they are and their message. It often allows the performer to swing wide, freeing up their inhibitions to access their best. If you've ever sat on the other side of the interview or audition desk, many times you can feel the palpable nerves of the people auditioning. Don't you just want to tell them to relax! If you're this nervous, there's no way we're going to get the best of you. In **Chapter 4,** we focus on The Job of Getting the Job. We also talk about the ideal connection between host and guest expert having to create a safe and warm environment for the audience. Not a *lullaby* safe but more in terms of a normal, buoyant and neighbourly chat.
Scarcity	During the 2012 London Summer Olympics, as many of us watched the excitement and even became familiar with the various athletes due to the vast number of interviews, Ryan Lochte (Olympic gold and multi-medal winner in swimming) talked about his workouts and how he designed a program for anyone to benefit from. Well of course, I was interested to see what it was, only to find a message on his website www.ryanlochte.com that read: "During the USOC blackout period, Ryan is not allowed to sell Lochte tee shirts or Lochte glasses on his website due to Rule 40 of the USOC. These products are not sold out, but we had to post that they are sold out in order to prevent anyone from purchasing due to this rule. Thanks and come back on Aug 16, 2012 and we will have all the products up again!" The way the message was crafted and the fact that I couldn't even put the product *on hold* until a certain day made me want the product even more. When August 16 came around, I purchased it.

INSPIRE your way with TRUST

ACTION WORD	HOW IT APPLIES TO YOUR PITCH
Security	In **Chapter 2**, *The Guest Expert*, we highlight many imperative qualities required to be a great on-air seller. There are some pros in the industry that would say that familiarity = security. If you're looking to last within the media market today, build your familiarity through engaging meaningful interactions with your customers and entire network. Familiarity is recognized with a matrix called the Q-Score which was highlighted earlier in the chapter. The Q-Score is a proprietary "...metrics that measure the likeability, popularity, and appeal of athletes, celebrities, and brands. Marketing Evaluations claims that the Q-Score is more valuable to marketers than other popularity measurements, such as the Nielsen ratings, because Q-Score indicate not only how many people are aware of/or watch a TV show, but also how those same people feel about the TV show. A well-liked television show, for example, may be worth more as a commercial venue to an advertiser than a higher-rated show that people don't like as much. High emotional bonding with a show means strong viewer involvement and audience attention." Source: http://en.wikipedia.org/wiki/Q_Score
Self-Reliant	You are out there alone with all eyes on you. **Chapter 9**, *The Lily Pad Strategy*™ helps to ensure you are ready to perform with confidence.
Sense of Humour	If you've got a great sense of humour, use it. Be ready to laugh at yourself too. It's an endearing quality that is always welcome in any arena. Consider some of the best comedians today. They'll use self-deprecating humour in order to relate instantly to their audience.
Sensitive	A great synonym for sensitive is - alive to. Become **alive to** all of the current changes in the market you are working within and the advances to technology. This additional material and heightened approach will deepen and expand the reach of your selling message.

CHAPTER 8 — DIET YOUR WAY TO SALES SUCCESS™

INSPIRE your way with TRUST

ACTION WORD	HOW IT APPLIES TO YOUR PITCH
Silence	This can be a very powerful attention getting tactic. You only get one moment of silence during your show. If you choose to use it, know how to hit it out of the park. The reason why it works is when listeners tune-in; they all expect to hear a voice and someone chiming in words and phrases. When all of that stops for even a second or two, the pattern is broken and people want to know what happened.
Surpass	If you are a runner or cyclist, you know exactly what the merits of cresting the hill does for an athlete. It pushes you beyond expectation and through your own limitations. When you run through the peak of the hill, it strengthens belief in yourself and prepares you for the times when you want to give up. Not giving up and cresting the hill past the top incline gives the confidence to move past challenges more easily. **Surpass your own expectations any time you have the opportunity to do it. This is at the root of true growth for any professional.**
Surprise	If you want to experience one of the best examples of using surprise as a meaningful tactic to gain credibility and attention: log onto Hugh Laurie's audition (he was hired to play the coveted lead role of Gregory House in the TV hit series *House*). Watch this audition! The video is only a few minutes long and worth your time. I don't want to spoil the surprise but you have to experience how he uses all of his talents in one quick moment that is the perfect *call-to-action* for the part he was auditioning for. http://www.youtube.com/watch?v=UqHh6TvGQIQ
Stake	What's at stake today? Assessing what you need to do in order to impel and inspire people to take action is part of your work. If you are not feeling the urgency of why your pitch is worth listening to, no one else will care. Think about your Anchor Seven™ anytime you can't figure out why your message is important. It will keep you honest and grounded because you know who your customers are and what their needs are.
Stories	Think about why a well-told joke works so well to break the ice with a group of people that don't know each other well. There's a strong set up, a story and a punch line. It's a great sales tactic. If you have a story to tell that fits with your style, product and pitch, do it. But make it quick!

INSPIRE your way with TRUST

ACTION WORD	HOW IT APPLIES TO YOUR PITCH
Surrender	There is a marked difference between *making* it happen vs. *letting* it happen. When your career seems like it's on the line, you just want to force the right events to happen the way you think it should. Right? Circumstances like waiting to hear if you got the high paying, high ranking, high opportunity job is gut wrenching when you know you are ready for this job and there is no one more qualified to do it. It is sometimes the most difficult endeavor in the world to surrender to trusting in the big picture plan that is in place right now for you. We all want the crystal ball to tell us what is coming up next. Give them all you have to give without looking back. And then let it go. The *Tao of Pooh,* written by Benjamin Hoff, is a wonderful book that employs the fictional characters of A. A. Milne's Winnie-the-Pooh stories to explain how to just *be.* If you've never read this charming book, add it to your bedside as a must read.

CHAPTER 8 — DIET YOUR WAY TO SALES SUCCESS™

EXECUTE your way with **TRUST**

ACTION WORD	HOW IT APPLIES TO YOUR PITCH
T	
Team member	You have to trust that everyone who is responsible for getting your product out to market will bring their A+ game. Depend on each other's expertise and let them do their work while you do yours. In an interview with Basketball player Grant Hill on the television show, The Next Chapter on *OWN* with Oprah Winfrey, he shares the following story about trusting in his team: 1991-92 Duke University vs. University of Nevada/Las Vegas lead by 1 point. There's only 2 seconds left on the clock and only a hail Mary shot left to make. For months prior, Duke coach Mike Krzyzwski would have his team do a baseball overhand throw from one side of the court to the other to the bewilderment of the team member. In basketball, this is not a common shot. This championship day, however, the coach needed Hill to deliver that overhand shot with accuracy. He told Grant this was the only shot they had to win the game. Grant Hill relays the story. *"Our coach asked, 'Can you make a pass all the way down the court?' I said, 'Yeah, I can do it.' Then he asked teammate Christian Laettner, 'If Grant makes the pass, can you make the shot?' Christian said, 'I'll make the shot if Grant makes the pass.'"* *"We walked out of that team meeting (and I've talked to the guys twenty years later and we've all said that we believed we were going to win). I just knew that I was going to do my part and Christian was going to do his. And we did. We won back-to-back championships."* The 2013 World Series winners, The Boston Red Sox is another great story of overcoming all odds to work as a unified team in order to triumph in the greatest baseball arena in the world.
Testing	This is elementary advice: Be sure to test and test and test your product and your demonstration. Leave nothing to chance. If you can do the same demo ten times in a row without one mistake, you are ready. Never settle for good enough.
Thick-skinned	When you are the product, you have to be able to separate responsibility to yourself and to other people's opinion. Being thick-skinned means you have a tremendous amount of integrity and focus with the work you do.

EXECUTE your way with TRUST

ACTION WORD	HOW IT APPLIES TO YOUR PITCH
Through-put	*"Through-put is the rate at which the system generates money through sales."* Page 61 of *The Goal: A Process of Ongoing Improvement* written by Eliyahu M. Goldratt and Jeff Cox. What's one of the biggest concerns when it comes to moving business along? It's identifying the log jams or what Mr. Goldratt refers to as the 'constraints' to get the information you need in order to do your job. There is a lot of information that will need to be exchanged between the network, vendors and you. Pre-empt as many of the possible log jams as you can foresee in order to do your job to your best ability. This includes getting samples well in advance, programming notes, contact lists, getting scripts, demo materials, sales reports, technical information, getting paid in a timely fashion, and every other element required.
Time Management	The 3-minute loop is all you get to complete your pitch at least twice. Watch the countdown clock in the studio and stay on message. One side-step like a missed demo or too many ums or ah's, wastes your valuable time.
Time Contraints	Time constraints provide pressure to create results. In **Chapter 10**, *Practice*, we will deal a lot with time. Recently I heard a phrase on TV, *"Time is oxygen."* When you only have a few seconds to ignite someone's interest, don't waste it.

CHAPTER 8 — DIET YOUR WAY TO SALES SUCCESS™

EXECUTE your way with TRUST

EXECUTE

ACTION WORD	HOW IT APPLIES TO YOUR PITCH
Time-Limited	Here's a fun example taken out of the home shopping structure for a moment but applies the same emotion of urgency that home shopping channels do so well. On a local radio station my husband and I listen to a fun promotion called *"Every second counts."* They play one second of a song (extremely **un**recognizable) and have people call in at certain times of the day to catch a different demographic. The 107th caller or the 200th caller would have their chance to guess the correct answer. With every wrong answer, $100 is added to the pot. One afternoon, we were found madly redialing and redialing on two cell phones, hoping to get the chance to answer. It's fun, you get caught up in the excitement and in some odd way, you grow an allegiance to the contest format and perhaps even with the radio station itself. You can't wait for the next time slot to try again - particularly if you think you know the correct answer. ***We don't want to be left behind if there is a chance that we could be a part of something special.*** I was at a real estate open house event in our neighbourhood looking to purchase a new home. It was Sunday and the open house was getting ready to wrap up. The real estate agent announced every time someone new entered the front door that new bids would be taken only until 8pm that night and not a minute later. She created this frenzied excitement by making it seem like this house was the most desired home for sale that day. Her pushy tactic garnered ten bids that night all before 8pm and the house was sold that same night.
Training	If you can repeat your demonstration 10 times in a row and not make one mistake, you are ready. Ill prepared guest experts won't make it long-term. There are too many good ones out there waiting in the wings.
Turnover	Speed of turnover is one of the keys to keeping the message fresh and interesting. Refer to **Chapter 12**, *10-Point Checklist*. It will train your mind and mouth to turnover information quickly and succinctly.

EXECUTE your way with TRUST

ACTION WORD	HOW IT APPLIES TO YOUR PITCH
R	
Raise your game	If sales are flat or if things are not happening the way you envision they should be, raise up the level of your game. Use whatever is happening in the moment and change it up. Do something a little different to shake things up. You only have a few minutes to succeed. Always keep pitching it out there.
Recall	In *Chapter 12*, *Camera Ready 10-Point Checklist*, we have included tactics to help you speed your turnover of recall from the Italian rehearsal to the at-a-glance script.
Record	Record your shows on your PVR consistently. It helps to catch and address ways you can improve your pitch. It may also help you to pick up on habits you've perhaps added unknowingly. It helps you to focus on your body language, your wardrobe choices and helps you to assess your success in a retrospective manner in order to make changes for next time, or to confirm that you are on the right track.
Recover and Rebound	No matter what happens, the show must go on. It's important to know how to adjust and recover constantly during your shows. (As if you are skiing a black diamond mogul run. Knees limber and ready to absorb the bumps with resolve.) Many unexpected events can occur which may challenge your ability to capitalize on doing the best performance you can. Lights can go out, your microphone may not work, the host may talk all over you, interrupting your flow and thought pattern. You may all of sudden have a cough, the stagers may have mistakenly shortchanged your product set-up etc. Forgive yourself and the situation and get on with it. Remember, the customer who just tuned-in has no idea what has gone on. They are expecting to know why your product is so great and why they should stick around to find out.
Re-energize	You play a part in re-energizing the host. Sometimes they can feel a little flat. This may be their 'Friday' and the week may have been a long and exhausting week. By coming in full of energy with an attitude that lifts the spirit, you'll often get the best out of the host and more from the show itself.

238

EXECUTE your way with TRUST   EXECUTE

ACTION WORD	HOW IT APPLIES TO YOUR PITCH
Relentless	To remain determined and unyielding with respect to your vision and career path and what you want to get out of life is a requirement. Being relentless with your determination to achieve all that you can is a gift given to us. Most of the definitions of relentless seem to be negative and uncharacteristic of the positive nature and intention of this book it is, however, a word that has earned an important spot. Refer to the quote from marathon runner Bill Rodgers at the very beginning of the book, *Setting The Scene*.
Reset	Practice re-setting your three-minute loop. Practice getting distracted and having to reset your train of thought. Refer to ***Chapter 10***, *The 3 P's*.
Results	*"Life is serious. We are judged by our results."* Dr. Phil McGraw *"The only success in DRTV (and all home shopping) is the success of the show. Is the CPO (cost per order) in the range to break even or make a profit? If the show doesn't work, no matter how great it looks, then it's a show that has failed."* Linda Brooks, Director, DRTV Operations at Monte Media TV
Return Policies	The return policy is a very important element for the customer to feel comfortable with their purchase, particularly with a higher-ticket item. This is normally only something that the host will say but I have heard guest experts use it as a sales tactic. When a guest expert uses these types of corporate directives, it appears to look more like an apology begging the customer to buy. Yes, it's an important part of the transaction, but let the host take that role. Your job is to keep lobbing great reasons to buy for people to catch. Help inspire them to place the order!

EXECUTE your way with **TRUST**

ACTION WORD	HOW IT APPLIES TO YOUR PITCH
Reward	In his book Drive, Daniel H. Pink explores what motivates us to work beyond what we're capable of doing. Is it only the rewards? Is it the accolades that drive us? In a song called *"Another National Anthem"* from Stephen Sondheim's musical *Assassins,* the cast members sing about how they are all obsessed by needing a prize for what they have done. *"What's my Prize?"* is the common question that never seems to get answered. I believe that rewards, medals, and acknowledgement of a job well done are important components, but can't be the whole story. They are the markers of excellence and stepping stones signifying you are on the right path. They acknowledge work well done and this often strengthens our allegiance to what we are doing. **The ultimate prize is the work you do, the subtleties you learn about yourself and the reputation you build.**

U

Urgency	The last two minutes of any public auction draws most of the action and bidding. Home shopping also creates a sense of urgency with just minutes left to sell. One of the three best visuals on the television and computer monitors seen by our customers at home are: the countdown timer, the items left graphic and the units sold counter. The host and guest expert use these visuals to their full advantage to push the urgency to act now: *"We only have a handful left." "If you are looking at the screen right now, I guarantee that by the end of this hour, we will be sold out."* All great examples of a call-to-action! More in **Chapter 9**, in the section *Ask for Business*.
Utilize	Utilize as much from your life experience as you can as long as it is relatable to the product and your customers. For instance, if you sell waterproof cameras or a heart rate monitor that measures altitude or a waterproof watch and you also do some extraordinary activities like scuba diving or jumping out of planes, these experiences are viable examples worth sharing. If however, you are selling fashion wear, scuba diving may not have the same impact or relevance to furthering your expertise or the overall sales message.

CHAPTER 8 — DIET YOUR WAY TO SALES SUCCESS™

EXECUTE your way with TRUST

EXECUTE

ACTION WORD	HOW IT APPLIES TO YOUR PITCH
S	
Sales	This is a sales job! No matter how pretty, famous, rich or poor you are, if you don't have the skill to sell, your career will be short on a shopping channel. Learn how to sell if you want to last in this industry.
Self-Motivated	Fear can sometimes be a great motivator. Fear that this may be your last job, last performance, etc. In **Chapter 10,** *The 3 P's,* I talk about a seasoned actor who keeps a list of ten action words that have great meaning to him. There is no such thing as phoning a performance in. It is hard work to get it right and takes a different amount of focused discipline to keep delivering excellence consistently. If you want to have a long career, figure out how to do that because that is your job.
Sell	Above all else, this is a selling role. No matter what else you have going for you, if you don't know how to sell and ask for business, this is not the job for you.
Sell Yourself First	People buy *you* first. Later in this chapter we'll talk about the power of your anchor statements to start out strong. People are attracted to confident people who have something important to share.
Social Media	According to Donny Deutsh, *"Social media is the technical articulation of democracy."* It can be used for tremendous good – like the outpouring of support from 1000's of people during the November 2012 Hurricane Sandy storm victims. *No matter how you use this mandatory platform of communication, ensure that with every tweet, poke or post that you know your reputation is built upon the trail you leave behind.*
Speed	The only way to achieve speed is through a solid foundation, which is made up of precise technique. Whether you're a runner, cyclist, boxer, tennis player or skier, when you add the element of speed or full-force intensity, you have to have good technique or you'll get injured or your mind will burn out. The same principle applies to on-air selling. The nature of the medium is speed, therefore you have to be fully charged and plugged-in or you'll get left behind. There is no time for tripping or grabbing for words and there's definitely no room for playing small. ***On your mark, get set, GO!***

EXECUTE your way with TRUST

ACTION WORD	HOW IT APPLIES TO YOUR PITCH
Stamina	If you are doing a GVS, you have to train yourself to switch 'on' and 'off'. Having the stamina to sustain your energy level is a skill. You may be working all hours of the day or night. Practice resting in action to maintain stamina.
Success upon Success	Anything can slow you down. Anything is possible and you have to be ready. Therefore, we have to plan for success in every possible way and that includes setting attainable goals. Big sky thinking is great but you have to have a few other goals where you'll have a pretty good chance of achieving. Build success upon success. (Refer to *Chapter 11, Assess Your Success* for some helpful strategies.)
Summarize	Part of the host's job is to summarize what you are saying. They listen for strong sound bites of your pitch to summarize for those customers who have perhaps just joined the network on TV or online. The act of summarizing is part of asking for business or closing. Both you and the host can play a part in this.
Surround	When you are rehearsing, surround yourself with both visual and audible distractions. This will help you compartmentalize your attention and abilities and will keep you focused on the task at hand.
Sustain	Sustain *dis*belief is a phrase often used in theatre. Every possible technique goes into capturing the imagination of the theatregoer. From the plush seating, to the set decoration to the wardrobe, lighting, sound, etc. In the home shopping world, we too use many levels of beauty to capture our customers' imagination with one exception: We want to sustain *belief* by keeping it real and relatable for our viewers. They chose to tune-in, now it's our job to sustain their attention and interest.

CHAPTER 8 — DIET YOUR WAY TO SALES SUCCESS™

TRUST your way with TRUST

ACTION WORD	HOW IT APPLIES TO YOUR PITCH
T	
Trust	Trust in your preparation and in all the work you have done that it is in place and ready to be called up when needed. Trust too that all the trials and challenges you've faced along the way have prepared you for your big day. Trust in yourself, trust your partnerships, your products, the network and alliances you've created and nurtured. Trust your training, trust your instincts and your intuition and finally trust that your customers will be thrilled to get your product home and will use it with delight for years to come. ***It all has to work together, and trust is the glue that binds success.***
Trusting	Gaining a trusting and trustworthy reputation is earned, not assumed.
R	
Referrals	Receiving a good review from your peers, customers, critics and bosses is currency and can never be taken away. It belongs 100% to you and is earned through your exceptional action. One of the tests (or rewards) of achieving trust is receiving a referral. If other people say that you are worth hiring or the product is worth buying, it makes for a much more direct route for you to enjoy further growth in your career. Because receiving excellent feedback and endorsements is an important part of our work, use social media platforms and others to build up your portfolio. In this highly competitive world, when there are thousands of candidates equally qualified for the same job, what people have to say about *you*, matters. ***Make yourself stand out based on your work ethic and reputation.***
Relationships	In ***Chapter 12***, *Have you Got Your Game Face ON?*, The three keys to success are identified.

TRUST your way with TRUST

ACTION WORD	HOW IT APPLIES TO YOUR PITCH
Reputation	Reputation is tied 100% to what you do. It is perhaps the most powerful of all currencies in that without proper management, one wrong move can irreversibly damage your reputation. What you do today creates your future for tomorrow. Every connection, every action and reaction plays a part in affecting in real time your reputation and your ultimate professional growth.
Retention	Customer retention should be as important as gaining trust with your peers. It is one of the paramount goals in business and in life. It can be difficult to maintain one good friendship/one good customer. Establishing a great relationship with one friend/one customer presents the enormity of care and attention required if you want to gain more.

S

Sincerity	No matter how much you talk the talk and walk the walk, if you are not believable and do not believe in the value of your product, you'll have little chance of succeeding long-term. People can see through dishonesty and *'acts of sincerity'*. They will choose to go elsewhere and have every right to do so.

T

Thank You	**Standing on the shoulders of giants.** "The metaphor was first recorded in the twelfth century and attributed to Bernard of Chartres. He used to say that we are like dwarfs on the shoulders of giants, so that we can see more than they, and things at a greater distance, not by virtue of any sharpness of sight on our part, or any physical distinction, but because we are carried high and raised up by their giant size." Source: interpreted from: http://en.wikipedia.org/wiki/Standing_on_the_shoulders_of_giants

Acknowledge everyone who has brought you to this point in your career and life. Know how they contributed to your pathway to success along the way. Include your partners, customers, mentors, competition, network of peers and team members and most importantly your family and friends. |

CHAPTER 8 — DIET YOUR WAY TO SALES SUCCESS™

SOURCES

1. http://www.imdb.com/title/tt1568150/
2. http://www.davidkhurst.com/#
3. http://hbr.org/1984/05/of-boxes-bubbles-and-effective-management/ar/1

CHAPTER 8
DIET Your Way to Sales Success™

1. This section is the nuts and bolts of the entire book. If you read nothing else and want to fast-track this book, read this section. I guarantee you'll want to read other sections because of it.

2. No's save you $, Yeses make you $, Maybes cost you $.

3. Sales success depends on how well we *listen* to our *listeners*. The principles of DIET and the Anchor Seven™ all apply here.

4. At-a-Glance charts provided for your reference:

    a. DIET Leads to TRUST

    b. Sales Equation DIET Funnel

    c. TRUST Chart of Action Words

CHAPTER 9

THE LILY PAD STRATEGY™

Performance is anything but a linear experience. There is no clear path of progression and everything happens simultaneously. You realize that in one second, twenty equally important things are happening all at the same time and sometimes they are as unpredictable as you could ever imagine. It is always the way we respond to the challenges that keep us getting better. In the world of turtles and frogs, each waxy leaf of a lily pad is a useful surface to seek shelter and sustenance. The instinctive creatures that depend on the lily pad jump from one to the other, reacting to their surroundings as they need to. As performers, we have to rely on our instincts and develop our own show plan adapting to whatever happens on-set. One can easily get lost without having a strong pitch structure. Just like the jazz musician who may work only from lead sheets, there is a lot of improvisation. Within that fluidity there is structure and rooted principles. That is what **The Lily Pad Strategy**™ is all about. It allows you to bridge gaps, dance and pop onto any rooted platform giving you the confidence to fly from one thought to another effortlessly.

"There is a vitality, a life force, an energy, a quickening that is translated through you into action, and because there is only one of you in all of time, this expression is unique. And if you block it, it will never exist through any other medium and it will be lost. The world will not have it. It is not your business to determine how good it is nor how valuable nor how it compares with other expressions. It is your business to keep it yours clearly and directly, to keep the channel open."

-*Martha: The Life and Work of Martha Graham by Agnes De Mille*

CHAPTER 9 — THE LILY PAD STRATEGY™

Picture used with Andrea Boyle's permission.

Fact about the Lily pad:

"Characteristically round, flat and waxy, a lily pad is designed to **repel** moisture from its surface. Though lily pads appear as if they are simply floating atop the water, the stem that they are attached to may extend many feet down to the bottom of a pond or lake, where it takes **root**."[1]

Repel
Definition: To drive back or away
Synonym: Put to flight

Root
Definition: The fundamental tone of a compound tone or of a series of harmonies, to implant or establish deeply
Synonym: Support, Bolster

Formulating Your Pitch

> "The key is you have to hit people in the face with a cream pie — you have to get their attention. And then you have to say something smart."
>
> **-James Patterson**

If I gathered six experts in the field of pitching and asked them to watch what was considered to be a very successful pitch, each of them would have their own slant on why that pitch worked. That's the beauty of the creative process. There is however one common theme of a good pitch. The ball never hits the ground. The pitch person and host are continually floating and popping out ideas that reach a mass market in milliseconds.

As we established in Chapter 7, Your Customers, unlike most other sales environments, you do not get the opportunity to look or talk with your customers directly. You have no idea if they are kicking tires and new to the network or are so familiar with your product category that they don't even need to hear your pitch. You also have no idea whether the person on the other side of the screen has a learning style that is more analytical, outrageous and/or has expertise in your field. The conventional sales principles of *close early and close often* are not as important as 'always hook them!' In this section, we're going to put all of the best sales principles together using the same Sales Equation DIET Funnel we've been developing throughout the book. We will also create your script, establish your voice, style, your technique, brand, and add wings to your message to help you create the highest sales turnover and buzz every single time you get the opportunity to sell.

Pitch Pad

There are seven major pitch pads to structuring your script. We will develop each one independently, but first, let's look at how it works within our Sales Equation DIET Funnel:

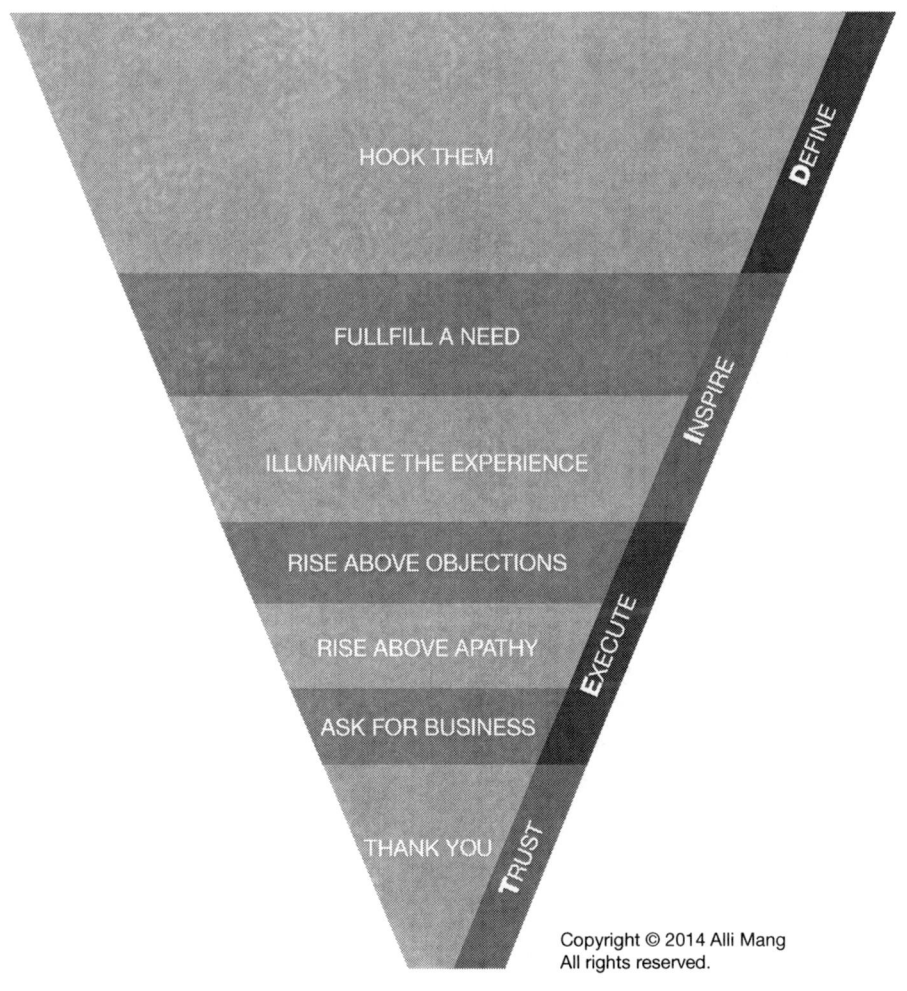

Breaking Down Each Pitch Pad

The best pitch people in the business can easily do three complete pitches within seven minutes. This chart shows you how they do it. They launch from one Pitch Pad to another with fluidity and ease because they always have a plan that is dependent on what is happening in this moment and three moments from now.

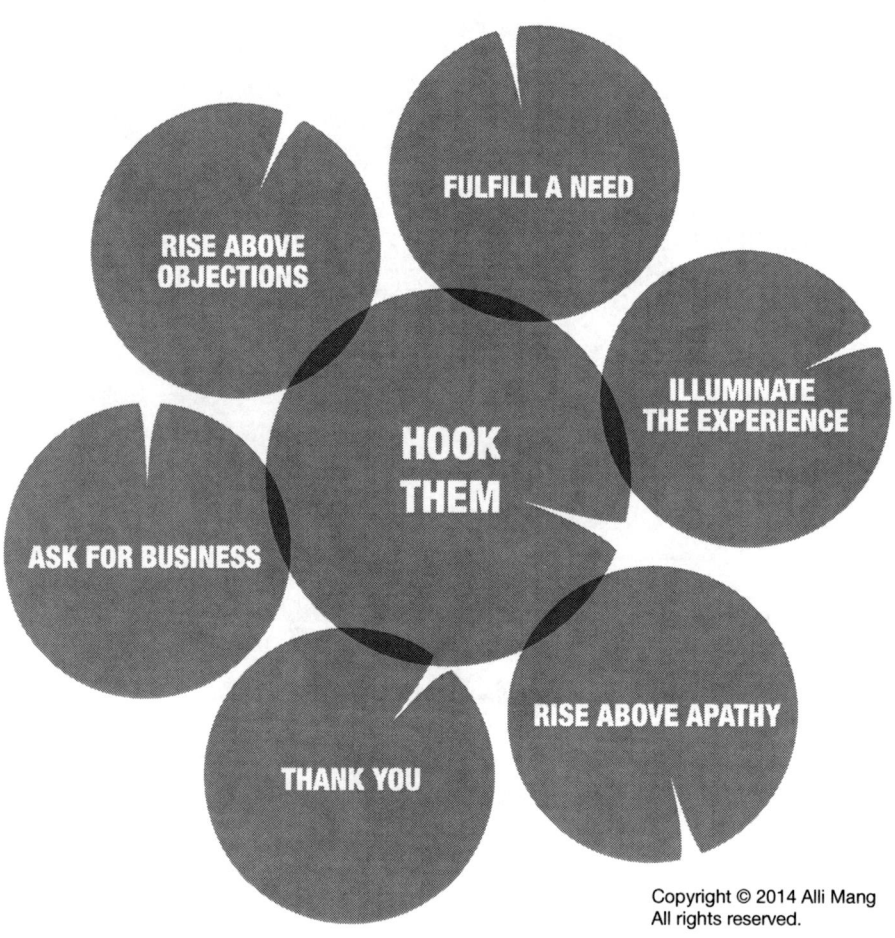

The Lily Pad Strategy™

Overall Tactic:

Set the stage for exciting expectation. Create first impression fireworks with the power of the One Image. Use your Leadership and Imaginative skills to electrify them. Find ways to solve your customers problems. Put them at ease. Charm and enchant them.

Viewers are tuning-in every minute of your pitch. Therefore you must hook your audience throughout the length of your pitch, not just at the beginning. You set the stage by crafting your messaging to relate to each individual you are talking to. In theatre, no performance is done without a deliberate stage set and lighting. The set defines the genre and vision of the director and writer and should tell the audience immediately what they are in for.

No matter what else you are doing, whether demos, introductions or instruction, you have to find a way to hook your customers with an exciting message. This is where heightened creativity, imagination and detailed knowledge of your customers will help you tremendously.

Stick around because on the next few pages, you will have a handful of meaningful opening statements to hook your customers!

The Host Has Introduced You, Now What?

In sports, starting out strongly sends a message that you are here to play and stay. The key is to find the way that will plug you in immediately in order to engage your audience with optimum impact. Go out boldly and claim your space during the first minute. It is not about being cocky or obnoxious, it's about making a strong first impression coupled with that quiet confidence that you are in charge, and when introduced, you will deliver.

You're standing just off camera ready to be introduced by the host. The monitor shows that the host is teasing products that are coming up within the hour and then highlights the very first product in the program. The host sets the scene for what the viewer is about to experience and they encapsulate all of the important points within thirty seconds. You stand there with your glossy lips and blank mind wondering what you're going to say now. "The host hit all the key features and benefits of this product perfectly and I really have nothing to add!"

"And now, I'd like to introduce _____who is our resident _____." You smile to the camera and shake your host's hand, (or not – depending on what the rules are at the particular network) and you have to have a launch line. Something that will anchor your thought process and the viewers' willingness to stay tuned-in for one more minute.

Opening Statement

Dancers on pointe have to be in touch with their centre of balance and line at all times. There are constant minor adjustments the athlete needs to make to adapt to the terrain in order to execute high performance. The same is true for a figure skater, skier or snowboarder. The phenom professional golfer Tiger Woods, has so much control and awareness of his body and technique that he can stop the momentum at any point during his swing. This power gives him the flexibility to reset and adjust as needed in the moment.

The selections of opening statements are endless. The ones you choose will be personality driven and need to suit your category, style and comfort level of showmanship but also need to represent the clearest path to your pitch. Similar to the importance of making a solid serve in a tennis match, opening statements are intrinsic to every part of the pitch. The opening statement is tossed up, and as the racket directs the ball to the line or just over the net, a positioning point is made. The ball is returned and you have to make another shot with a different spin on it to land in a different area of the court. It establishes you as a leader and helps the host, the producer, the buyer and the camera crew to feel confident that you've *got this*. You can be relied upon for taking the baton when you are invited to, and more importantly, you have some unique ways of selling and talking about your product that no one else has. (Brand yourself and your style.) If you establish yourself early, you will be given the room you need to sell and perform.

Personality Driven Opening Statements

Always acknowledge the host. It's just plain courtesy and if in their introduction they said something that seemed relevant to expand on right from the beginning, use it. Remember, the host is the winner/hero in the viewers' eyes no matter what. Use that as a jumping-off point. It immediately connects and **unifies** (synonyms of 'hook') you to the host, and allows you to take an **angle** (synonym of 'hook') quickly.

In Chapter 2, in the section Know Your Entertainment Style, we focused on identifying your own personal vision statement. The clearer you are in identifying your strengths and quirks, the more fun you'll have in coming up with opening statements that work for you specifically.

Here's an example of a strong personality opening statement. Can you *hear* his personality?

"…Honey, I know *you* know exactly what I'm talking about. Listen to me – you don't need anything else but what is in this package. Trust me darlings. All the girls in my salon fall over backwards to get this product."

On the next few pages, there are some real-life opening statements and other helpful guidelines that have been used by some of the best guest experts in the business. Allow the lists to inspire strong opening statements for you that mirrors your personality too.

OPENING STATEMENT GUIDE		
• What are your biggest frustrations when it comes to cleaning up the garbage?	• In less than 1 minute, I'm going to show you five simple ways you can achieve an expensive look with this product and for less than the price of a boutique coffee!	• In 30 seconds, here are five of the most important tips you need to know to keep your house clean and free of allergens
• I'm going to give you five reasons you and your family can't live without this...	• And today is the only time in the history of our company that you will get it at this price	• Everyone who is watching right now: I want you to raise your hand if...
• Stop whatever you're doing for a moment and take a look at this	• I want you to open up your ___ and come clean about the shape of your ___.	• For under ___, you can...
• Today is your day to make it happen and we're going to show you how easy it is to get started...	• This ___ will change your mind about...	• Do you want something that is beautifully designed, enhances any décor, is extremely lightweight, a baby could lift it, and keeps the bugs away...
• We've been around for fifty years because...	• People love it so much because...	• You've probably noticed that...
• Be sure to stay tuned-in to the end of this hour when we reveal...	• Check out our five-star ratings on our website for yourself. Our customers tell it like it is and they love it!	• Don't turn away because in 30 seconds you'll see exactly how this works
• It's not every day that you...	• Imagine being able to get back...	• Today, I'm going to change your mind about...
• Within thirty days from today, you could be...	• Are there times when you...	• Often spells the difference between failure and success

CHAPTER 9 — THE LILY PAD STRATEGY™ — Hook Them

OPENING STATEMENT GUIDE		
• If you're like most people, you probably…	• Women our age are looking for…	• You're in for a pleasant surprise, stick around to see this demo
• It's never too early to… • It's never to late to…	• Every once in a while you come across a…	• Today, more than ever…
• We've got the solution to your…	• We've sold over one million of them and here's why…	• It's hard enough… without having to worry about…
• Don't you love it when…	• Can you imagine never having to ___ again?	• Did you ever stop and think about ___?

Anchor Yourself

In Chapter 7, Your Customers, we started the principle of anchoring with the development of your Anchor Seven™. As discussed earlier, anchoring yourself grounds your message in the real world. It forces you to stay in this moment while connecting with your customers and thinking globally. On the next few pages, you will see a chart that will help build your anchor statements.

ANCHOR YOURSELF GUIDE		
CURRENT EVENTS	**EXAMPLE FACTORS**	**HOW YOU CAN CAPITALIZE IN A FEW SECONDS**
Time of day	• Day or evening or middle of the night?	• Your wardrobe
Season and current weather	• Check out the weather station to find out what is happening in the country (Not just where the network is based). • Snowstorm (for instance) – if I'm selling something to do with cocooning, home entertainment, dry skin due to weather conditions, comfort, warmth and safety- this is a great situation to use.	• People and regions love being recognized as a whole. It's the same tactic as when rock stars shout out – "I love New York" (or wherever they are playing). • Don't miss the opportunity to use what is actually happening right now for the audience to relate to immediately. *It also shows this is a fresh performance and not 'canned'.
Current News	• As above, by all means use appropriate newsworthy events if it suits your pitch and approach. Examples are infinite but may include: presidential elections, space launches, Diamond Jubilee, Royal Ascot, Super Bowl, Veteran's Day and Remembrance Day, etc	• As an example, in Canada we wear poppies on our left chest lapel in the weeks leading up to November 11 – Remembrance Day to salute our war veterans and soldiers currently fighting for our country. It's a heartfelt gesture for out-of-town guest experts to consider wearing as people relate positively and quickly to this symbol of honour. • Be careful to not be too real about current events (Sandy Hook tragedy, celebrity deaths, disease talk, war, etc.). People may often tune-in to escape their own world for a while and you want them to enjoy their time spent with you.

ANCHOR YOURSELF GUIDE		
CURRENT EVENTS	EXAMPLE FACTORS	HOW YOU CAN CAPITALIZE IN A FEW SECONDS
Trendy Talk	• Know the pulse of your customer as it relates to your category. As an example, if you are selling aromatic fragrances which are meant for the older generation, consider the sophistication of your pitch. Adding younger "colloquial language" (like, hot, OMG, you know…) might be considered off-the-mark for your category.	• No amount of trendy talk is appropriate on-air. There is a certain amount of formality balanced with relatable language that you must be aware of when choosing your words. • It is amazing how certain choices of words and adjectives can influence your image in one moment – even if it is meant to be fun or 'hip'. Be very clear on how your word preferences could be perceived.

Chase Thought

The anchor statement sets you up for your chase thought. Use the Lily Pad Strategy™ to decide where you are going next. Will you thank the audience, acknowledge the buying team, satisfy a need, demonstrate something or overcome indifference? Keep your path simple and deliberate. Most times, your chase thought is predicated by what the host has just said. It gives you a nice opening from which to jump off from. Part of *their* role is to speak for the audience to benefit the customers and in turn, you. You are having a conversation with the host and the listening audience will notice if you don't acknowledge the question. If the host doesn't say anything back, then jump to the next thought. The host will give you room if he/she hears and feels you have a plan that is working.

The Out of Town Guest Expert Advantage

If you are from another country, this is a great opportunity to endear the audience to you instantly. Japan, France and Germany (to name only a few) love English speaking guest experts. This can be the same in other countries as well. It adds a perceived exotic and authentic element that overseas customers love. Compliment the country, the people you've met, the time and experiences you've enjoyed. Mention the provinces or states or regions too. If you reference things that mean something to your audience, it sets you up as the metropolitan traveler who's been around and loves learning about their country as a visitor. It's your opportunity to position yourself as the expert having the worldwide eye on the pulse of current and future trends. It is a paramount opportunity for you to capitalize on.

CHAPTER 9 — THE LILY PAD STRATEGY™ — Fulfill a Need

Overall Tactic:
Make the connection with your customers. Uncover problems and provide solutions to satisfy their needs. In order to cover all of your bases you need to think in terms of multi-level functionality of your product, multi-level usefulness of your product and multi-level audiences. Let *them* know *you* know exactly who you are talking to.

This is your time to **inspire action** with your audience with as much personality, speed and pizzazz as you can muster! You must uncover unrealized needs in your audience in order for them to get over the *so what* syndrome. The most effective way to do this is to get them thinking about their own life and circumstances and/or their loved one's lives. Asking open-ended questions peaks the curiosity of your audience and that is what gets them engaged to find out more about what you have to say about your product. Examples may include:

"Do you ever wake up with itchy watery eyes and wonder why?"

"Can you imagine finally putting on your makeup without having to keep re-applying the entire day?"

"How old looking are your towels? Are they even drying you at this point, or merely pushing water around? Are you embarrassed to put them out for your guests? Are you so resistant to change that it took selling your house and having your real estate agent to tell you it's time for new towels?"

"Go up to your bedroom and fold your pillow in half right now. If it springs back quickly, your pillow is still in good shape. If it stays in a fold or slowly rights itself, it is time for a new pillow."

Overall Tactic:

Think globally, regionally, locally, short term and long term to illuminate how your show will appeal to the multi-level masses within milliseconds. Tie your message up with hope and the assurance that the viewer will have an entertaining and unexpected experience as well as answer the questions your customers have.

Viewers are looking at your pitch and wondering, "What's in it for me?" Your job is to illustrate and tell them exactly *what's in it for them*. People aren't going to buy this product just because it's available to them. With all of the many options of shopping we now have at our fingertips, you have to WOW them in order to attain and maintain their attention. The features of your product must benefit the buyer. A bath towel is just that until you illuminate what kind of value it will bring to the buyer. Will it absorb lots of water like a thirsty sponge? Will it save you time and money on laundering because it dries so quickly? Will rolled towels and face clothes create an inviting, peaceful scene in the powder room for your guests to use or for home stagers to dress up a home to sell? Will it be soft enough to wrap your baby in and large enough to wrap your spouse in as he walks out of the hot tub or lake?

Features and benefits go hand in hand

Example 1:

Feature - The television has one-button technology

Benefit - It will keep it simple for anyone to use. The less buttons to worry about, the less can go wrong with the technology, and the easier it is for your grand parents to use.

Example 2:

Feature - This tunic was designed with a longer hemline in the back

Benefit - The tunic covers the derriere, providing extra options to accessorize and wear leggings, etc. The resulting benefit will give you more confidence for those who are self-conscious in any way.

CHAPTER 9 — THE LILY PAD STRATEGY™ — Illuminate the Experience

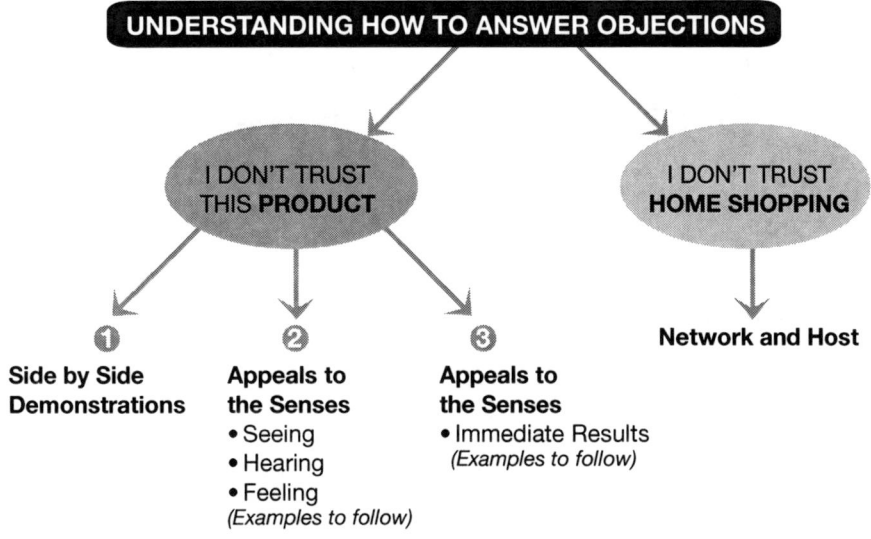

| Side by Side Demonstrations | Appeals to the Senses
• Seeing
• Hearing
• Feeling
(Examples to follow) | Appeals to the Senses
• Immediate Results
(Examples to follow) | Network and Host |

I DON'T TRUST THIS PRODUCT	I DON'T TRUST HOME SHOPPING
❶ Seeing demonstrations appeals to *define* dominant customers ❷ Hearing appeals to a blend of *define* and *inspire* customers ❸ Feeling appeals to *inspire* dominant customer (Refer to Chapter 8 for a full explanation of the *define* and *inspire* customers)	The overall corporate structure coupled with the role of the host plays the leadership role here. Among the most important network factors will include: Promoting hassle free customer service, 100% reliability, and the guarantee of quality from the entire sales throughput, from initial order to delivery and beyond. *(Examples provided next)*

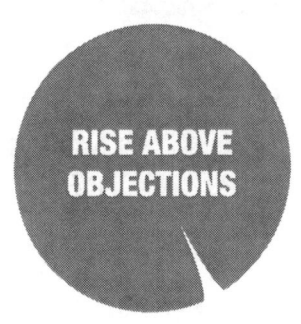

Overall Tactic:
Answer why it is a stand-out product, why it improves, decreases, elongates, softens, clears up, relaxes, quiets, eases, fixes, reforms, revives, lifts, gains, loses, shortens, darkens, illuminates, etc. Demonstrations play an enormously influential role to rise above objections. The define customers are particularly watching and waiting for you to prove it.

You may note that in this next section I have expanded to a much larger degree compared to the previous pitch pads. The main reason for this if you can't rise above objections quickly, there's no chance of a sale, let alone a sell out.

Overcoming legitimate objections is a major constraint in any sales environment but it is made much more difficult much more difficult when you can't see the person or hear their objections. In Chapter 7, Your Customers, we explored identifying the intricacies of exactly who your customers are. Dealing with each objection they have becomes an extension of *that* work.

No matter how well the guest expert does at convincing the customer to buy the product, the real test is still once the customer gets it home to use it. That is where the demonstrations can help any customer rise above their objections when they can *see* it work with *their own eyes*. Real-time visual selling plays a huge role in the switch from NO to YES, I'll buy!

COMPONENT I: I Don't Trust the Product

Engaging all three senses is important to overcoming objections as they play a major factor in the decision-making process.

In an article for *SUCCESS* magazine in January 2011, Kevin Harrington (highlighted earlier) shares, **"People don't buy fluff; there has to be a viable explanation of how and why the product works. Be prepared to back up your claims."**

At the beginning of this book we talked about how the home shopping business officially started back in the early 80's. As stated, in 1977 the first actual *at home shopping* network was on a radio station that discovered they could sell consumer products over the airways and proved to be a surprising success. Why? Because the radio station had enough listeners to appeal to a broad audience and the radio personality did such a great job at getting the listeners to *imagine* how helpful and useful the product would be with the addition of a good value equation. He was forced to explain in inspiring and delightful detail how simple and easy it was to work with and to buy.

Igniting The Three Major Senses Deepens the Connection

1. Seeing

Painting pictures and showing your audience how well it works pushes many people to the 'yes' side. If you can show the audience how great this product is without saying a word, that is the ideal situation. This type of message packaging appeals to everyone who is looking for answers that speak to them. Particularly, it appeals to a more logical, 'define' listener. They have certain tendencies towards problem solving and they base their knowledge in fact finding and 'proof getting'. It's important to identify them as part of your script building no matter how soft and cuddly your product may be.

2. Hearing

This is an extension of seeing. You have to become even more detailed in the description of how it will meet the visual needs of the lives of your customers. This type of message packaging appeals to everyone who is looking for quick and easy transformations.

3. Feeling

This type of emotional *message packaging* appeals to everyone concerned with safety, fulfillment, guarantees, environment, expense and so on. Using authoritative endorsements is a huge plus if you are selling a product that has many claims of transformation. If you can secure endorsements from recognized or certified professionals like doctors, chiropractors, NASA, the military or navy seals or celebrities, it will greatly support the credibility and legitimacy of your product. The use of quotes or recommendations from other authorities like associations and experts in the field also helps to drive that feeling of trust. (Toothpaste manufacturers do a great job at that. For example, "This plaque-busting toothpaste is dentist recommended.")

Category: In the Kitchen

Specific Concern: I just bought these baby back ribs because I'm trying to impress the new in-laws. We're hosting our first potluck lunch with *his* family. Will the baby back ribs that are being sold online make me look like I made them myself?

EXAMPLE PRODUCT	SEEING *Define* Dominant Customer	HEARING *Define* and *Inspire* Customer	FEELING *Inspire* Dominant Customer
Gourmet Baby Back Ribs with 4 different sauces	• Provide multiple demonstrations on all kinds of ways the ribs can be cooked to save you time and money with the highest return on taste and accolades! The camera professionals are working all the angles right along with you!	• Sound of the food being cooked and sauce being poured upon the ribs • Timbre and levels in your voice – to bring your customers right into your kitchen so they are almost smelling the ribs themselves	• Connect the food to the familiar experience of special life events, family reunions, holiday get-togethers, 'just like mom used to make' memories, Sporting events - Super Bowl, Grey Cup, celebratory events - July 1st and 4th, Martin Luther King, Christmas, anniversaries, birthdays, New Year's eve, etc.

Category: Skincare

Specific Concern: I want to buy this line-erasing skin cream with the promise that when I wear makeup, the creases around my eyes and laugh lines will be less prominent for longer than a few minutes compared to the others I've tried before. I have a family reunion coming up and want to look my best. Is this product worth the money?

EXAMPLE PRODUCT	SEEING *Define* Dominant Customer	HEARING *Define* and *Inspire* Customer	FEELING *Inspire* Dominant Customer
Line Erasing Primer	• Multiple demonstrations of real-time before and after shots • Working on the models • Showing the silkiness of the product and that a little, goes a long way	• Using different timbres of your voice to build excitement	• Connecting trust to this product to the hope of how it will benefit. Hours will pass by and no touch ups will be required. • Connect the hope to an event – school reunion, job interview, first date where you want to look your natural best without looking like you've had to 'try' very hard. • It will work with any makeup you apply on top • You'll see results without any makeup

Immediate Results Demonstrations:
Side by Side Comparison

Recently I witnessed one of the best comparison demos that I had ever seen. This guest expert hooked us immediately by pointing out that the product he was selling was the most sought after, top-of-the-line camera available in the world today. "And today is the only time in the history of our company that you will get it at this price," he stated proudly.

He then proceeded to compare all of the most important capabilities the camera had compared to the very limited capabilities that the best cell phones with photo and video capabilities had. The merit for the comparison to a cell phone is that we could all *relate* to the limitations of the cell phone as a camera. He spoke directly to us by comparing his product to something we use every day. "It's the same size, width and weight, and that's where the similarities end." The side-by-side comparison of the exact same photos taken with both the cameras – with his product and then the best cell phone camera – made the difference obvious. Then he showed the capabilities of the zoom lens and the ability to do panorama vision on his camera. He also asked all of the hosts to take their own personal pictures. A very smart tactic, as we know that the host is the *hero* in every show. So, if you can get genuine buy-in from the host, it can buy you more time to sell. It was an extraordinary comparison demo, and what's even better is he barely spoke and allowed the strong demo to sell his product for him. Those numbers at the bottom right of the screen began to march up and up and up. He leaned on the power of all three senses to sell-out his product.

Immediate Result Demonstrations – Before and After Comparisons

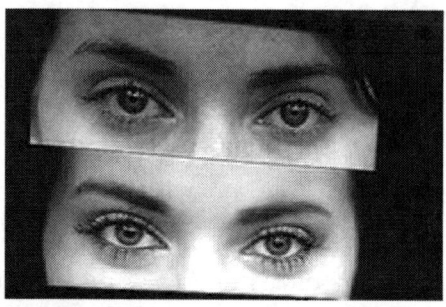

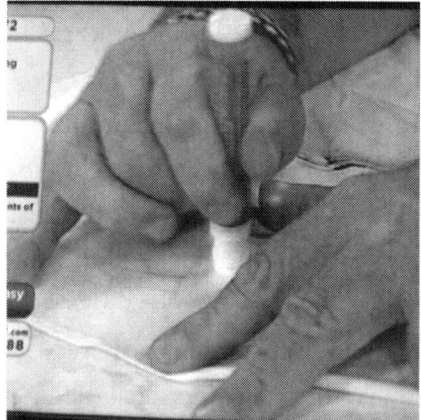
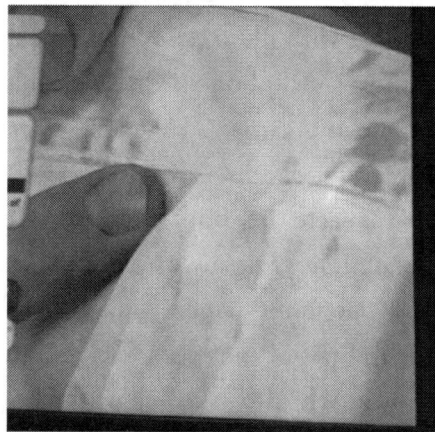

The above before and after pictures illustrate how, in one quick moment, you can *see* the difference the product has made. The after shot is a power punch and is satisfying because the customer gets to see it for themselves to make their own decision on the merits. If the sound were turned off with these demos, would the viewer still be able to *see* what a stand out product it was quickly and easily? Demonstrations whether they are side-by-side comparisons, before and afters or straight demos (like a vacuum cleaner picking up crumbs and candy) are your best friends for removing doubt from your viewers' minds. The more familiar your customers are with competitive products, the closer they will be able to make an educated purchase for themselves. Remember, they've already tuned-in and now they can relate more clearly to the current problems and will be looking for this new product to solve it for them.

Here are four more immediate result examples:

1. Power of Home Theatre Speaker Technology:

The guest expert will show the power of the base sound by placing lightweight fabric in front of the speakers. When the speakers are in use, the limp fabric perks up immediately and starts to sway like a flag. It is an instantaneous change you can see and hear. That, coupled with how the guest expert explains all of the stand-out features, easily turns any doubt into clear understanding of why the technology is superior and the product is so terrific.

2. Hand Towel Absorption:

This is a product I personally love selling because it is quick, clear and the results are evident. With 750 ml of water poured into a clear bowl, an unwashed hand towel will be tossed into the bowl and we all get to *see* the water get soaked up like a sponge by the towel. The cameras are always focused in very tightly to the towel to see it in action. It's instant and it immediately shows the thick and thirsty qualities of the towel without having to say a word. I'll make sure that the viewers see that no water is dripping either, from the towel itself or the bowl. Any time I do this demo, our sales spin up and up.

3. Beauty Transformation in *Real Time*, Right Before Your Eyes:

Used with Stacey's permission

Stacey Schieffelin, the founder, President and on-air personality for *ybf* beauty has engineered an eighteen-year track record of success in direct sales. For almost two decades, Stacey demonstrates how to transform a look from bare faced to perfectly polished on live TV at QVC UK, HSN, TVSN (Australia) and TSC. In my opinion, the way she has crafted her show line up building to the big reveal at the end of the show is as good as it gets in this business of selling on-air. Then there is the power of her demonstration that starts with the fact that you can turn the sound off and still *get* everything she is telling us. This is how Stacey sets the scene: She begins the show with curlers in her hair and doesn't wear one stitch of makeup – it is very real and transparent to the viewer. During her show, she sells her product in the order she puts on her makeup. It is a highly relatable message because it's how every female approaches her beauty routine when getting ready for work or a night on the town. It is a magnificent example of the perfect hook! Right before the show is over, Stacey takes out her curlers, fluffs up her beautifully styled locks, and voila, you have this fabulous looking woman who transformed herself right in front of the viewer's eyes…you too believe you can master the makeup magic! The big *reveal*, together with the before and after comparison, is highly convincing which is why she sells out a lot! By the way, her products are fantastic![2]

4. Using Your Creativity and Knowing Exactly Who Your Customers Are Works!

Sandie Savelli (highlighted earlier) is a model and fashion designer as well as being one of the most exceptional and experienced guest experts in the business. In the fashion category on any shopping network, models wear the garments while the guest expert sells the product. Looking at any garment hanging flat on a hanger or dressed on a Judy mannequin doesn't bring it to life the way a professional model does. If Sandie doesn't have models to work with in some of her segments, she shows photos that were taken of her, wearing the fashions in various ways and in different situations. This demonstrates the enormous variety that customers have and it gives them ideas of how they can incorporate an item into their existing wardrobe. This also ties her to the product in a very strong way. A savvy move that every exceptional guest expert knows how to capitalize on.

Used with Sandie's permission

Take a look at the picture above. This was taken from the television set, (notice her finger holding the picture on the left of the screen). In her demo, Sandie will scroll through ten to fifteen photos, creating a virtual fashion show for the viewers. Every time she does this particular demo, the sales immediately spike because people relate to her and her message. They see all the possibilities that will work for them as they picture themselves wearing the product, which is the most important aspect.

COMPONENT II: I Don't Trust Home Shopping

The host is there to help the audience overcome these objections by talking about what the network is willing to do to ensure that purchases are risk-free through hassle-free 30-day return policies, shopping and gift giving options with easy pay and ship-to-bill-to options (to name only a few).

You would be surprised how many people watch and never buy from home shopping. Studies have shown that the average person who eventually purchases has visited the station and watched the same pitch between six and ten times before they actually bought anything.

Here is a selection of some common customer incentives most networks offer to build the urgency and trust for new and returning customers to purchase with confidence:

- 30 to 60 day money back guarantees
- Affiliate marketing
- BOGO – Buy one get one
- Cash and other gift rewards
- Competitions for a chance to win or meet one of the hosts and/or celebrities
- Extended Holiday Returns
- Flash Sale - 4 hours only
- Free shipping and return shipping
- Gift with purchase
- Home shopping credit card with low interest
- Hot Picks, Hosts Picks
- Last Chance
- Lifetime of the garment guarantee
- Model for a day competitions and other customer involvement promotions
- No interest easy pay programs
- No-risk shopping, hassle-free, no questions asked, money back guarantees with free shipping
- OTO – One time only
- Rewards point programs and loyalty programs
- Risk-free exchange policy, repair or replace
- TSO - This show only
- TVO –This visit only
- Warranty programs

CHAPTER 9 — THE LILY PAD STRATEGY™ — Rise Above Apathy

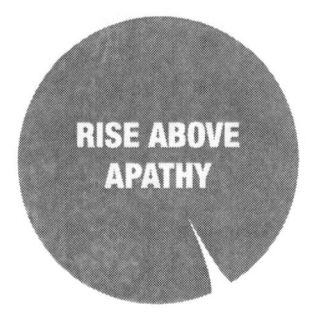

Overall Tactic:
Builds from the Pitch Pad, Rise Above Objections, but is packaged in a more lyrical and personable manner while at the same time answering all questions and speculations with the personal proof that the product is as good as the pitch is.

Has it occurred to *you* as the guest expert that the customer who just turned to your show is looking to be uplifted and you may be the best thing in that person's life currently? You may be playing a significant part in making their day a little brighter just by being there. It gives us a whole new assignment and reason to be fun, excited, funny, personable, real and enjoyable to spend time with.

Rising Above Apathy is a specific directive to the guest expert to ensure that you are keeping the selling message light hearted and entertaining as well as credible.

Apathy can have a negative connotation if taken out of context. Therefore, before this section is developed, let's take a few moments to address the meaning of the word. (Both definitions and synonyms are according to *Webster's Encyclopedic Unabridged Dictionary of the English Language* and *The Synonym Finder* by J. I. Rodale cited in Chapter 2, The Guest Expert).

Apathy
Definition:
1. Absence or suppression of passion, or excitement
2. Lack of interest in, or concern for things which others find moving or exciting

Synonym:
Impassivity, dispassion, lack of feeling or emotion, coolness, indifference, disinterest

By referring to the meanings and synonyms of apathy, it may give you a deeper understanding of the word and tell you why I have used it. Inspiring action and reactions can happen in all kinds of ways other than just the hard-hitting selling techniques. Telling stories, being highly personable and relatable and having a tremendous amount of empathy to see life in other peoples' shoes are all part of it. These are the key elements to Rising Above Apathy.

Most of us as children grew up listening to stories and it is virtually hard-wired into our pattern of learning. The beautiful feature about our selling platform is *if* we're given a few minutes of our customers' time, we can touch the hearts of many. We know that people are more likely to be convinced of the merit of any product or idea if they perceive that the expert is truthful, credible, sincere, relatable and also provides logical information.

Have you ever had to deal with a teenager who just won't do anything you say: Stay in school, bring the car back clean, catch the bus on time, be home for dinner, kiss your grandmother goodbye? As a parent, you do almost anything to get them to do what you want. You throw your hands up in exhaustion, you plead, bribe or punish. Let's face it, sometimes, none of those tactics work. That exact same frustration is felt when there is no movement of sales. You are screaming inside, why is no one budging to buy? What am I doing wrong? Is anyone out there?

Have you ever had to take care of an aging parent? It's a tough assignment because this person who has helped raise you and nurture you is now needing your strong direction and authority in order for them to make any movement or changes. They are often too proud to ask for help and too stubborn to want to do anything you suggest. You then have the special assignment of changing your packaging in order for them accept your message without changing your intention. (For more insight on how to package your messaging, refer to the section, Sales Success Depends on How Well We Listen to Our Listeners in Chapter 8.)

Intention and Pace

Apathy is probably one of the most difficult challenges to overcome. What is going to motivate people to take action? You can't reach through the TV screen to will people to move, so how do you do it? Many times it's not what you say but *how* things are said and the *pace* at which you say them.

Pace is one tactic that sometimes wakes people up. As well as the audience, this can also include the host, production and camera crew (at times). One strategy to change the pace is to alter your volume and the timbre of your voice. Another is to provide some quick facts that you can blurt out like a ten-round shotgun. It shakes up the predictable rhythm of the host and expert.

One cautionary note if you choose to use this technique - Make sure you are grounded and not sounding like the auctioneer who has said this 5,000 times before. Tie this message back to your intention of why your customers would benefit from knowing this information:

- 1 in 10 people suffer from asthma in this country alone
- 1 in 4 people suffer from allergies, seasonal or chronic
- Up to 10 gallons of perspiration settles in mattresses over eight years old
- Up to 20,000 dust mites can exist on a large paper clip

Too much of a good thing is too much so you must listen for the right timing to bring this boil of a pitch down again. Otherwise, you can quickly become the seedy nightclub act on the Lido deck desperately reminding the audience that you'll "be here all week and be sure to check out the midnight buffet..." ☺

Overall Tactic:
Act Now. Close the sale this minute. Find meaningful ways that are in the customers' best interests to inspire and motivate them to make a move to buy. Urgency, curiosity, candor and conviction are leading persuaders and motivators.

Asking for business or the *close* is a sacred part of the sale and if you don't know how to inspire action, you won't be selling for long. I'm not talking about the greasy snake oil salesman approach; I'm talking about a very professional call to action. As mentioned earlier in the book, the close is like the magician's secrets. Tradeshow professionals who pitch companies for new business will pitch everything else but the close to the panel of decision makers. The close is one of the most important elements and needs to be crafted to suit your category, your style and your customer. You have to ask for the business. Without a call to action, there will be no action.

Successful Call-to-Action

Make it personal, and again, think specifically about who your customer is. You can't allow yourself to generalize who you're talking to. You are required to be extra firm and concise with your close.

People need to know *when* it is their turn to act:
1. They must be reminded of how the product will benefit their lives, and
2. Why they need to act right now. (The host plays a leading role here.)

In a traditional sales environment, the conventional sales close may be:
"I'm happy to set aside this inventory while you write up your P.O. (purchase order) on Monday." OR
"We've scheduled the entire afternoon at the showroom for you." OR

"All of your best selling items are ready and the prices are the same as last year."

The aforementioned scenarios will obviously not work on-air. To follow, we have some closing statements to help inspire you as you build your list.

A quick aside: Most networks do not allow the guest experts to make the hard close. However, there are ways you can mirror the intention of what the host is doing without crossing lines. On the next two pages I provide closing statement guidelines. Most, if not all of the statements have been part of a successful sell out pitch. They are actual guest expert closing statements recorded over the past two years from the big four networks.

CLOSING STATEMENT GUIDE

• If you are tired of hanging on to those last ten pounds, this product is for you. By Christmas, which is only six weeks away, you will be well in your way to losing that weight. All of the instructions are included to make it as simple as possible. We've also included a full eating guide, 24-hour access to my personal trainers, quick guide on what to do when you have cravings and an exercise guideline that will help speed up the process.	• The holidays keep us so busy with family and our kids coming and going. If you want to have time to sit with your guests without worry and guarantee the perfect thanksgiving dinner, this one product will do it for you. With one easy push of a button, in less time, for less money, it will produce the juiciest turkey. It will look stylish and won't take up valuable counter space either. This is the very last airing and has been our #1 most popular product of the holiday season.	• After this show, we are retiring this line for good. You will never see this timeless piece again. It's not a tactic, it's the truth. If you have been a fan of this line and this product, like the hundreds of thousands of savvy shoppers have been over the years, now is your last chance to pick up on it.
• The last time we were here, they sold out within the first thirty minutes. We never bring in enough.	• These are only here once per year. When they are gone, they are gone.	• As you can see on your screen, only one hundred left to go around for the entire country!
• You've seen how well it works right in front of your eyes. If you want to look more refreshed instantly, this will be the easiest call to make for yourself.	• If your head is nodding yes right now, you know exactly what I mean. This will keep your hair fluffed up for hours with no need to re-check every hour. Our product will do its job so relax and enjoy your event.	• Do you see how easy that was? Think about how your Super Bowl party will be simplified just giving us a call now. We've done all the prep work for you so you can finally enjoy the game too. You deserve that!

CHAPTER 9 — THE LILY PAD STRATEGY™ — Ask for Business

CLOSING STATEMENT GUIDE

• Can you believe what you just saw? In seconds it smoothed out the panty line, lifted her behind like a twenty-year old and got rid of the muffin top and you're still breathing and comfortable! You can wear any fabric you choose to wear with full confidence. Even fine silk, which you know shows everything. Make the girls at the reunion jealous! Give us a call this minute. The black is almost gone.	• Make this the day you decide to get in shape. The program is easy to follow and will only take fifteen minutes of your time once per day. Do this for yourself. There's nothing to stop you. Go for it and I'll be right there with you every step of the way.	• Do you want something that is beautifully designed, enhances any décor, is extremely lightweight that a baby could lift it, and keeps the bugs away…
• I know how many we were able to bring in this time and currently we are through well over 3/4's of our inventory. We only have two more shows. If you want your exact colour, order it now.	• I know these will sell out by the end of this show. The reviews we have received on this line have blown us away! We thank you for your feedback. If this is your first introduction to our line, let us to blow you away too!	• We have been in the business for over fifty years and one thing I can guarantee is our lifetime quality. Hollywood starlets wear our products all the time because they know they'll always look fantastic. So will you.

Maybe To Yes Transition

How well you ask for business can establish the frequency of the *maybe to yes* transition. The home shopping viewer is already being considered a potential buyer when they open up the page on their screen. They may be a returning customer, or perhaps they've happened upon it for the first time and are curious. Never let up, and keep tossing the ball up in the air in their direction.

The network and corporate structure plays an extremely important role in the maybe-to-yes transition. Buyers are always trying to tweak free shipping or other time-sensitive incentives to create real time urgency for people to purchase right now, this minute.

Recently, I received an email from a long-time viewer who said she had just purchased the mattress protector (I was selling on-air recently) for her university son. She explained in her letter that he has breathing issues and was finding it hard to live in his dorm room. She pointed out that she had been watching on and off all day and although she was interested, nothing seemed to strike her to want to move until I specifically brought up the dorm room old mattress scenario. She thought of her son and realized that the old unprotected mattress was probably contributing to her son's asthma issues. She shared that she picked up the phone at that moment and her son hasn't complained since. "NO WORD OF A LIE!" is what she shared. I was thrilled and realized that guest experts have to continually be lobbing many ideas and scenarios out there. Be flexible and change it up in order to catch the attention of as many people as you can. We all want to have our problems solved and the quicker the better.

Asking for business is not about what *you* want but what the *customer* wants. This is the time when you re-focus your pitch to access that next gear inside of you.

People want to be told what to do. Paint the perfect scenario for the choice to become obvious to say yes.

CHAPTER 9 — THE LILY PAD STRATEGY™ — Thank You

THANK YOU

Acknowledge who brought you to the dance. This involves your entire professional experience, your customers, the buyers, the network and the huge team behind the scenes. There is nothing more charming and endearing than when you see a guest expert acknowledge the contributions and brilliance of their team.

There is a lot of positive power and momentum we can take in and pass on when we say thank you. For centuries, the Bible and every great philosopher in the world have taught us how important it is to be grateful for where we are right now.

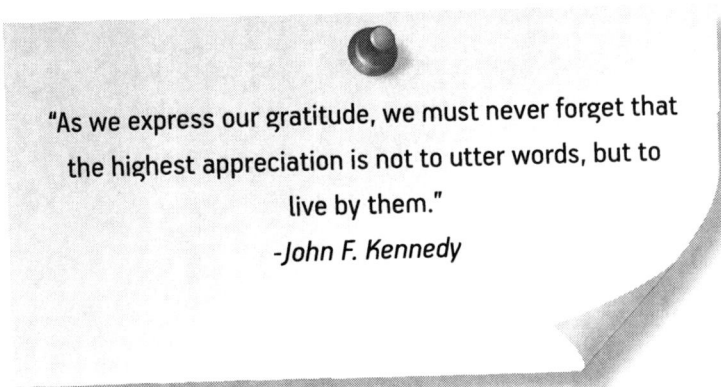

"As we express our gratitude, we must never forget that the highest appreciation is not to utter words, but to live by them."
-John F. Kennedy

SOURCES

1. http://www.ehow.com/list_7675959_lily-pads.html
2. www.ybfbeauty.com

CHAPTER 9
The Lily Pad Strategy™

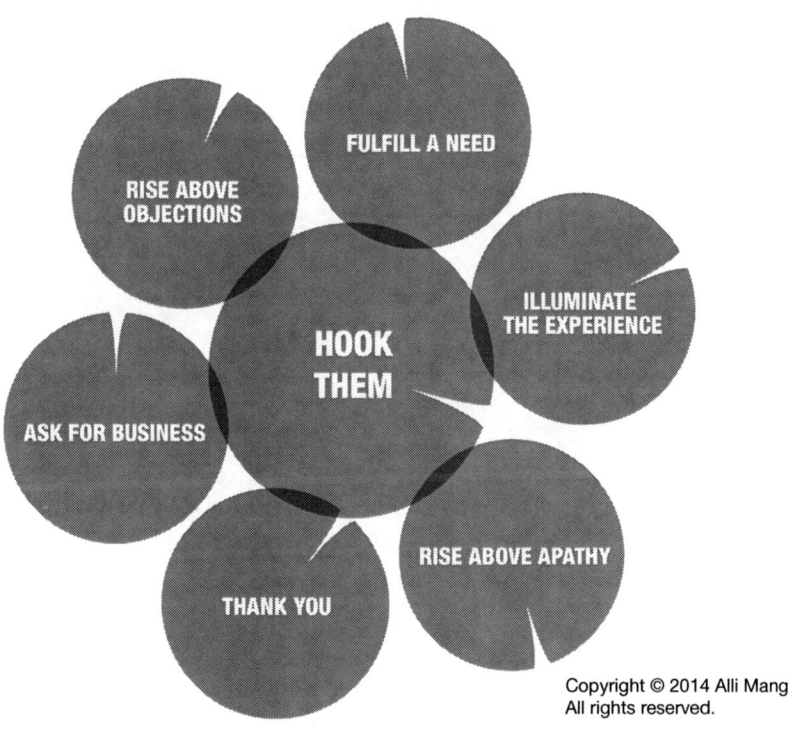

1. The Lily Pad Strategy™ is your key selling principle to successfully sell, excite and close the deal. Your customers can't feel or touch the product for themselves therefore they rely on your expertise and ability to enchant and captivate their curiosity and interest to buy. Charts and full explanations of all of the strategies are included.

SECTION III

ACHIEVING PEAK PERFORMANCE

This section is about performing at your peak ability. It is one of the most difficult skills to be able to capture in a tangible form, but this section does it for you!

It will involve the most important components of delivering excellence consistently with the 3 P's: Preparation, Practice and Performance, Assess Your Success and Have you Got Your Game Face ON?

CHAPTER 10

THE 3 P'S
PREPARATION, PRACTICE, PERFORMANCE

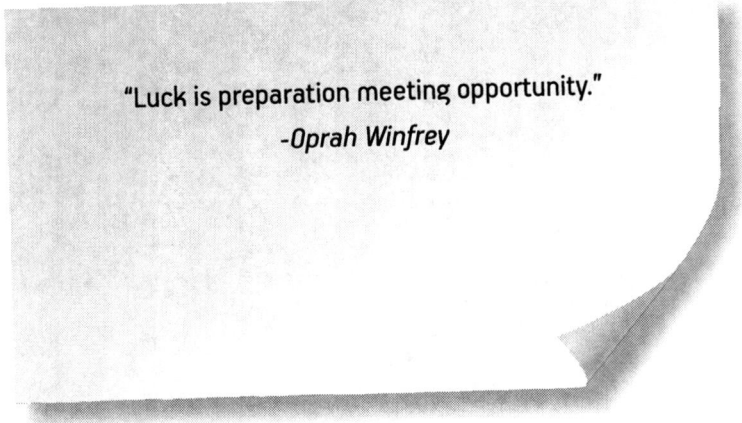

"Luck is preparation meeting opportunity."
-Oprah Winfrey

Earlier in Chapter 5, It's Showtime, Folks, I referred to the great Broadway and movie musical *Rent*. As stated earlier, it took seven years to create that show from concept to its first preview and in that seven years, there were many workshops, rehearsals, re-writes, cast changes etc. in order for it to be performance worthy. Most shows that you see in theatre whether it is Broadway, regional theatre or a tour has done a minimum of six weeks of rehearsals in order to mount the show. Not to mention the understudy and swing rehearsals done on a weekly basis while the show runs. That includes memorizing scripts, repeating, reforming, replaying, and learning blocking, choreography and music. All of this work is not just about getting it into our heads but rather the work is meant to penetrate into our souls because that is where the connection is made. This is *part* of the art and science of the professional performer.

Mark Cassius   Me   Darrin Baker

Recently, I held a round table discussion on the performing challenges entertainers experience when they are on stage. Included were my friends Mark and Darrin (in picture above). They both have multi-Broadway shows on their respective resumes and they are also concert and cabaret performers. The main difference between a cabaret performance versus a

CHAPTER 10 — THE 3 P'S PREPARATION, PRACTICE, PERFORMANCE

Broadway show is that cabarets generally have no scripts, no track to follow and the show plan is generally made up of only broad strokes. It's a lot like the principles of jazz wherein everyone is professional, knows the general idea of key, harmonics and *feel*, but within those perimeters, creative licenses are not only taken, but highly encouraged to inspire the creation of beautiful music

Used with Mark's permission

During the round table discussion, I asked Mark (above), "Does anything scare you when you perform?"

He paused and looked to one side then shared, "When I throw a thought or lyric out to the audience, the moment directly after that is what scares me. I have control over the choice of song and key, arrangement and tempo. I know what I want to say, how I move and how I look but I don't have any control over how it will be received or will *land* with the audience. We as performers feed off of what we receive from our audience. If we get a laugh, that is information we take in and we adjust accordingly. If we get silence, that is also information (usually a good sign they are engaged in the show). If I hear a cough, clearing of the throat or candy wrappers being opened, I know I've got some work to do. Sometimes, in some shows, we just run out of time trying to engage the audience. Not everyone may *get it* but my job is to connect with the stories and the audience to the best of my ability. If I concentrate on doing what I do best, most times the audience comes along for the ride." [1]

Used with Darrin's permission

Darrin, with six Broadway shows and multiple TV network drama roles to his credit added, "If you are grounded and you know your stuff inside out and backwards, you can make adjustments on the fly. This is the only way to stay in the moment. I often deliberately step on stage and throw out a light-hearted question or joke to the audience. It's my way of making a strong entrance and suits my casual personality. The responses I receive (or lack thereof) give me an indication of the pulse of the audience for that night and helps me to quickly assess the space. As I nod to the accompanist to start, I am already making adjustments to my tactics on how I plan on delivering the story based on the feedback I just received. We as performers know what we do well, but within that structure, we always have to adapt to what is needed during that moment."[2]

PREPARATION

SCRIPT WRITING

You may remember in Chapter 2, The Guest Expert, we spoke of many key qualities required to be a great guest expert. The second quality highlights having intense curiosity. It's a vital quality for many reasons but is essential for thoroughly investigating your product and category. Your curious nature will help guide your path of creating the script and everything that goes into your preparations. You will use the Lily Pad Strategy™, the Anchor Seven™ and the New DIET as a checklist to ensure you have fully described and touched on every angle that speaks to you, your customers and your product. This will also involve every phrase, note, close, anchor statement, opening and anecdote of your product and category.

You may find it seems somewhat overwhelming at the beginning. Have faith, once you chronicle your base of knowledge, it will only have to be maintained with additions the more and more experience you gain.

Key Words and Phrases

If you created the product or are the owner of the company and are also selling on-air, this section will not apply as directly to you. This section is specifically geared to helping the *hired gun* guest expert:

There are **keywords** and **phrases** that are applicable to any industry. One of the things you need to do in your preparation and rehearsals is to create a full list of these words that quickly position your credibility and industry knowledge.

For instance, if you have ever watched the great PBS television series *This Old House*, in one quick moment you know that one of the hosts Tommy Silva knows his stuff by the ease with which he works with his tools and with the terms he uses. He explains in one episode, "Because the walls of this one hundred-year old home have undulations and are not even or reliable enough to build frames to it, we have to build our own frames outside just enough to sit proud of the old existing wall."

Sit proud is a specific industry term that immediately plunks the listener and the expert into the world of home improvement and construction.

What are the keywords and phrases that are applicable to your category and industry? Make a list of them and include them at the end of your long hand script. If your industry has terms you aren't familiar with, it's your job to get comfortable with how to use them.

You will also add these words to your at-a-glance script (to be explained shortly).

The Voice Recorder is Your Best Friend

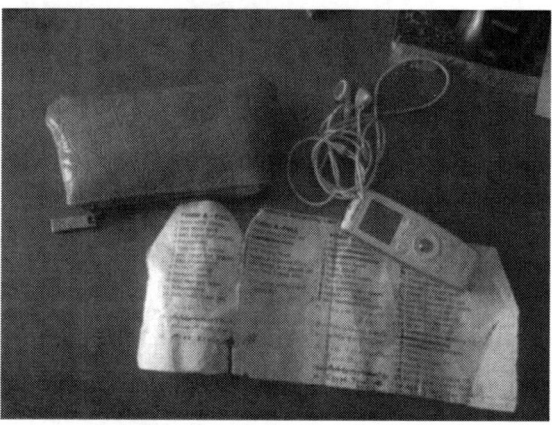

If you want to learn your script ten times more quickly while you work in the kitchen, rake the leaves, enjoy a cup of coffee, while getting your roots dyed, exercising or flying home for Thanksgiving, there is no better performance tool than the voice recorder. With the many years I have under my belt of selling, learning scripts and speeches, the voice recorder plops the pertinent information into my head quicker than anything else – including the at-a-glance script. It utilizes a minimum amount of time (when your time is so tight and precious) while fully maximizing the benefits. I highly recommend going to your local business supply store and purchasing a designated digital voice recorder. Some models even have a USB connection to download audio to your computer. They all can be pricey (around $80 - $150), but well worth the investment. I highly recommend to not skimp out on this valuable asset. Keep it separate from your everyday life. Using your iPhone or smartphone isn't a great choice. You can easily lose your phone and after a few years, you change phones; as a result data has more potential of being lost. I liken the value of the recording to your passport. You wouldn't carry it around unless you had good reason to do so as you never want to lose your passport. The same applies to your voice recorder.

When Do I Start to Record?

When you have exhausted all possibilities and feel you are ready to start committing the details to memory, record it. In order to perform well, you have to get *off book* and get on your feet as quickly as possible. Therefore, as great and interesting and funny as your written script may be, this is not a writing contest. It's all about getting it into your body and performing.

The act of recording your script gets you to start hearing the message. It is a time saver and definitely gets your head in the right frame of mind. Remember, the act of recording the material is another study tool so there is never any time wasted. You will also be recording your at-a-glance scripts (coming up next). As the inventory of your recordings grow, (I've actually run out of space from my first device and now have a second one), you will find you will have covered every aspect of your category. It will be your instant review tool and will contribute to getting yourself psyched up for the performance day quickly. As you gain more vendors to represent and products to sell, you'll have less and less time to prepare. This recording device becomes invaluable to fast tracking your readiness.

At-A-Glance Script

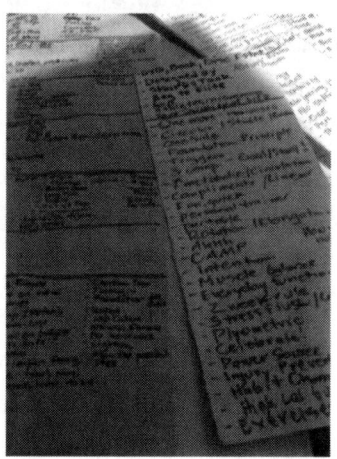

If ever there was an emergency at my house where I had to leave quickly, I'd take my husband, my two cats, the voice recorder with all of my scripts on it and my at-a-glance binder. They are that valuable to me. The at-a-glance workbook (or Cole's Notes version of your script) is your personal Bible of information and includes everything you need to know about your category, trends, product, and industry, including your Lily Pad Strategy™ in an at-a-glance format.

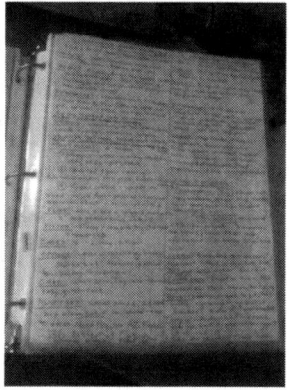

The at-a-glance script is a great tool that can be used to work on speeding up your recall, getting your words out quickly and efficiently and staying on track. The at-a-glance sheet is the only sheet of paper you should need on show day. If you are traveling, this is the only way to go. It's there to focus your thoughts before the show and to review after your show to ensure you hit all the marks you intended to in a quick point form manner. It also makes it simple to add notes and updates quickly and clearly.

Preparation Guide to Get You Ready for Your Show

- Always stay updated on potential show dates.
- Provide black-out dates to the buyer and planning departments as far in advance as possible to help them with programming.

Two to Four weeks prior to the show:
- Ask for all samples if you haven't already received them from your buyer or vendor. This may include asking for specific information including pantone colours, samples and swatches, testing and quality assurance sheets, legal notes on what can and cannot be said about your product.
- Pitching ideas and pertinent information the buyer used to pitch to the managers in order to get it on-air. It is helpful to see how your product is positioned in the eyes of network.
- Depending on the demos planned, ask for specific products that you will be using in order to have enough time to rehearse with them.
- Speak to the actual manufacturer if you can to gain intricate insights on the merits of the products.
- As soon as the product line up has been confirmed, ask for the forecasted sales targets for the day.
- After the show day, ask for the actual final sales report. Although ongoing sales are provided by each department throughout the sales day this report will provide the final numbers which will in turn help you to invoice with accuracy.

PRACTICE

Here is a typical rehearsal set-up in my bedroom at home. Well, minus the black tomcat. ☺

With hundreds and hundreds of live television hours, I still spend some focused time on my pitch and demos when prepping for my GVS shows. The images and demo props represent key parts of my script and acts as quick reminders. I can't afford to feel like I'm in the weeds and neither can you.

Rehearsing makes *rehearsal you* become the *studio performance you* within a snap of a finger. The main purpose is to free yourself up from remembering figures and facts and orders because it is all instantly available to you because you have *practised* it! You can then concentrate on connecting to your customers on a deeper level. Throwing three different pitches within your three-minute loop will be easy!

November 8, 2007 – Announced the fastest Multi-Million dollar deal world record was set by Donald Trump and Ricardo Bellino who, after a three-minute presentation, became business partners.[2]

In a quote from Donald Trumps' book, *Think like a Champion,* he shares, "Ricardo Bellino (author of *You have 3 Minutes! Learn the Secrets of the*

Pitch from Trump's original *Apprentice* and Founder and Entrepreneur in Chief of School of Life Academy) had exactly three minutes to give me his business presentation. I was extremely busy that day and not particularly in the mood for a presentation, so I thought he might decline, which would free up my day a bit. Not only did he not decline, he gave me such a great presentation within those three minutes that we became partners. It's surprising what people can do with a deadline."

Tools to Get You Show Ready

Refer to both of the pictures below. Notice the first picture and look at the bottom of the computer screen from left to right:

Price of item - $59.95

Quantity sold – 13,957

Time left to sell this product (Countdown timer) – 8:56

The picture on the right is what will help *you* to train your mind and body to work with a timer thereby mimicking the studio time pressure.

Whether you use a stopwatch or the second hand on your timepiece, get comfortable working with delivering your message within a finite amount of time. Referring to a timer sets the bar high during rehearsals and trains you to work under pressure when the stakes are high. I can't stress enough how important it is to practise working under the gun as much as you can. When the host passes the baton to you, you have to come out at top speed, and sometimes, it doesn't always come out the way you've rehearsed it in your cushy bedroom, dining room or basement with no distractions.

In Chapter 5, in the section Nerves Are a Good Thing, we talk about how it is almost impossible to know how your body will react to the anxiety of the moment until you are actually on-air. I call this the *nervous you*. We don't like nervous you because it often makes us overly self-conscious, inward focused, slow and clumsy. Speaking quickly and succinctly while the lights are hot provides a challenging unknown environment you can't really plan for completely. I've seen experienced and distinguished speakers, broadcasters and actors who are supposedly accustomed to this type of ad-hoc pressure buckle and get plowed under by the experience. No matter what's going on, the show must go on. If you don't show up in the eyes of the host, they'll take over instantly. There's no room for second chances.

Delivering within tight time constraints is especially important to such categories as jewelry, beauty, collectibles and fashion as many times they have up to twenty or more individual pieces to sell within the actual fifty-four minutes that makes up the show hour.

As illustrated with the Trump and Bellino deal, the three-minute loop is common everywhere in business. As we've been saying throughout this book, three minutes is all you will get in the world of home shopping too. Within this timeframe, you have to hit every key selling point, demonstrate, entertain, educate and connect with your host and viewers.

When rehearsing, start your timer off at three minutes and see if you can get through your entire pitch once. Chances are you won't be able to and that is okay. To be exceptional at this is not easy. It's designed to be challenging. You'll notice how perhaps the demo trips you up or the overall transitions to your specific sales points seem awkward. All this is good and essential to uncovering what may trip you up on set. You want to get rid of all of the roadblocks one by one until you feel you are ready. This is one of the many reasons why you can't cram in your work. Take the time to do it right.

Once you've got your flow down, find any opportunity to strike up your three-minute pitch. And by the way, you must have a pocket full of different pitches. Have a similar message with a slightly different dialect. If you're tired, grumpy or really do have a time crunch to deal with in your own life, this is even better. Do a quick rehearsal with the ten minutes you have to spare. It's all you need to get three or four loops in. These constraints will help you to figure out what your personal challenges and frustrations may be with the real pressure of time limits.

Are you challenged by:
- Getting the words out quickly?
- Hitting your key selling points?
- Setting up and doing your demo with accuracy within a short span of time?
- Transitioning from the host to your selling point with ease?
- Staying focused amid many distractions?

Remember, besides your own selling spiel, the host has a lot of business to do quickly eating up your time allotment. For example if you see, say, four minutes counting down on the timer, that tells you there is not much time at all to get people to rise to action. During the product introductions (done by the host), you may have to cull your entire pitch down to thirty seconds or less because you know the host will take up a certain amount of *your* time providing the necessary product information, 1-800 numbers, online addresses, sizes left, quantities left, etc. In this case, figure out what your top three most important points are and run with it.

This is your personal journey to figure out for yourself. Certain circumstances make some people feel safe and others completely off their game. The only guaranteed way to decrease some elements of the unknown is to make the *nervous you* a friend of yours. If doing your demo for instance takes too long, figure out in your rehearsal how to get to the nugget of the demo and cue it up to *that* point and then start from there.

Practice, Prepare, Rehearse. Practise, Prepare, Rehearse.

There's the famous story of how Tiger Woods' dad would prepare him for the pressures of competition. He would get right in his face and yell and scream at him during his toughest shots when he needed to have the most concentration. He knew that Tiger had to train his mind to stay focused and not be distracted no matter what kind of noise or visuals were in front of him.

The more you can create an uncomfortable rehearsal environment, the more prepared you'll be for show day. While you rehearse your pitch, I suggest turning up the volume of the TV or car radio. By creating audible and visual distractions, you are mirroring the type of environment you'll be facing in the studio. Tune-in to a talk radio or news show. Dialogue is often more distracting to deal with than music and is more relevant in this medium.

In the studio, lights are flashing, cameras are moving, camera crews are talking to each other on their head-sets, tours are happening, hammers are banging, the president of the company could have just walked in, sets and lights are being set for the next day and the producer who is talking in your ear continually updates you on how sales are going and what is coming up next among many other instructions. You have to be able to juggle all of the sounds and directions, knowing what to pay attention to and what not to and still keep your focus and attention on your customers and pitch.

On the next few pages are rehearsal tactics that deal with the most important rudimentary elements of performance.

If you are in the fitness or kitchen category, rehearse your pitch within your domain. Cooking or mixing while talking is a skill so do it every chance you get. One kitchen specialist friend of mine describes everything she is doing while preparing the meal for her family. Generally the kids roll their eyes but that just urges my friend to find ways to be more engaging. She loves doing it and it has given her more confidence when she gets on-air. Fitness experts are most often in good shape to begin with and more times than not they are either personal trainers, dancers and/or teach classes so they are accustomed to talking while doing the exercises. This is an important element to their success.

Next, get your message out of your rehearsal studio and off of the page as soon as you can. You must pull yourself away from any comforts because you won't have many in the studio. I'll quietly rehearse my closes and anchor statements standing in line at Starbucks or while walking down a bustling sidewalk or through a mall, all the while saying my pitch as I walk around the throngs of people. I actually don't mind if people notice I'm talking to myself. It trains my mind to not take in negative energy. Judge me all you want – you're helping me to zone into my confidence level. It may sound crazy and you may feel foolish at first, but you have to do everything you can to drop the message into your soul. I also think it's a very good idea to talk to a friend about your product. I suggested this for tradeshow sellers specifically in Chapter 2, The Guest Expert, but provide the suggestion for everyone here as well. This is often the toughest thing to do because you immediately hear your 'sell voice' and you realize how inauthentic it sounds. It's one of the best exercises to do and really brings your message down to earth taking away any insincere showmanship.

Visualize Success Throughout Your Day

Athletes who train for the Winter Olympic event of Luge, only perform up to two-hundred and fifty runs per year as the sport is extremely taxing on their bodies. As a result, an enormous part of their training is done through visualization and becoming intimately aware of every twist and turn required for that perfect run on competition day. Similarly, we as on-air guest experts may not always get to perform every day either. Therefore, visualizing the entire experience to prepare you for overall success makes a tremendous amount of sense. Visualize the day moving smoothly and harmoniously and see the sales numbers on the screen keep flying up every minute. Picture your customers welcoming you and picture them completely excited to get your products home. Visualize the SOLD OUT sign that crosses in front of your product on the screen. See the host, your buyer, the president, your team and the entire crew working harmoniously together. Picture yourself walking through the middle of the action with confidence, ownership and full receptivity.

This is obviously a highly personal exercise. Create your own script by visualizing other winning images that speak personally to you.

Preparing Your Voice

Earlier on in this book, I referred to your instrument. That's *you,* and you have to prepare it for the big game. There are various voice exercises that can prepare your voice and your tongue to work with you instead of against you. They are designed to help throw words forward in your mouth instead of stuck back in your throat. This will allow for more fluid speech and enunciation. We sometimes underestimate the need to limber up our lips, tongue and throat when talking for as many minutes as is necessary. If you spend only a few minutes per day as you rehearse your pitch, it will help make the entire script more available to you and will also help to release and free-up your pent up areas of stress. Most times, the camera will not be focused on your face but rather the product (aside from some beauty and fashion products). Therefore, your voice diction, pitch, pronunciation and animation need to resonate through your body. It is a very important selling tool. Take care of it!

To follow is a regime that will take you less than five minutes to accomplish. Do this during your rehearsals and/or sometime before every performance to not only engage these muscles, but also to check-in with your body. You can do this anywhere – driving in your car, sitting on the streetcar or in your dressing room waiting for your sound check:

1. Take a breath in for a count of 5, hold it for 5 counts and then let your breath out for a count of 5. Repeat 2 more times.
2. Now we'll work your lips a bit. While humming "Happy Birthday", blow air through your closed lips – like a baby does when she is learning

to blow bubbles. This may tickle your lips a bit. Go with it and let it flow easily through your lips as you hum the song. Take as many breaths as you need to.

3. Recite each phrase 10 times each as fast as you can:
   - Red Letter Yellow Letter
   - You Need Unique New York
   - Deputy Equity

(Ha! This one is for all of the Equity members reading this. It gets your lips moving and forces your voice out of your throat.)

Speed of Turnover

The best exercise to increase your speed of recall and performance is called the *Italian rehearsal*. I touched on it in Chapter 8 in the TRUST action words - Recall. This is a well-known theatre exercise where actors run through the play without emotion, spitting their words out as fast as they can. It is designed to not only get you out of your head, but also tells you where you are with your real working knowledge of the script. It will train your senses to work at a rapid fire rate so when you go back to normal pace, the words will fall out of you.

Your target will be to plow through your at-a-glance script within one minute or less. You can whisper the words or use your full voice but speak the words as quickly as you can. I tend to do something additional to throw my concentration off even more like ironing a shirt or folding laundry as I recite my script. Honestly, I'm terrible at it but it keeps pushing the bar of expectation, and that is good! If you can say your script in less than one minute while doing another engaging activity, imagine how well prepared you'll feel. You'll be ready to go and that confidence will 'read' on camera. It will allow you to be alive to react to the space, the people and whatever happens in the studio without concern because you know your script every which way. Again, certain categories force you to be tapping your head while rubbing your tummy and chewing gum. Good. Keep doing multiple activities every chance you get when you rehearse. You should be able to do ten absolutely clean performance rehearsals to confirm your readiness. Be hard on yourself. If you make a blunder, start again and count that as one again. *Have I convinced you yet?*

Stay Hydrated and Well Fed

Some say that water is the 'nectar of the Gods.' In Chapter 4, The Job of Getting the Job, I talk about the importance of hydration. Please refer back to it if you haven't read it yet. It is a very important tool!

PERFORMANCE

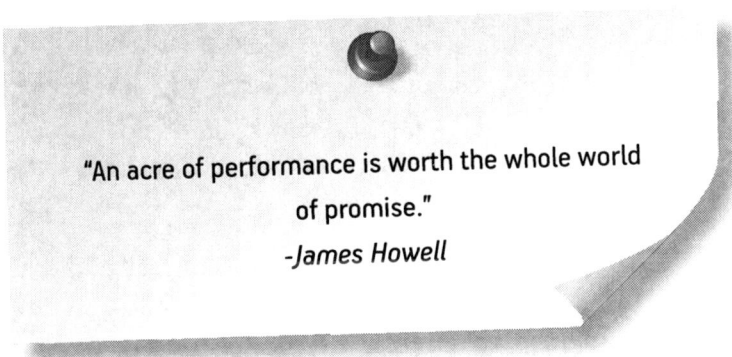

"An acre of performance is worth the whole world of promise."
-James Howell

It is your job to be prepared and ready to perform. To be a great performer means you left it all out on the stage or course, leaving nothing in the dressing room. To have the discipline and deep knowledge of yourself as the conduit is the ability to access your vulnerability. This is the true risk every great performer takes. To be vulnerable in performing is not to be weak but rather opens your soul to stand firmly on your foundation of technique and involves all that brought you to the arena that day. It allows the performer be it the athlete, actor or guest expert to surrender limits in order to push their capabilities to new heights.

Rosamund Stone Zander and Benjamin Zander in their book *The Art of Possibility* state, "Mistakes can be like ice. If we resist them, we may keep on slipping into a posture of defeat. If we include mistakes in our definition of performance, we are likely to glide through them and appreciate the beauty of the longer run."

Ryan Lochte (seven-time Olympic medalist for the US and counting), in his 2008 Beijing 200m backstroke race thought he had blown his chances at gold when he realized seconds before the gun had gone off that he had not tied his swimsuit tightly enough. He didn't have time to fix it, so when he kicked off the wall, his shorts filled up like a balloon – milliseconds of lag was the difference between gold and 4th. He couldn't believe that something so rudimentary could be the reason for his loss. It was distracting to say the least, but he relied on his training, his mental strength and technique and kept on pushing through four lengths of the pool. Ryan won Gold, beating defending champion Aaron Peirsol (seven Olympic medals, five of them gold), considered at the time to be the "greatest backstroke swimmer the United States of America ever produced."[4]

Habits are Habit Forming

"Toastmasters is an organization devoted to helping all of their members improve their speaking abilities, no matter what level they may be at." [5]

Within each weekly Toastmasters meeting, a handful of speakers are assigned to perform speeches with prescribed guidelines. Other assigned members are responsible for providing constructive feedback. They could be assigned to watch out for grammatical issues or the timing of the speech or they may be responsible for counting the number of 'ahs' and 'ums' each speaker utters in any given speech. What has made this group so long-lasting and successful (since 1924) is the discipline and consistency of the framework the organization provides. It is a great example of what consistent monitoring can do for subjective expressions of communication such as performance.

Guest experts have to become their own evaluator, coach and critic when it comes to their performance. You may remember in Chapter 8 under the action word Record where I suggest you consistently record your shows on a PVR. The best content and pitch in the world can get lost with a guest expert who isn't aware of their habit of continually pausing, or using distracting terms and/or gestures such as:

"Ummm"

"Ah…"

"Do you know?"

"Do you understand what I'm saying?"

"And that's just great."

"It's fabulous."

 "You have to understand"

"Like, like…"

Pointing to the camera or the host

Any term used occasionally during your presentation is perfectly fine and is a part of your personality and style. What you need to be aware of is the overuse of repetitive terms. You don't want to become a caricature of yourself. Odd habits can creep up without notice. At one point, I somehow started doing this weird noise with my throat (almost like a hungry cookie monster like grunt). I identified that I did it when I finished a point and was waiting for the host to say something back. It was dead air filler and was strictly a nervous reaction on my part. Once I became aware of it, I stopped it. It's like weight gain. Sometimes it's easy to put on, and without notice you're ten pounds heavier. It's often harder to take it off and takes some awareness but is easily maintained if you stay informed of your habits.

Performing Demonstrations

Some products have to be demonstrated in order to sell product. Recently I was filling my truck up with gas and this very nice young man came walking toward me with a spray can, microfiber cloth and a smile. At first my response was rather impolite. I thought to myself, *I'm just getting gas, don't bug me.* A clever sales tactic though, as I had already started filling up therefore was forced to stick around for a moment. He wasted no time and gave me his thirty second pitch, which didn't impress me.

"I'm not a car person. I don't care about shiny cars or tires," I said over the loud noise of the gas station.

He smiled and proceeded to show me how it worked and shared, "In seconds, with no water, no streaks, anyone can have a clean car. But you can also shine up stainless steel appliances."

Oh, oh... now he hooked me. He listened to my objection and directed his pitch in a different way! After paying almost $90 for the gas, I paid another $30 for one can with a BOGO offer and two microfibre cloths!

Well done, Tommy in the red shirt. Now I have a shiny car that repels rain AND my appliances (including my new industrial range) have never looked better!

Demonstrations are a black and white function based on tangible facts. The products we sell are our co-stars. There is so much opportunity to have fun with the function of demonstration. It gives you a chance to be personable with the viewers while showing off how the product works. We explored the power of the demonstration earlier in the chapter – highlighting the utmost importance of how it contributes to overcoming indifference and objections. Now we will deal with the performance of the demonstration.

You have to know how to move it around for the camera to capture every side of it and the skill cannot be over-rehearsed. An ill-prepared demonstration is a red flag. If you are bumbling and dropping things, it may negatively affect the sales you do that day and perhaps even your reputation. When you only have a few minutes to keep the attention of your viewers, a misstep during the demo can ruin your flow and potential for solid sales.

Pre-Show Set check

Move around all over the set to ensure that your shoes don't slip and you can walk comfortably. Check that you can pass through all areas with ease and that your demo material and any other material are close at hand to ensure economy of motion.

Two Dimensions of the TV Screen II

In Chapter 3, To Wear or Not to Wear, That Is the Question, we talked about working within the limits of the two dimensions of the TV when you make choices on your wardrobe. If you don't provide some type of taper or dimension to your shape, the camera will make you look wide and flat – even if you're not. Similar principles apply to our products. If one of your selling features is size or dimension or refers to scale in any way, be sure to put it in perspective for your audience with something they can relate to. The ruler is used frequently for this very reason. More details in the section, The Camera and You, coming up shortly.

(Refer to Chapter 3, the section Two Dimensions of the TV Screen I)

When Demos Don't Go According to Plan

After all the preparations and work you've done, unforeseen things can still happen. You could make a flub of some kind, drop something, soak yourself with water, or worse, the host. If something does go wrong during the show, be warned: the producer may ask you to not do the demo again if it was a total disaster or took focus away from the merits of the product in any way. You may very well be judged not as much on the demo itself, but how you handled the flub. This is particularly true if you are new to the scene and have no record of success. If there is a mistake, forgive yourself quickly and get on with it. Edit any move that seems troublesome. Get back to this moment right now. No matter how great you think your props and ideas are, don't take any chances. You have to be able to walk in knowing that every possible demonstration and prop you use looks great at every angle. We wrap a lot of confidence and selling features around our demos. Don't take away a valuable asset because you didn't do a thorough job in rehearsal.

Your rehearsal process is an important factor to flush out any potential problems. The idea may be great but the execution of certain demos may not be. Here's a perfect example of what *I thought* would have worked well only to realize during my rehearsals that it did not. My demo illustrated the unique construction of the varied length of fibres of a highly absorbent towel.

As you can see in the pictures, I used nautical rope to depict the varied heights. The problem with rope is it frays. So when I created it, I thought well, I can't use a lighter on the end to bind it because it will appear burned. So I chose to seal the ends with a glue gun. The problem was, even with my glasses on and a bright light shining down upon it, I didn't realize how UGLY this yellow and white thing was until I filmed it on my iPad. Refer to the picture again and take a look at all the globs of glue on the tips. If I had brought this to the studio to use on-air, it would have been a deal-breaker mistake on my part.

I had to go back to my favourite nautical store, find better rope to recreate a new and improved demo. It took another day but it was well worth my time and effort. During my show, it worked like a charm! It gave me the confidence to show every side of it to the camera and it allowed me to make my three second point and then move on. Had I walked in with the first version, the producer would have pulled it.

The Camera and You

In Chapter 6, There's No 'I' in Team, we talked about the fourth wall, which is the audience. The camera is actually your third and fourth wall. The third is your ability to work with the camera to show off your product using the correct angles, pace and movement to capture and how you frame up your *ask*. The fourth wall is your customer.

- Connect yourself to the product at all times. Always have your product in your hand or be in contact with it if possible.

- Think about how the camera is going to focus in on your product. If your head is directly behind the product, it makes for an awkward camera angle and pulls focus away from the product and onto your body or nostrils or gums. When the camera focuses on the product, stay out of the way *favouring* one side or the other (Vanna White style from *Wheel of Fortune*). This also helps when they pull back to a wide shot. The camera crew is highly capable of working around you but you can make it a bit easier for them. It ultimately makes a larger impact to the overall look.

- Always put the scale of the product in perspective. Help the viewer understand what he is seeing. The clearer you can do that with the camera, the more sales you'll get. When selling jewelry, the host will use rulers so people can relate to that. If you are showing the size of something, use a common product that we are probably all familiar with to frame up the point quickly. If you can help the viewer understand what he is seeing, the more connection you'll make with your customers. (I often bring a dress maker's tape measure to show the deep pockets of the fitted sheets. People like it when you take the time to clarify things with simple visuals that they can relate to).

- If you are kneeling or bending over in some way, ensure that what you choose to wear allows you to move the way you need to without any wardrobe malfunctions. Refer to Chapter 3, To Wear or Not to Wear, That is the Question, for all wardrobe recommendations. Always remember to kneel sideways to the camera. If you kneel front facing towards the camera (whether you are wearing a skirt or not) it's not an attractive angle. Sharon Stone has already done it.

- Work and move in what you will perceive to be slow, slow motion. Watch the monitor and dance with your camera people. When you decide to move the product away to another shot or angle, do your camera crew and producers a favour to slow down your movements to a molasses crawl. Remember, think in terms of what shot the camera is getting, not what you are doing. I will sometimes do the entire rehearsal through my iPad in front of me. The TV and computer is a frame and you have to understand how that can work for you. One seemingly minute movement of one inch translates to one quarter of the diameter of a camera lens so take it slowly. When you look at the camera, it is actually backwards. It's a little like driving a boat – when you move the tiller to the right, the boat moves left. Similarly, on camera, you appear to move in the opposite direction. Practice your demos by facing a mirror and working by looking into the mirror, not at the product.

Visual Tools

In visual media (including home shopping), there are certain designations given to the names of footage in the world of journalism, film and TV.

Generally, **A-roll** is the main footage of the broadcast – when the main characters and plot are captured.

B-roll is the supplementary media that supports the main footage. For instance, CNN, when reporting from the Gaza strip will use a lot of B-roll shot earlier that day to support what the journalist broadcasts later in the day. In a movie, they traditionally have second and third camera crews shooting B-roll to establish where the scene is happening. A front shot of a house, traffic on the highway, perhaps a long shot of a rainy street scene or an overhead travelling wide shot which could be used to roll the credits at the beginning or end of the movie.

A and B-Roll in Home Shopping

A-Roll is actual video footage that adds another layer driving the sales message forward even more. There are many options within this realm including an edited version of the infomercial, which is usually a variation of the complete pitch. A-roll could also be interviews from experts, chiropractors, athletes, etc. who endorse the product. It could also be product footage if the product is too large to show its full capacity within the limits of the studio. This might include a sprinkler with fire hose strength, LED Christmas lights or solar panels (to name only a few).

B-Roll is behind-the-scenes visual only footage that often shows how and where certain products are manufactured. It can play a fantastic accent role to support what the guest expert is pitching. For instance, when a guest expert sells jewelry, it is interesting to see where the gemstones are being mined. This can often help certain viewers decide to buy because they now understand why a rare gemstone is so expensive. As a customer, I also like to see shots of the actual product being made. When the beautiful Royal Doulton figurines are sold, they often share with us what the first sketches look like and introduce us to some of the artisans. They often capture the evolution of the process of creating these signed pieces of art. If B-roll is done well, it can be a captivating ingredient that gives the expert more to talk about and may also play a role in building the customers' allegiance to the product, the guest expert and the network itself.

To Use Cue Cards or Not to Use Cue Cards

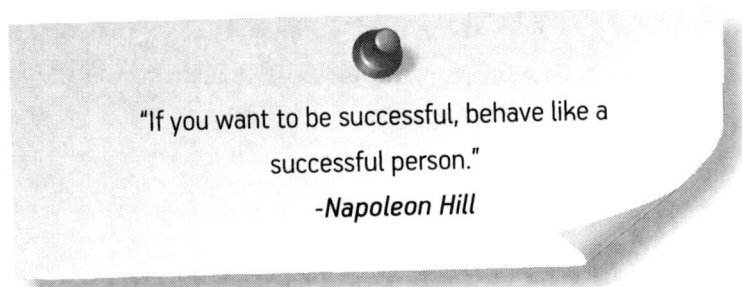

"If you want to be successful, behave like a successful person."
-Napoleon Hill

When opening night comes, no actor comes on any stage holding his script. It is show time and the rehearsals are over. As a guest expert, the same principles apply. Remember the image you are painting on camera. If you have notes in your hand, it looks like you are ill prepared or you look old and cannot remember anything. I have used notes on occasion when I just wasn't comfortable with my knowledge. I found it limited my flow and my choreography around set. It also left me feeling very self-conscious instead of focusing on the product and the viewers. The host is generally the only person who should be referring to notes. You should be the expert and the expert in my books does not need notes. There are a number of exceptions, however, including when you're filling in for another expert. Using notes is permissible, but try to remember at least the most important points *off book*. Referring to notes rather than connecting with your message and your customers will not get you closer to sell out performances.

If you choose to use them, hide them from the camera as best you can and *rehearse* working with them.

Use of Large Visual Boards

There is a great alternative to using cue cards, and that is poster size easel boards which can be set just off camera. Many guests work with them well and on a regular basis. There's one high energy expert who speaks a mile a minute who relies heavily on them because of the pace he speaks at. One of his sales tactics is to fire out multiple stats and this gives him the ability to instantly recall without worry. It helps him to stay on track without missing a beat. The audience would never know and that is the point. If you are working with easels, rehearse working with them. The camera crew will tell you where you can place them so they won't create shadows or interfere in their track.

There's only one major potential negative issue using large cue cards, and that is they can be read by anyone. Hosts (particularly if they are unfamiliar with the product or are new) will steal your words. They don't do it in a malicious manner, but if there are selling points directly in front of them that they haven't used before (or thought of), they are going to weave them into their pitch too. And hosts can do ten things at once and end up spinning your whole easel of words into one beautiful minute of inspiration. When I was new to the circuit, I used easels to help me feel more confident, only to be standing in awe and shock that my entire shtick had just been said by the host. "Well, I couldn't have said it better myself. Thank you for wrapping it all up so beautifully." Hey, it's fair game. If they use your words, consider it a compliment and be ready to vary your manner. You always have your demos. What you will find, if you do end up bringing your large cue cards, more times than not, you most likely will forget to refer to them. If you need them for your own security, go for it. It is still my preference to leave all crutches in the dressing room or at home.

Pace Yourself on a Long Show Day

"One of the many challenges of being an ER nurse is we never know when an emergency will be coming in, so when there are down times we take them."

-Louise Careford, 16+ year veteran

Registered Nurse

If you are selling a GVS, you will be at the studio for a long time and you need to be able to access your energy stores efficiently. The sign of a veteran guest expert is one who knows how to pace their day and their energy.

I think of veteran athletes who you see standing on the podium consecutively. One of the many factors to their success is they know how to pace themselves before, during and after a race. In track and in the swimming competitions for instance, many athletes will have perhaps completed one race and have to turn around to do another equally as important race thirty minutes later. Pacing is a skill that athletes learn how to manage in their training. Performers must do the same. If your blood sugar is down, your mind can't work as efficiently. When long distance athletes are in the middle of a race and they are feeling negative or sluggish, coaches will tell them to take in fuel. Be informed and plugged-in to what you need and put your feet up when you get the chance. When you are on, rest in action!

Phone Calls to Air

It is one of the greatest examples of how a perfect stranger can sway the opinions of others in a heartbeat. In the world of loyalty marketing, tens of millions of dollars are spent trying to get across great messages of support from their potential customers. Home shopping does this every day without spending one dollar more than they have to because their customers do it for them. It is the quintessential example of the 'neighbourly chat over the fence.' Often times, the networks have in place many types of reward programs for providing a testimonial of support and review of their products. It creates that interactive experience for everyone involved.

Every shopping channel weighs the importance of the value of call-ins. Therefore, depending on what network you work for, you may have many or very few to participate in. QVC and HSN build a certain amount of programming time around talking directly to their customers because it works from an experiential level and has the potential to build sales momentum. It is a great way to extend loyalty as well. Most networks have some type of hotline where customers can leave messages of support.

Phone calls to air is a layer that adds to the live element and the excitement. The main focus of the calls is to ask as many relevant questions that spark ideas and questions to benefit the entire listening audience. The host is responsible for handling the direction and length of the phone calls. The guest expert generally follows the host's lead, even if you're a celebrity. Again, network culture is different in every studio. When you receive your guest package, they will mention how they prefer phone calls to be handled. If not, ask prior to your arrival. The idea is always to keep it light, honest and fun. As the host and guest expert, remember that everyone has a personality. Since you don't have the luxury of reading faces, it's important to listen to the tone of voice as much as anything. Learning to control phone calls and use them to your advantage is a crucial part of selling.

The New World Approach

The New World Approach sets the tone for a buoyant performance that easily allows you to bend in one direction or the other depending on what you and the host do together. If you find that you are feeling rigid and stiff and can't roll with the punches, find a way to loosen that knot. Your performance will benefit greatly! It is an effective *grounding strategy* that places you in a neutral frame of mind and body. This state of readiness allows a performer to embrace each moment as it happens and gives him/her the heightened ability to react honestly to anything that comes along – whether it be person, emotion or circumstance. The new world happens every time you either change directions, intentions or someone or something else enters your space.

> "Staying present in the moment with my scene partner(s) is my main focus while onstage. In the wings I focus entirely on my *onstage life*. I make certain my energy level is appropriate for the upcoming scene and I think only about why my character is entering the scene. The lines, the blocking, the high C's are all givens at this point in the process. It is the degree of vulnerability and willingness an actor has to listen and to be willing to react to everything that they are given that can transcend a performance from being just fine, to being truly magical."
> **-Rebecca Poff,** *28+ year veteran performer and vocal teacher*

I first learned about the concept of New World through acting classes taken with Patsy Rodenberg from the Royal Shakespeare Festival in London, UK. With over thirty years of experience working with actors and public speakers, she is perhaps Britain's most highly regarded voice coach. The actors on her formidable roster of 'have-taughts' include Oscar-nominees and winners such as Dame Judi Dench and Sirs Ian McKellen and Daniel Day-Lewis (to name only a few).

Outwardly, one would never recognize that the performer was practicing 'new world' strategies. It might appear as if nothing is happening, just as the lily pad appears floating effortlessly on the surface of the pond. (Refer to Chapter 9, The Lily Pad Strategy™.) As the pads sway with the current flowing all around, the lily pads remain as they are, but rooted yards beneath the surface. This foundation allows them to stay in place no matter what is happening around them. It is one of the secrets of any great performer. If you've ever experienced a great performance in film or theatre that moved you to tears or laughter inexplicably, this was most likely an actor living in the moment 100%. We as audience members feel it, and are moved by it. Eckart Tolle and many other great writers, poets and leaders speak of this power to embrace the now. In the on-air sales medium, it is not a philosophy; *it is part of our work.*

We've all entered the studio with a grocery list of to-dos between shows or remembered the disagreement you shared with your spouse earlier that

CHAPTER 10 — THE 3 P'S PREPARATION, PRACTICE, PERFORMANCE

day. On the set, our mind wants to jump ahead, (particularly if the day is a tough one) or we want to regress back to re-living the demo that didn't work moments ago. It's because we are perfectionists on some level and we want every moment to work. All of this "noisiness" can be read on some level on screen. These things happen and it's life, but here in the theatre, in the studio or on stage there is nothing more important than *this moment right here, right now*.

Earlier I talked about how an actor has the potential to be a solid guest expert. The best actors are exceptional at honing their new world approach to the work they do. The performance has to seem fresh, energized and inspired every moment the camera is on you. There's a term called *locking it in* in theatre that occurs when the director puts his final stamp on the overall performance of the cast and crew right before opening night. This level of performance is expected to be held up from the first day until the close of the show. It's then the stage manager's job and the dance captain's job (in larger shows) to ensure that this level of performance doesn't lessen. If it does, performers are given notes on what they need to do to bring their level of performance back up to what the initial *locked in* performance was.

Many years ago, there was a young on-air guest selling front door floor mats. The unique thing about the fibres of the carpet was their ability to soak up any dirt and the demonstration proved it worked very well. On-air, the guest expert would soak his boots in wet mud and would walk on a regular door mat and then walk onto a clean sheet of paper that instantly became soiled by his muddy boots. It clearly showed that the comparative mat did nothing to soak up the mud. Then, he'd repeat his move by going back to standing in the mud and then would stand onto the magic carpet. He'd wipe his boots as before and then stood on a new clean white sheet of paper. The paper remained completely white with no trace of dirt. It proved in one quick image that the magic carpet soaked up all the dirt. This was a great before and after comparative demonstration. You could see why this product would do well in many selling environments. The issue was he never varied his pitch, his tone, pace or his demonstration one bit. It was boring, monotonous and the carpet after one show was sooooooo dirty that it was hard to watch if you sat for more than one demo. The product was great but never sold particularly well because I believe the guest locked himself into a performance that he felt comfortable with and never considered the audience and the elements of levels and entertainment required to inspire action. That's where the 'new world approach' layered in between the rest of the sales tools in this book allow you to sell with results. You always have to be re-inventing and renewing your approach during your shows.

Two Fantastic Guest Experts Who Are New World Specialists

Tune-in to watch the magic of Jamie Kern Lima and Marc Gill. Let me introduce them to you:

Used with Jamie's permission

Jamie Kern Lima is probably best known for being the co-founder of IT Cosmetics. She is a dynamite guest expert who truly knows how to relate to her customers! Jamie performs the same demo and has the camera focused only on her face for minutes on end and never once do you see her lower her energy or excitement of what she is talking about. She has found a way to engage that continual new world attitude while remaining relaxed and

CHAPTER 10 — THE 3 P'S PREPARATION, PRACTICE, PERFORMANCE

real. No matter when you see her in the afternoon or in the wee hours of the morning, her smile and bright eyes and personality remain consistent with her desire to inspire us to understand why the products are great. I want to purchase her products because watching her makes me happy and hopeful. Her products are exceptional too.[6]

The other Fantastic New World Specialist is none other than Mr. Marc Gill.

Used with Marc's permission

Marc Gill is HSN's Kitchen Authority. He also appears on TSC and many International infomercials. He's a tremendously strong pitchman and sells every kind of kitchen-related item imaginable from knives, to slow cookers to tasty sauces, treats and recipes. Marc has to do the same exact demo and talk about the same exact techniques well over fifty times per show. Any time he does a demo, it's as if he just thought about doing it for the first time. It's not shtick. It's his high performance standard. He maintains a level of discovery with everything he does and that is why he is one of the most sought after pitch specialists out there today. He also has a great social identity providing lots of recipes and tips to his customers. People love him and so do the network buyers.[7]

Find a way to access your New World Approach. It will keep your versatility high and help you to maintain flexibility. It is a technique that will keep you fresh, and interesting during the 11th hour of your sales day, which many times can be your best hour.

When the Unexpected Happens

Approaching your work with a new world consciousness applies not only to what you are saying and doing but also to your attitude toward what is going on during every moment. Personally, as long as the anchors of my performance are solid, I love it when unexpected things happen. It's the pizazz and charm of live performance from lights falling directly in front of you, to another upcoming guest bouncing on the bed during your show (without being invited). If you don't like something that has happened during the show, regardless of why it happened or who is responsible, don't punish your viewers for it. Park the issue for when you can deal with it off camera.

I've witnessed guests spoil their valuable air time, literally shaking their heads at whomever caused the mistake or referring back to a demo that completely failed three minutes ago. Too bad for you and get over it! It's important to keep in mind that thousands of people have just turned off their TV and computers before your blunder and thousands more have just clicked to the airing for the first time completely oblivious of the past blunder.

Stay in this moment right here, right now.

CHAPTER 10 — THE 3 P'S PREPARATION, PRACTICE, PERFORMANCE

SOURCES

1. http://markcassius.com/
2. http://www.imdb.com/name/nm0048370/
3. http://www.worldrecordacademy.com/business/fastest_deal_world_record_set_by_Donald_Trump_and_Ricardo_Bellino_70919.htm
4. Wire Sports http://3wiresports.com/2011/05/12/aaron-peirsol-swim-ambassador-and-waterman/
5. Source: http://www.toastmasters.org/Members/MembersFunctionalCategories/AboutTI/History.aspx
6. http//.www.itcosmetics.com
7. www.butimnotstoppingthere.com

CHAPTER 10
The 3 P's – Preparation, Practice and Performance

1. This chapter is the heart and soul of implementation and putting on the show. It coaches you to get up on your feet to be ready for show time.
2. Prepare – includes all of the tools that will get you ready for your show day including:
   a. At-a-glance script
   b. Tape recorder of all scripts
   c. Industry lingo
3. Practice – concentrates on speeding up your recall and your ability to float from one thought to another no matter the distractions around you. This includes:
   a. Three Minute Loop
   b. Repetition 10 x
4. Performance – Deals directly with how to perform at your best and flushes out any issues that may impede your ability to successfully do your job including:
   a. Dealing with annoying habits
   b. Perfecting your ability to demonstrate
   c. Considering how the camera is capturing your message from all sides
   d. Using performance aids, or not
   e. Pacing yourself to always be *on* when you need to be
   f. Keeping your message fresh, exciting and compelling
   g. Maintaining your communication with your Anchor Seven™ customers.

CHAPTER 11

ASSESS YOUR SUCCESS

The business of performance and on-air sales is like every business. It is driven by the measured tangibles – sales, margins, dollars per minute, inventory turnover, returns, numeric quality reports, testing results, 30-day money back guarantees, easy payments and so much more. The bottom line reporting measures are imperative for sure, but your ability to perform at peak depends on how well you manage your responses to the reports. When you are in the middle of a show day for instance and the sales are soft, you have to have a plan of attack that helps you to rise above negative responses to them. Control how well you manage the intangibles of your profession. You have to be able to be your own judge and jury without the added pressure of the bottom line to give you a passing or failing grade. Yes, within certain boardrooms at certain times and moments, sales is the only element that matters, but a cold hard number can't tell the whole story of our achievements.

In this chapter, you will leave with four tangible rating systems that measure the intangible elements of *achievement*. Every time you work, rehearse, prepare, train, you can walk away knowing how well you did that day without anyone else's feedback. This certainly is not meant to make you the difficult diva and untouchable, but rather a way to measure how well you are managing your work day to day. We will delve into finding ways you can make a difference today.

Years back when I started in the business of acting, this was the one element I couldn't quite figure out. How may one rate their work and measure improvements made when the reality is we are not always employed and our bank accounts and cash flow sometimes show it. How can one *literally* assess their own success when one doesn't always get the desired short term or long-term, hardline results expected?

When you think of it, the pressure to perform applies to all of us. I think we can all relate to losing out on what we thought should have been ours, the win, the raise, the job, the sell out. People lose jobs and solid presentations in the corporate boardrooms are often passed up. Champion athletes sometimes don't even make it to the finals let alone the podium. These are all the tangible realities and sometimes life just isn't fair. At times there is nothing more to say than learn from this opportunity and get on with it.

In order to gain some insight on how some expert performers deal with these real issues, I asked pro endurance athletes, actors, entrepreneurs and commission sales people all the same question:

"How do you keep on going out there when you don't always get the results you intended to receive?"

They all answered with the same conviction:

"What else would I do?"

"This is what I do."

"I have no choice but to do this."

These thoughts were chased with the fact that they *never stop* auditioning, running sprints, knocking on doors for parts and/or listings. I noticed again and again this tremendous belief in themselves knowing that there *is always a plan* that far exceeds whether one gets this job, that win or that booking. There seemed to be an inherent and overall trust that the right path of work will find them, if they keep moving forward on their own path, not stopping to wait for directions but building their portfolio of experience and achievement.

As guest experts, you will not always sell out your product, but that must always be *one* of your goals. Keeping this as your constant, it forces you to remain poised, continually refining, improving and building on your successes each time you take a swing.

Control what you can control. Show up being your best and the right jobs and desired outcomes will attach themselves to you.

Understanding the Long-Term Process of the Goal to Sell Out

Have you ever had to lose weight and chose to join a group to help you get it done? There are so many wonderful weight loss programs to follow, but there is a common theme running through most of them. If you lose weight, you are winning and if you don't, you are losing. Now, I know, that is not the only intention and there are many other aspects to the benefits of weight loss. This may include: living a healthy lifestyle and moving your body more and educating yourself on making better choices. They are all certainly part of the success plan, but let's face it, you've gone to the trouble of signing up with one goal in mind, to lose weight! So, if you don't get that done, it's well…a failure.

I have stood in line ups to get weighed in and as you're taking off your heavy belt, the security FOP and your chunky necklace to lighten the load a bit you hear from the other side of the table:

"You're up two pounds, did you have a bad week?" OR

"Good for you, you're down five pounds. What did you do this week that worked so well?"

You walk away from that meeting either dismayed as to why you gained when you did everything right or laughing that you got away with eating those three extra pieces of pizza and an extra beer the night before and *still* lost weight. As you get in the car with your new booklets to inspire your upcoming week of activities you wonder will I be able to repeat what I did this past week again? What should I stop doing and what should I continue to do? It's this vacuum-like bubble that is frustrating when all you want to know is how to lose the weight and *keep it off.*

In the on-air world, well-intentioned people might pass you in the hall and throw out comments like "You were great" or "Great show." This is all nice to hear and it's a lot better than hearing that you stunk, but either way, it doesn't help you understand what you are doing well and not so well.

Have you ever felt that way after a job interview? Or a date?

Looking back at the experience you ask yourself, "What didn't work and how could I have done better?" OR "What did I do to get this outcome?"

It's baffling sometimes to understand the process of achievement because the tangible signs sometimes don't come fast enough for our comfort level. As a guest expert, when your show day is going well (i.e. you are hitting or crushing the sales targets), you will notice that there won't be too much said to you. Smiles may be exchanged, other guests may thank you for setting the tone for a strong sales day for them as well, but for the most part everything will be quiet and you will be free to go about your day.

There are times however, when you will be doing everything you possibly can to hit your targets ensuring that the through-put is solid but the signs *still* don't show marked progress. When sales are soft, this is the time to swing wide and apply all the skills and technique you have built up. On a GVS day particularly, there is pressure like you can't believe. Closed door meetings, bottles of Tums are popped by the buyers, stagers come to fix the look of the set, lists of modifications and wide eyes are directed right at you. Whether the sales are high or low, it is not the whole story most times. It could have been a long holiday weekend or your show was scheduled right after Christmas when everyone has perhaps spent their money. It could have been poor timing, the offer may have not looked good enough, seasonality could have been the issue, the product may not have looked good enough or the price might just have been too high for the consumer.

Regardless of the pass or fail, the performer still needs feedback to know how to adjust each moment in order to continue to get better and keep getting hired back. You end up putting a lot of stake in other people's reactions and reviews and that can't be something you can rely on. So what can be relied on? You'd love to be able to lock in your sell out performance, but how?

The answers are in this next section:

Feedback from Your Measurements

Measurements provide immediate feedback on how we can fix, improve, confirm and continue. With athletes, statistics act as coaches as they measure what parts of the race need to be worked on. In swimming, cycling and track and field, coaches and athletes will work on the power output, strides and turnover at the start and throughout the race. In 1000m sculls (in rowing), the first one to hit the last 500m marker historically wins the race outright. These stats are all known commodities and help relay meaningful information to the athlete in order to make minute improvements.

Identifying INtangibles You Can Measure

Do you want to know how *you* can encompass the totality of the selling experience and be directed on how to use your abilities to your maximum value today? Would you like to know how to identify, lock in and activate your best performance skills?

On the next number of pages, there are four different formats that will contribute to filling your toolbox with all you need to assess your INtangible success. Format #1 is a fluid list of scenarios. Format #2 and Format #3 are quantifiable charts giving you *tangible* ratings for many INtangible functions. Format #4 provides a framework to set good, better and best goals.

The scenarios in Format #1 will also help you to customize the Format #2 and #3 charts that follow. *How well* you deal with the changing issues of the selling day is critical because everything can be considered a building block even if sometimes you feel you are being pushed backwards. Picture the spirit of behavior your hungry dog or cat has when the food bowls haven't quite reached the floor. The animals are right there ready tails wagging and bodies purring to do their job. Every time you push them away because *you* aren't ready, their faith is renewed and are right back to try again. They know if they stay close and ready to act when the bowls go down, they will be fed *soon* if not right this second.

It is this spirit of perspicacity that is needed at all times in our work of selling and performing. If you hit many of the intangible markers with consistency, you end up putting yourself in a stronger position to be ready for a sell out when the opportunity arises.

This winning mindset may be the difference between preparing to do a fair show to preparing to do your best sell out show ever.

Format #1:
HOW WELL did you manage the following scenarios:

- Your ability to recall intricate details, relay applicable statistics and product information.
- Your professional performance level with transitions, distractions and changes the host throws at you.
- How successfully you prepared yourself in order to peak at the right time for thirty-six hours straight.
- Hitting your opening statement and your chase thought.
- Your recovery when six things went wrong at the same time.
- Your show performance itself. Did you successfully hit the key features and benefits at the right time in the right manner in a succinct three-minute bundle.
- Demonstrating the product and working well with the camera.
- Maintaining an entertaining and seamless flow between the host, camera and the audience.
- Dealing with the pressure of a soft sales day and the criticism that seemed to be directed at you.
- A professional demeanor with colleagues and team members.

- Adjusting to producers barking orders with last minute instructions or changes.
- Dealing with camera operators and others directing your every little move.
- Dealing with your microphone pack needing to be changed on the fly seconds before or during the show.
- Working alongside the stagers who were late to set up your set.
- Solving and dealing with dirty or ripped merchandise you only discovered the last minute before you started your show.
- A calm and focused energy that was ready to entertain and live in the moment.
- Working with a host that would rather be anywhere else but with you.

The previous list of INtangible measurements can easily be used to customize your measurements in the charts Format #2 and 3 to follow:

Quantifiable Matrices

These two matrices help you rate your performance as often as you need to. After years in this business, I still use both formats on a regular basis because the data captured on one page can be easily transferred into quarterly and annual reviews and for marketing purposes as well. This type of meaningful data is most helpful when you need to capture a snapshot of the progress of the brand(s) you represent.

Blank templates and examples of both Format #2 and Format #3 charts can be downloaded and customized to suit your needs.

Go to: www.allimang.com/vip

Format #2 - Self-Evaluation Performance Checklist Template

Quantifies and measures *how well* the show-day went and is based on all the performance elements we covered in Chapter 2, The Guest Expert. It forces you to rate the intangible skill set. It doesn't matter whether you are a *tough* marker or an *easy* marker. The fact that you are the only person marking will keep your rating consistent every time you do the exercise. It helps in so many different ways, particularly if you are just starting out and want to get-to-great as fast as possible. You may have great sense and muscle memory, but for those of us who don't or who are too busy to brush our hair, this list is a great resource to quickly plug you in. You can use it as often as you feel the need.

Format #3 - Sales Tracking Worksheet Template Tracking your sales per minute, per show, per day, per quarter, per year, other products with similar average ticket prices and how the best value of the day went. It keeps me focused on how well I am doing and keeps me motivated and charged up for the next show. Every green room is equipped with real time sales figures of all the products you are responsible for selling that day. A computer program allows you to access your sales figures. There is nothing more thrilling than to reach and exceed your target numbers and to see the graphic sell out covering some or all of the products you have sold that day! You want to bottle that feeling, but since you can't, these reporting systems are the next best thing! I use this sales tracking sheet to keep track of the sales per day. It is also an important business practice as a cross check for when you invoice your vendor or buyer. It will help to confirm that the sales numbers you recorded coincide with the final sales numbers your buyer will give you after the show day is over.

CHAPTER 11 — ASSESS YOUR SUCCESS

PERFORMANCE SELF-EVALUATION TEMPLATE

PRODUCT:				
DATE OF SHOW:		SHOW TYPE:	# OF SHOWS:	TARGET SALES $:
ACTUAL SALES $:		$ DIFFERENCE:	COMMENTS	EVALUATION %:
ACTION	RATING 1-10		COMMENTS	IMPROVEMENTS & COACHING NOTES
Demonstration 1. Was it smooth and clear?				
2. Did you successfully make the connection between the demo and how it adds value to your customers?				
3. Did you work well with the cameras?				
Product Knowledge 1. Did you hit all the important points?				
2. Were you able to complete your loop at least 3 times? (dependent on the time allotted)				
3. Did you handle host and audience questions with ease and confidence?				
4. Did you add new material?				

PERFORMANCE SELF-EVALUATION TEMPLATE (Continued)

ACTION	RATING 1-10	COMMENTS	IMPROVEMENTS & COACHING NOTES
Communication			
1. Did you seamlessly play with pace, vocal and energy levels?			
2. Did you connect with the camera and the host?			
3. Did you stop your um's, ah's, stutters?			
4. Did you surprise and create suspense and a sense of grand occasion?			
NUMERIC SCORE:		**TOTAL PERCENTAGE:**	
TOTAL POINTS: 111		%	

CHAPTER 11 — ASSESS YOUR SUCCESS

SALES TRACKING WORKSHEET TEMPLATE

DATE OF SHOW:		SHOW TYPE:		TOTAL POSSIBLE $:		TARGET SALES $:	
ACTUAL SALES $:	AVERAGE TICKET $:	SALES DIFFERENCE $:		GROSS LEFTOVER $:			

OVERALL WINNING COMMENTS:
1.
2.
3.

IMPROVEMENTS FOR NEXT SHOW:

TIME ON-AIR	PRODUCT 1		PRODUCT 2		PRODUCT 3		TOTAL $
	# OF UNITS	AVERAGE TICKET	# OF UNITS	AVERAGE TICKET	# OF UNITS	AVERAGE TICKET	
START TIMES							
TOTALS:							
ITEMS AND $ LEFT:							
TAKE-AWAY FOR EACH PRODUCT:							
						TOTAL ACTUAL GROSS SALES:	

If you are paid by commission, you can easily plug in your commission rate based on the gross sales amount.
*(For more information on negotiation and rates, please refer to **Chapter 4**, in the section, Negotiation Guidelines).*

How Did the Numbers Help You? What Did You Get Out of It?

If you truly scored high marks on performance measures and feel you're doing all you can to pull out your best performance and the sales are still not climbing, it provides feedback that you need to pursue to get answers perhaps elsewhere. Use the 3 Questions in Life captured in Chapter 4 as another tool. You may need to talk to the vendor, the buyer, the producer and other experts to gain some insight on what, in their opinion, is happening. They have the history and the expertise and if a product fails, it's their job to report their findings as to why it is failing. We know when we're in the zone, and oftentimes the climbing numbers on the screen point to that fact. But when the numbers are different than what you are expecting based on your solid execution, you need to work with your team to make any necessary adjustments accordingly. Take advantage and look at it as an opportunity to push you to identify where you can do something a little different to change the game.

Establishing Your Good, Better, and Best Goals

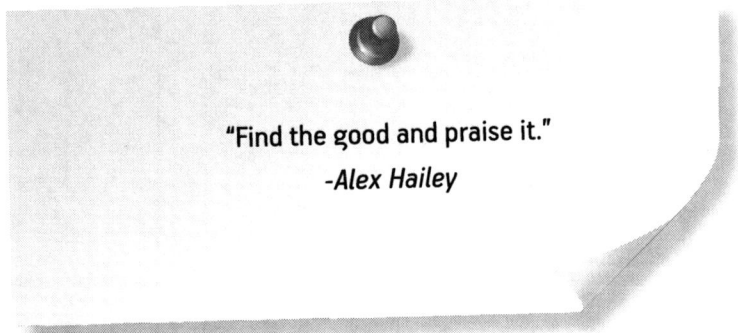

"Find the good and praise it."
-Alex Hailey

At the beginning of the book, I shared my own good, better and best goals for a marathon I had run. It is a fantastic strategy that puts us in the driver's seat and sets us up for more successes. Nurturing the habit of succeeding trains your mind to expect success. Come up with your three good, better and best goals the next time you sell. It will provide a framework that will help you to stay fighting and fresh, up until the last minute of your last show. You'll also be able to walk away from an exhausting day knowing you hit the milestones you set out to do at 100% effort. In this section, we'll establish your own set of goals.

With three gradient goals, the goal setter is bound to walk away with helpful information about themselves that will set him up better for the next opportunity as he moves forward from this experience. Goals bring order and awareness to our work and that is why they work. Setting goals is just as important as the other two tracking systems we just laid out. Set out a plan to achieve attainable goals including lofty, big sky goals. When you run out of time on your show day, either because you sold out, or you were yanked off early (because of soft sales), it is your professional duty to walk away feeling that you accomplished at least one of your goals whether it was goal 1, 2 or 3. It forces you to commit to your ongoing growth no matter what happens.

Format #4 – Establishing your Good, Better and Best Goals

Here are three examples for illustration purposes:

The first two examples will compare the differing goals of an Olympic marathoner and an average everyday marathoner. The last example will illustrate the goals set by an on-air guest doing her first GVS:

I)   Multi-gold medal Olympic marathoner

Scenario: Olympic marathon race (he is the favoured athlete and most likely to win)

Goal #3: Perform strongly (within his current time range) in order to maintain current sponsors and attract new sponsors

Goal #2: Place within the top 3 winners

Goal #1: Win the race

Why is it important to have at least three different goals for an athlete of this caliber? Nothing in racing is ever guaranteed. Even though he may be the favoured athlete, the race still needs to be run and anything can happen on race day and usually does. The wind could be much stronger than expected, there could have been a forest fire nearby that affects the ability to recover and breathe normally. The athlete could have a leg cramp that slows him down, they could have planned their nutrition incorrectly somehow or a lace could have broken off one of their shoes. Things happen and if we don't prepare our minds to manage the unknown with a degree of focus, we'll walk around feeling disappointed a lot more than is necessary.

II) Middle of the pack average marathoner

Scenario: Running the local marathon in his hometown for the fourth time

Goal #3 Qualify for the Boston Marathon (which does require finishing a previous marathon within prescribed time restrictions)

Goal #2 Manage his pacing well and run a strong finish

Goal #1 Cross the finish line healthy, upright and smiling

III) GVS Day

Scenario: First time she has done a GVS

Goal #3 Perform strongly with the host, the demonstrations and provide high turnover pitch delivery in order to confirm a future booking date

Goal #2 Surpass all sales target goals

Goal #1 Sell out

Come up with your own good, better and best goals. You'll love the focus it provides for you during the day and will give you the freedom and flexibility to deal with anything that's thrown at you like a champion!

CHAPTER 11
Assess Your Success

1. Selling out is the result of a long-term commitment to excellence. This chapter provides ways to measure how well you are managing all the stresses and implementation of your profession, no matter what the bottom line says. It will keep you on track to building a portfolio of sell out performances.

   They include:

   Format #1 - Identifying Intangibles You Can Measure

   Format #2 - Performance Self-Evaluation Template

   Format #3 - Sales Tracking Worksheet Template

   Format #4 - Establishing Your Good, Better and Best Performance Goals

*Blank templates and examples of both Performance Self-Evaluation and Sales Tracking charts can be downloaded.

Go to www.allimang.com/vip

CHAPTER 12

HAVE YOU GOT YOUR GAME FACE ON?

What you do today creates your future for tomorrow. Every connection, every action and reaction plays a part in affecting in real time your reputation and your ultimate professional growth. Many people are invited but the truth is, not everyone shows up. As a pressure performer, you have to know how to access your best performance, which goes beyond just hitting your mark and doing your best because in this world, that level is expected. It is the ultimate state of performance readiness. That ***game face*** is put on every time a surgeon works on a patient and when the paramedic and first responders are first to the accident scene. This sense of heightened presence and ability never leaves completely until the job is done. I use the term deliberately in our home shopping sales environment because this term explains the intensity and focus required to only bring your A-Game.

CHAPTER 12 — HAVE YOU GOT YOUR GAME FACE ON?

Used with David's permission [1]

David Rogers (above) is one of the most electrifying performers. When he sings it's like a high powered waterfall that floods your soul. He shares, "A professional who lasts in this business is the person who consistently delivers their best every single time, from the very first show to the 3004th. This is our work to do and is the only element that really counts. We have a huge responsibility to our audience. They have paid to see us on our best day. Give them all you have to give."

Give Them All You Have to Give

Throughout this book, I've provided tools to arm you with the most important elements to bring out the absolute best in you. We all have the potential to perform at the top of our profession. Every time you get the opportunity, go out there giving the best effort you can. The potential exists that you can achieve something that is amazing. If you have an extraordinary brand and it is delivered by the right person, at the right time, in the right moment, the buzz spreads like wild fire and all you have to do is get out of the way and watch the magic happen. Offer the most you can give us. You deserve it and so do your viewers.

In September, 1989, when *Phantom of the Opera* first debuted at the Pantages Theatre in Toronto, Canada (renamed as the Ed Mirvish Theatre in 2012), I spent a lot of time watching backstage and sitting in the dressing rooms. My best friend David (shown in the photo earlier) first understudied the lead role of Raoul to the late great Broadway star Byron Nease. After taking over his role, David toured with the National Company only to come back to Toronto to perform both roles of Raoul and the Phantom of the Opera, clocking in well over 2000 performances before it closed in 1999. Playing these two vastly different roles is something extraordinarily rare. In fact, the infamous director Mr. Hal Prince only granted a handful of gentleman in the world permission to do this during those early years of the production.

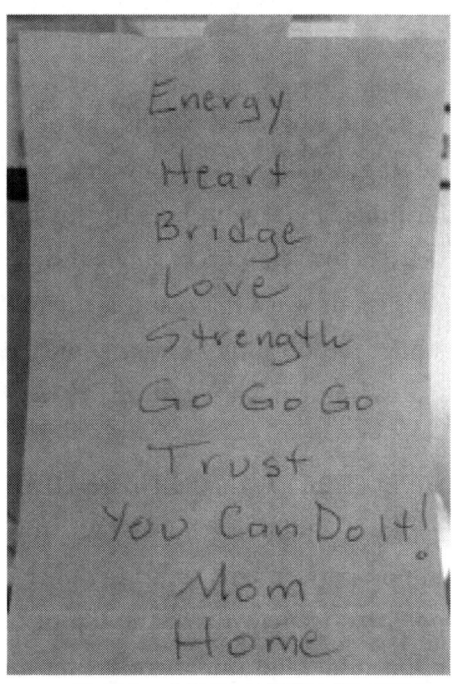

One matinee day as I sat backstage watching David's makeup artist transform his beautiful features into the hideous scars of the Phantom, I noticed this sheet of paper taped to one of the other lead actor's dressing room mirrors. It was placed right by the door. I assumed that every time the actor exited his room, he would see it. This was his private checklist of coaching words and grounding thoughts. It made me realize that even when you are at the top of your game, you have to keep reaching for more. This sheet of paper with one quick glance zoned his thought past the groceries purchased that morning and the tennis match lost at lunch and into the theatre where people were paying to see him play his role. That personal list represented him on his best day and reminded him where that behavior came from. The honesty and the integrity of what that list represented to me was breathtaking. I wondered if this was a list that changed every show, every week or whether this list was dragged around all over the country for all of his shows. It changed me, and from that day on, I realized the level of deep, thoughtful action and perseverance it takes to remain at the top of your profession. You can never take it for granted.

A fun story of a well-known British actor named Sir Derek Jacobi is worth sharing here: Born in 1938, he has played the greatest leading roles in the most important and beautiful theatres in the world. In 1985, the Royal Shakespeare Company (RSC) production of *Cyrano de Bergerac* was brought to Broadway. He was being interviewed by one of the big newspapers and when he and the reporter sat down, the reporter noticed that Mr. Jacobi had a terrible cold coughing and sniffling as they talked. The reporter shared with him that he was sitting in the second row and didn't notice any signs of this seemingly very sick person sitting in front of him. Mr. Jacobi replied, "My boy, the audience didn't come to see Derek Jacobi with a cold; they came to see Cyrano de Bergerac."

When you have your next great show, along with your vision statement (from Chapter 2, Guest Expert), identify some words that represent the feelings and images you experienced that day. They may very well help you to recall that level of excellence again. Find out what ten words have meaning to you and post them on your mirror.

No matter which network you work at, as you become more familiar with the faces and names at reception and throughout the building, your state of high intensity may lighten somewhat but **the game face will remain**.

10-POINT CHECKLIST

#	WHAT IT IS	WHERE CAN I READ MORE ABOUT IT?
1	**Italian Rehearsal** - Repeat 10 x accurately and consecutively *with* distractions.	Chapter 10 Speed of Turnover
2	**Demonstration rehearsal** - Repeat 10 x accurately and consecutively *with* distractions.	Chapter 10
3	**3-Minute Loop** - Repeat 10 x consecutively *with* distractions.	Chapter 10 At-a-Glance
4	**Voice is prepped** - Be hydrated and feel warmed up.	Chapter 10 Preparing Your Voice
5	**Anchor Seven™** - Know specifically who you are talking to today and that what you are saying will benefit them.	Chapter 7 Anchor Seven™ and Anchor Seven Discovery
6	**Update your social media platforms** - Promote your show times, your products and tell us what is special about them. Ensure the sharing is meaningful and a strong takeaway for your readers.	Chapter 12
7	**Visualize success throughout your day** - Visualize the day moving smoothly and harmoniously and see the sales numbers on the screen keep flying up every minute. Picture customers excited to buy your product and you. Visualize the red line that crosses in front of your product signaling a sell out. Picture yourself walking through the middle of the action with confidence, ownership and full receptivity to success.	Chapter 10 The 3 P's: Preparation, Practice, Performance
8	**Pre-show set check** - Move around all over the set to ensure that your shoes don't slip and you can walk comfortably. That you can pass through all areas with ease. That your demo material and any other material is close at hand to ensure economy of motion.	Chapter 10 The 3 P's: Preparation, Practice, Performance
9	**Bring energy into your body** - Just before sound check, (approximately 15 minutes before your show) do something physically vigorous for a minute. Do push-ups, jump up and down, shake your entire body, run a flight or 2 of stairs, take a quick walk outside. Anything to bring blood into your head and trunk. It makes a world of difference to get your blood flowing and to get your head in the game.	Chapter 10 The New World Approach
10	**Vision Statement** - Be sure you know exactly what your overall passion and goals are for today before you take off.	Chapter 2 Finding Your Own Unique Voice

Pre-Host Meeting

This meeting is part of your pre-game set up. You will be meeting with the host(s) you'll be working with. It's an important piece of the puzzle. When you receive your guest package, information about where and when this meeting will take place should be included. If not, check with your buyer or guest services manager beforehand. The host will most likely have already talked to the buyer about your upcoming products so will have a fairly decent idea about them already... or not.

This meeting is not about your product as much as it is about you. They are interviewing you to get a feel for your personality. This is your chance to set the tone of your professionalism and preparedness. One way you can set this tone is to write your own introduction on a piece of paper they can take with them. Make it short. Three or four lines in length and ensure the font is large enough to read from a distance. Make a few copies as well so that you always have another to give to the next host. They are extremely quick reads so don't worry if they seem to only glance at your intro. They will place it together with the rest of their product information notes and will use it. Never miss the opportunity to be very specific on how you want to be introduced, particularly if you are brand new to the network. The customers are loyal to the host and will take note of what is said about you. Ensure the message is simple, interesting, brief and consistent with your brand identity.

The Power of the Green Room

The green room is the place where we all kick back a bit between shows. It is also the place where many deals and alliances are created. Think about it, nowhere else do prospective buyers and guest experts get to mingle on such a level playing field. We all get to see each other work in real time. It's the greatest opportunity to extend your reach of connections. If you align yourself strategically by staying connected with the professionals you meet here, it has the potential to positively affect your career moving forward. Many guest experts get many, if not all, of their vendor contacts through meeting the right people in the green room.

Relationship Capital II

In Chapter 6, There's No 'I' in Team, we spoke about relationship capital. To me, it is one of the most important elements to achieving long-term success and bears further development in this chapter. Whenever you get the opportunity to meet new people within your industry, take note of who you met. The business card takes care of the usual information but the more important information is what separates you from being just another sales person. Take note of what that person was wearing and the discussion shared, the date you met them, whether they have a family and a pet, have taken any vacations lately, and anything else you can think of to remind you of that person. That information gives you meaningful information to help you to become a strong connector and better communicator. Why? It is because you took the time to notice that person and to find the common ground between the two of you. People want to be recognized and feel special even for a moment. Go beyond just remembering a name.

(Refer to Chapter 6, Relationship Capital I)

With permission from my friend Dennis, I share his sales follow-up letter. It's personable with a folksy style that suited the lighthearted conversation and shows he was listening to his customer. Here is an excerpt:

Dear Michael,

It was a pleasure talking with you yesterday about your interest in our show. I am glad to learn about how you're a life-time fan of Frank Sinatra's music and how your father also was an aficionado as well.

It's interesting to learn about your market and how enthusiastic audiences are to embrace the wealth of entertainment offerings. It's also good to learn about the various venue options in your city. Based on our conversation, I would recommend 2 performances in one of the smaller seat venues rather than the larger 5,000 seat recreational centre. I think your patrons would have a richer experience in a smaller, more intimate environment. As you suggested, it would be wonderful to coincide our show with your 25th Anniversary of the aviation museum and the planned reunion of all the 1,500 aviation graduates?!

On a personal note, in our conversation we briefly discussed the origins of our surnames. Your name must be pronounced Del Fre and not Del Free...right? I assume your parents are of northern Italian extraction like mine? I am Pellarin but pronounced in Italian...it's Pellahreen What a small world it is.

The Keys to Success

My business partner and I recently had a meeting with the largest retailer in the world. The product we were pitching was a product I was very familiar with, as I had sold a similar product on-air. The thirty-year veteran buyer seemed genuinely interested in the product. Knowing she was tight on time, I pitched hard and fast, highlighting only the standout features of each product. Without delay, she then said, "I'll send you a complete deck tomorrow and we'll get you set up as a vendor as soon as possible."

As my partner and I walked out of the head office, a smile came over my lips.

He coached, "Wait 'til we get in the car."

I then asked him, "It can't be that easy to get in. How did we do it?"

He smiled and said, "I've known that buyer for almost twenty years and I've been waiting for the right product to bring to her."

One of my fondest memories was attending a twenty-five year awards ceremony honouring my father and the other inductees celebrating this significant milestone. Dad was the president of a North American Steel Service Centre at the time and had the pleasure of congratulating all the award winners for their years of devoted service in his keynote speech address. He was also a Toastmaster and was an electrifying orator. He shared that in the future we will no longer *have* jobs but rather we'll *do* jobs and as such, working at the same company for twenty-five years will never be the norm anymore. How studies have shown that most of us only use 10% of our brainpower and it is our challenge in life to harness as much out of the opportunities that life presents to us as possible. His speech was heartfelt and filled with pearls of wisdom to last the audience a lifetime. As he wound up his speech, he closed with the following few thoughts.

"Being an instant success takes a lifetime to achieve." (This was decades before *instant success* TV shows like *The Voice* and *American Idol* became common entertainment. In the 80's it hadn't become engrained in young minds that we *could* stumble upon fame as instantly as it seems we can now.)

He went on to say, "The key to success can be captured in three words." There was a respectful hush among the 100's of listeners glistening in black tie attire. He paused and then continued…

"Relationships. Relationships. Relationships."

Anyone who has achieved great success knows they could never have done it on their own or alone. In fact, the more successful you are, the more contacts and colleagues you have to lean on because highly successful people know the secret to success. And now, you do too.

SOURCES

[1] www.davidrogers.ca

CHAPTER 12
Have You Got Your Game Face ON?

1. What you do today creates your future for tomorrow. Put your game face on and never take it off until you're back on the plane or driving to go home.

2. Give them all you have to give, your customers, show crew, buyers and the entire team behind the scenes.

3. Use your 10-Point Checklist to maintain your sharpness as a performer.

4. Nurture your professional relationships as you grow within your career. They are your keys to success.

GO BEYOND THE FINISH LINE

In closing, I wanted to share a little story with you. My dear friend recently finished thirty-nine radiation treatments for cancer. For eight weeks, I proudly escorted him to the hospital every single day walking side by side. We put one foot in front of the other knowing the promise of the *last treatment* was in sight. The radiation therapists affectionately call the last day, *graduation day*. On our graduation day, I stood (as I always did) with childlike anticipation in front of the roped off doorway marked **Do Not Enter**. His grey golf jacket was draped over my arm as I held my tangerine clutch in the other hand watching for him to come out. It held a half drunk water bottle, his money clip, cell phone and credit cards. As tears streamed down my cheeks, the lights in the hallway flipped back on, signifying his last treatment would soon be a distant memory. One of the therapists (Marie) kindly escorted him out. He walked towards the doorway, stopping to honk the patient horn which was attached to the wall right at the threshold of the doorway. It was an old style bicycle horn with a black rubber rounded end – large enough to squeeze with ease. The honking of the horn signified the last trip for every single patient and believe me, it was always a triumphant sound. Any time throughout the day, no matter what anyone was doing within the waiting area – patients, employees, ambulance drivers and family members would drop everything to clap for that person. My friend gave the horn a few honks. As we stopped our lives to applaud, he walked over that threshold for the last time. His eyes and body smiling. He had made it. I hung a medal (seen in the picture) around his neck signifying his forward journey. "We've done our job, sir," Marie said. "Now its your turn to use everything you've learned and to live your life to its fullest. Walk past us and keep on going."

With my friend's blessing, I use our highly personal story to illustrate the requirement to go beyond the finish line in thought and action in everything we do. Be consistent, don't allow yourself to settle for good enough. Go beyond what you think you can do because I guarantee the experience of striving for better will never leave you where it found you. If I have learned anything from this recent life experience and my entire life in the world of performing it would be this: Never take your life and the gifts you have been given for granted. Develop them, nurture them and hone them to work in your favour to benefit others too. There are no short cuts or quick fixes to becoming an overnight sensation and that is the best part about it.

I began the book with the intention to inspire exceptional sales execution and to train you to be able to access your best performance every single time you have to show up! I posed the questions: What kind of work has to be done in order to deliver that sell out performance and how can it be repeated? How is one able to access their best on command? Is there a switch that great performers have inside them and are there similarities with every high achieving professional at the top of his or her game? I also wondered if this could be identified and packaged in such a way that would allow we regular people to somehow learn, emulate and apply this focus and drive to our own careers.

Did I accomplish the goal sufficiently answering the questions to your satisfaction? That is ultimately up to you to decide. I do know this: What I attempted to do was package a solution-based how-to platform that was designed to be simple enough to grasp for anyone interested in sales and peak performance no matter their depth of experience. I used my own experience and the experience of as many experts as possible to convince you that pressure performance is teachable. I developed the most important aspects to excelling at selling and included ways you can tangibly measure the *in*tangibles of performance and modelled the funnel for training and running a marathon as a guide to the Sales Equation DIET Funnel. It is a sound and reliable tool that I have used for many years. Without following a plan to get you moving in a proven direction, getting to the start line is one great accomplishment but crossing the finish line is dependant on how well the principles of training were applied. This principle is often the difference between finishing strongly versus finishing at all.

If you read the book and applied some or all of the tools, I know it has illuminated the path to free up your natural sales abilities in order for you to fly without a net. You've completed all the due diligence on competitors, sales tactics, relationship building, preparations, practice and you will have discovered how to achieve your peak performance, chosen the best strategies to suit your selling style and learned exactly who your customers are. Now, just as Marie intimated to my friend, TRUST that all of your knowledge and abilities will always be available to you and if managed well, will continue to grow and flow through you like a funnel. Your hours and years of work are forever in place and operating together for a common good, for not only yourself, but for all.

I wish you much success in everything you do!

Your Best Friend Seller,
Alli Mang

CPSIA information can be obtained at www.ICGtesting.com
Printed in the USA
LVOW12s0953130514

385463LV00008B/21/P

9 781628 650884